1st Workshop on Evaluating Vector-Space Representations for NLP 2016

Held at ACL 2016

Berlin, Germany
7 – 12 August 2016

ISBN: 978-1-5108-2770-7

ACL 2016

**The 54th Annual Meeting of the
Association for Computational Linguistics**

**Proceedings of the 1st Workshop on Evaluating Vector-Space
Representations for NLP**

August 7-12, 2016
Berlin, Germany

Introduction

This workshop deals with evaluating vector representations of linguistic units (morphemes, words, phrases, sentences, documents, etc). What marks out these representations - which are colloquially referred to as embeddings – is that they are not trained with a specific application in mind, but rather to capture a characteristic of the data itself. Another way to view their usage is through the lense of transfer learning; the embeddings are trained with one objective, but applied to assist some others. We therefore do not discuss internal representations of deep models that are induced by and applied in the same task.

The Problem with Current Evaluation Methods

Since embeddings are trained in a generally unsupervised setting, it is often difficult to predict their usefulness for a particular task a priori. The best way to assess an embedding's utility is, of course, to use it in a "downstream" application. However, this knowledge tends not to transfer well among different tasks; for example, a 12

To avoid these issues, many papers have chosen to concentrate their evaluation on "intrinsic" (perhaps the more appropriate word is "simple") tasks such as lexical similarity (see, for example: Baroni et al., 2014; Faruqui et al., 2014; Hill et al., 2015; Levy et al., 2015). However, recent work (Schnabel et al., 2015; Tsvetkov et al., 2015) has shown that, just like sophisticated downstream applications, these intrinsic tasks are not accurate predictors of an embedding's utility in other tasks.

One notable issue with current evaluation options is their lack of diversity; despite the large number of intrinsic benchmarks (23 by some counts), and their many differences in size, quality, and domain, the majority of them focus on replicating human ratings of the similarity or relatedness of two words. Even the challenge of analogy recovery through vector arithmetic, which seemed like a more nuanced metric (Mikolov et al., 2013), has been shown to be reducible to a linear combination of lexical similarities (Levy and Goldberg, 2014). As a result, many other interesting linguistic phenomena that are inherent in downstream applications have not received enough attention from the representation learning community.

Goals

New Benchmarks This workshop aims to promote new benchmarks or improvements to existing evaluations that together can address the issues with the existing collection of benchmarks (e.g. lack of diversity). Such benchmarks should fulfill the following criteria:

1. Be simple to code and easy to run

2. Isolate the impact of one representation versus another

3. Improvement in a benchmark should indicate improvement in a downstream application

Better Evaluation Practices The new benchmarks enabled by the workshop will lead to a well-defined set of high quality evaluation resources, covering a diverse range of linguistic/semantic properties that are desirable in representation spaces. Results on these benchmarks will be more easily understood and interpreted by users and reviewers.

Better Embeddings In the long run, the new tasks presented, promoted, and inspired by this workshop should act as a catalyst for faster both technological and scientific progress in representation learning and natural language understanding in general. Specifically, they will drive the development of techniques for learning embeddings that add significant value to downstream applications, and, at the same time, enable a better understanding of the information that they capture.

Submissions

We received 39 submissions, of which 26 were accepted.

Organizers:

Omer Levy, Bar-Ilan University
Felix Hill, University of Cambridge
Anna Korhonen, University of Cambridge
Kyunghyun Cho, New York University
Roi Reichart, Technion - Israel Institute of Technology
Yoav Goldberg, Bar-Ilan University
Antoine Bordes, Facebook AI Research

Program Committee:

Angeliki Lazaridou, University of Trento
Ivan Vulic, Cambridge University
Douwe Kiela, Cambridge University
Torsten Zesch, University of Duisburg-Essen
Preslav Nakov, Qatar Computing Research Institute
Peter Turney, Allen Institute for Artificial Intelligence
German Kruszewski, University of Trento
Manaal Faruqui, Carnegie Mellon University
Karl Stratos, Columbia University
Oren Melamud, Bar-Ilan University
Minh-Thang Luong, Stanford University
Yulia Tsvetkov, Carnegie Mellon University
Tamara Polajnar, Cambridge University
Laura Rimell, Cambridge University
Marek Rei, Cambridge University
Roy Schwartz, Hebrew University of Jerusalem
Georgiana Dinu, IBM
Omri Abend, Hebrew University of Jerusalem
Antoine Bordes, Facebook AI Research
Mohit Bansal, Toyota Technological Institute at Chicago
Diarmuid O Seaghdha, Vocal IQ
David Jurgens, Stanford University
Alona Fyshe, University of Victoria
Mohit Iyyer, University of Maryland, College Park
Sam Bowman, Stanford University
Neha Nayak, Stanford University
Ellie Pavlick, University of Pennsylvania
Gabriel Stanovsky, Bar-Ilan University

Table of Contents

Conference Program

Friday, August 12th

09:00–09:15   *Opening Remarks*

09:15–10:00   **Analysis Track**

Intrinsic Evaluation of Word Vectors Fails to Predict Extrinsic Performance
Billy Chiu, Anna Korhonen and Sampo Pyysalo

A critique of word similarity as a method for evaluating distributional semantic models
Miroslav Batchkarov, Thomas Kober, Jeremy Reffin, Julie Weeds and David Weir

Issues in evaluating semantic spaces using word analogies
Tal Linzen

10:00–10:20   **Proposal Track 1**

Evaluating Word Embeddings Using a Representative Suite of Practical Tasks
Neha Nayak, Gabor Angeli and Christopher D. Manning

Story Cloze Evaluator: Vector Space Representation Evaluation by Predicting What Happens Next
Nasrin Mostafazadeh, Lucy Vanderwende, Wen-tau Yih, Pushmeet Kohli and James Allen

10:20–10:45   *Coffee Break*

Friday, August 12th (continued)

Evaluating Informal-Domain Word Representations With UrbanDictionary
Naomi Saphra

Thematic fit evaluation: an aspect of selectional preferences
Asad Sayeed, Clayton Greenberg and Vera Demberg

12:30–14:00   *Lunch Break*

14:00–15:30   **Proposal Track 2: Word Representations**

Improving Reliability of Word Similarity Evaluation by Redesigning Annotation Task and Performance Measure
Oded Avraham and Yoav Goldberg

Correlation-based Intrinsic Evaluation of Word Vector Representations
Yulia Tsvetkov, Manaal Faruqui and Chris Dyer

Evaluating word embeddings with fMRI and eye-tracking
Anders Søgaard

Defining Words with Words: Beyond the Distributional Hypothesis
Iuliana-Elena Parasca, Andreas Lukas Rauter, Jack Roper, Aleksandar Rusinov, Guillaume Bouchard, Sebastian Riedel and Pontus Stenetorp

15:30–16:00   *Coffee Break*

Intrinsic Evaluation of Word Vectors Fails to Predict Extrinsic Performance

Billy Chiu   Anna Korhonen   Sampo Pyysalo
Language Technology Lab
DTAL, University of Cambridge
{hwc25|alk23}@cam.ac.uk, sampo@pyysalo.net

Abstract

The quality of word representations is frequently assessed using correlation with human judgements of word similarity. Here, we question whether such intrinsic evaluation can predict the merits of the representations for downstream tasks. We study the correlation between results on ten word similarity benchmarks and tagger performance on three standard sequence labeling tasks using a variety of word vectors induced from an unannotated corpus of 3.8 billion words, and demonstrate that most intrinsic evaluations are poor predictors of downstream performance. We argue that this issue can be traced in part to a failure to distinguish specific similarity from relatedness in intrinsic evaluation datasets. We make our evaluation tools openly available to facilitate further study.

1 Introduction

The use of vector representations of words is now pervasive in natural language processing, and the importance of their evaluation is increasingly recognized (Collobert and Weston, 2008; Turian et al., 2010; Mikolov et al., 2013a; Faruqui and Dyer, 2014; Chen et al., 2013; Schnabel et al., 2015). Such evaluations can be broadly divided into intrinsic and extrinsic. The most common form of intrinsic evaluation uses word pairs annotated by humans to determine their degree of similarity (for varying definitions of *similarity*). These are then used to directly assess word representations based on how they rank the word pairs. In contrast, in extrinsic evaluation, word representations are used as input to a downstream task such as part-of-speech (POS) tagging or named entity recognition (NER). Here, good models are simply those that provide good performance in the downstream task according to task-specific metrics. Intrinsic evaluations are typically faster and easier to perform and they are often used to estimate the quality of representations before using them in downstream applications. The underlying assumption is that intrinsic evaluations can, to some degree, predict extrinsic performance.

In this study, we demonstrate that this assumption fails to hold for many standard datasets. We generate a set of word representations with varying context window sizes and compare their performance in intrinsic and extrinsic evaluations, showing that these evaluations yield mutually inconsistent results. Among all the benchmarks explored in our study, only SimLex-999 (Hill et al., 2015) is a good predictor of downstream performance. This may be related to the fact that it stands out among other benchmark datasets in distinguishing highly similar concepts (*male, man*) from highly related but dissimilar ones (*computer, keyboard*).

2 Materials and Methods

2.1 Word Vectors

We generate word representations using the *word2vec* implementation of the skip-gram model (Mikolov et al., 2013a), which can be efficiently applied to very large corpora and has been shown to produce highly competitive word representations in many recent evaluations, such as sentence completion, analogy tasks and sentiment analysis. (Mikolov et al., 2013a; Mikolov et al., 2013b; Fernández et al., 2014). We induce embeddings with varying values of the context window size parameter ranging between 1 and 30, holding other hyper-parameters to their defaults.[1]

---

[1] The default parameters are size=100, sample=0.001, negative=5, min-count=5, and alpha=0.025.

Proceedings of the 1st Workshop on Evaluating Vector Space Representations for NLP, pages 1–6,
Berlin, Germany, August 12, 2016. ©2016 Association for Computational Linguistics

Name	#Tokens	Reference
Wikipedia	2,032,091,934	Wikipedia (2016)
WMT14	731,451,760	Bojar et al. (2014)
1B-word-LM	768,648,884	Chelba et al. (2014)

Table 1: Unannotated corpora (sizes before tokenization)

Name	#Pairs	Reference
Wordsim-353	353	Finkelstein et al. (2001)
WS-Rel	252	Agirre et al. (2009)
WS-Sim	203	Agirre et al. (2009)
YP-130	130	Yang and Powers (2006)
MC-30	30	Miller and Charles (1991)
MEN	3000	Bruni et al. (2012)
MTurk-287	287	Radinsky et al. (2011)
MTurk-771	771	Halawi et al. (2012)
Rare Word	2034	Luong et al. (2013)
SimLex-999	999	Hill et al. (2015)

Table 2: Intrinsic evaluation datasets

2.2 Corpora and Pre-processing

To create word vectors, we gather a large corpus of unannotated English text, drawing on publicly available resources identified in word2vec distribution materials. Table 1 lists the text sources and their sizes. We extract raw text from the Wikipedia dump using the Wikipedia Extractor[2]; the other sources are textual. We pre-process all text with the Sentence Splitter and the Treebank Word Tokenizer provided by the NLTK python library (Bird, 2006). In total, there are 3.8 billion tokens (19 million distinct types) in the processed text.

2.3 Intrinsic evaluation

We perform intrinsic evaluations on the ten benchmark datasets presented in Table 2. We follow the standard experimental protocol for word similarity tasks: for each given word pair, we compute the cosine similarity of the word vectors in our representation, and then rank the word pairs by these values. We finally compare the ranking of the pairs created in this way with the gold standard human ranking using Spearman's ρ (rank correlation coefficient).

2.4 Downstream Methods

We base our extrinsic evaluation on the seminal work of Collobert et al. (2011) on the use of neural methods for NLP. In brief, we reimplemented the simple *window approach* feedforward neural network architecture proposed by Collobert et al., which takes as input words in a window of size

Name	#Tokens (Train/Test)
PTB	337,195 / 129,892
CoNLL 2000	211,727 / 47,377
CoNLL 2003	203,621 / 46,435

Table 3: Extrinsic evaluation datasets

five, followed by the word embedding, a single hidden layer of 300 units and a hard tanh activation leading to an output Softmax layer. Besides the index of each word in the embedding, the only other input is a categorical representation of the capitalization pattern of each word.[3]

We train each model on the training set for 10 epochs using word-level log-likelihood, mini-batches of size 50, and the Adam optimization method with the default parameters suggested by Kingma and Ba (2015). Critically, to emphasize the differences between the different representations, we do *not* fine-tune word vectors by backpropagation, diverging from Collobert et al. and leading to somewhat reduced performance. We use greedy decoding to predict labels for test data.

2.5 Extrinsic evaluation

To evaluate the word representations in downstream tasks, we use them in three standard sequence labeling tasks selected by Collobert et al. (2011): POS tagging of Wall Street Journal sections of Penn Treebank (PTB) (Marcus et al., 1993), chunking of CoNLL'00 shared task data (Tjong Kim Sang and Buchholz, 2000), and NER of CoNLL'03 shared task data (Tjong Kim Sang and De Meulder, 2003). We use the standard train/test splits and evaluation criteria for each dataset, evaluating PTB POS tagging using token-level accuracy and CoNLL'00/03 chunking and NER using chunk/entity-level F-scores as implemented in the `conlleval` evaluation script. Table 3 shows basic statistics for each dataset.

3 Results

Tables 4 and 5 present the results of the intrinsic and extrinsic evaluations, respectively. While the different baselines and the small size of some of the datasets make the intrinsic results challenging to interpret, a clear pattern emerges when holding the result for word vectors of window size 1 as the zero point for each dataset and examining average differences: the intrinsic evaluations show higher

---

[2]`http://medialab.di.unipi.it/wiki/Wikipedia_Extractor`

[3]For brevity, we refer to Collobert et al. (2011) for further details on this method.

Dataset	Window size								
	1	2	4	5	8	16	20	25	30
WordSim-353	0.6211	0.6524	0.6658	0.6732	0.6839	0.6991	0.6994	**0.7002**	0.6981
MC-30	0.7019	0.7326	0.7903	0.7629	0.7889	0.8114	**0.8323**	0.8003	0.8141
MEN-TR-3K	0.6708	0.6860	0.7010	0.7040	0.7129	0.7222	0.7240	**0.7252**	0.7242
MTurk-287	0.6069	0.6447	0.6403	0.6536	0.6603	0.6580	**0.6625**	0.6513	0.6519
MTurk-771	0.5890	0.6012	**0.6060**	0.6055	0.6047	0.6007	0.5962	0.5931	0.5933
Rare Word	0.3784	0.3893	0.3976	**0.4009**	0.3919	0.3923	0.3938	0.3949	0.3953
YP130	0.3984	0.4089	0.4147	0.3938	0.4025	0.4382	0.4716	0.4754	**0.4819**
SimLex-999	**0.3439**	0.3300	0.3177	0.3144	0.3005	0.2909	0.2873	0.2811	0.2705

Table 4: Intrinsic evaluation results (ρ)

Dataset	Window size								
	1	2	4	5	8	16	20	25	30
CoNLL 2000	**0.9143**	0.9070	0.9058	0.9052	0.8982	0.8821	0.8761	0.8694	0.8604
CoNLL 2003	**0.8522**	0.8473	0.8474	0.8475	0.8474	0.8410	0.8432	0.8399	0.8374
PTB POS	**0.9691**	0.9680	0.9672	0.9674	0.9654	0.9614	0.9592	0.9560	0.9531

Table 5: Extrinsic evaluation results (F-score for CoNLL datasets, accuracy for PTB)

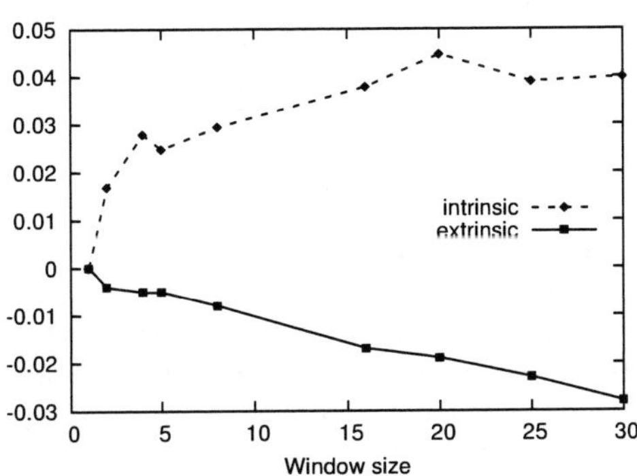

Figure 1: Average difference to performance for window size 1 for intrinsic and extrinsic metrics.

	CoNLL 2000	CoNLL 2003	PTB POS
WordSim-353	-0.90	-0.75	-0.88
MC-30	-0.87	-0.77	-0.90
MEN-TR-3K	-0.98	-0.83	-0.97
MTurk-287	-0.57	-0.29	-0.50
MTurk-771	0.28	0.37	0.27
Rare Word	-0.57	-0.29	-0.50
YP130	-0.82	-0.93	-0.50
SimLex-999	**1.00**	**0.85**	**0.98**

Table 6: Correlation between intrinsic and extrinsic measures (ρ)

overall results with increasing window size, while extrinsic performance drops (Figure 1).

Looking at the individual datasets, the preference for the smallest window size is consistent across all the three tagging tasks (Table 5) but only one out of the eight intrinsic evaluation datasets, Simlex-999, selects this window size, with the majority clearly favoring larger window sizes (Table 4). To further quantify this discrepancy, we ranked the word vectors from highest- to lowest-scoring according to each intrinsic and extrinsic measure and evaluated the correlation of each pair of these rankings using ρ. The results are striking (Table 6): six out of the eight intrinsic measures have *negative* correlations with all the three extrinsic measures, indicating that when selecting among the word vectors for these downstream tasks, it is *better to make a choice at random* than to base it on the ranking provided by any of the six intrinsic evaluations.

4 Discussion

Only two of the intrinsic evaluation datasets showed positive correlation with the extrinsic evaluations: MTurk-287 (ρ 0.27 to 0.37) and SimLex-999 (ρ 0.85 to 1.0). One of the differences between the other datasets and the high-scoring Simlex-999 is that it explicitly differentiates similarity from relatedness and association. For example, in the MEN dataset, the nearly synonymous pair (*stair, staircase*) and the highly associated but non-synonymous pair (*rain, storm*) are both given high ratings. However, as Hill et al. (2015) argue, an evaluation that measures semantic similarity should ideally distinguish these relations and credit a model for differentiating correctly that (*male, man*) are highly synonymous, while (*film, cinema*) are highly associated but dissimilar.

This distinction is known to be relevant to the effect of the window size parameter. A larger window not only reduces sparsity by introducing more contexts for each word, but is also known to affect the tradeoff between capturing *domain* similarity

Dataset	Window Size								
	1	2	4	5	8	16	20	25	30
WS-Rel	0.5430	0.5851	0.6021	0.6112	0.6309	0.6510	0.6551	**0.6568**	0.6514
WS-Sim	0.7465	0.7700	0.7772	0.7807	0.7809	**0.7885**	0.7851	0.7789	0.7776

Table 7: Intrinsic evaluation results for WS-Rel and WS-Sim (ρ)

vs. *functional* similarity: Turney (2012) notes that with larger context windows, representations tend to capture the *topic* or *domain* or a word, while smaller windows tend to emphasize the learning of word function. This is because the role/function of a word is categorized by its proximate syntactic context, while a large window captures words that are less informative for this categorization (Turney, 2012). For example, in the sentence *Australian scientist discovers star with telescope*, the context of the word *discovers* in a window of size 1 includes *scientist* and *star*, while a larger context window will include more words related by topic such as *telescope* (Levy and Goldberg, 2014). The association of large window sizes with greater topicality is discussed also by Hill et al. (2015) and Levy et al. (2015).

This phenomenon provides a possible explanation for the preference for representations created using larger windows exhibited by many of the intrinsic evaluation datasets: as these datasets assign high scores also to word pairs that are highly associated but dissimilar, representations that have similar vectors for all associated words (even if not similar) will score highly when evaluated on the datasets. If there is no need for the representation to make the distinction between similarity and relatedness, a large window has only benefits. On the other hand, the best performance in the extrinsic sequence labeling tasks comes from window size 1. This may be explained by the small window facilitating the learning of word function, which is more important for the POS tagging, chunking, and NER tasks than topic. Similarly, given the emphasis of SimLex-999 on capturing genuine similarity (synonyms), representations that assign similar vectors to words that are related but not similar will score poorly. Thus, we observe a decreasing trend with increasing window size for SimLex-999.

To further assess whether this distinction can explain the results for an intrinsic evaluation dataset for representations using small vs. large context windows, we studied the relatedness (WS-Rel) and similarity (WS-Sim) subsets (Agirre et al., 2009) of the popular WordSim-353 reference dataset (included in the primary evaluation). Table 7 shows the performance of representations with increasing context window size on these subsets. In general, both show higher ρ with an increasing context window size. However, the performance in the relatedness subset increases from 0.54 to 0.65 whereas that in similarity only increases from 0.74 to 0.77. Thus, although the similarity subset did not select a small window size, the lesser preference for a large window compared to the relatedness subset lends some support to the proposed explanation.

5 Conclusion

One of the primary goals of intrinsic evaluation is to provide insight into the quality of a representation before it is used in downstream applications. However, we found that the majority of word similarity datasets fail to predict which representations will be successful in sequence labelling tasks, with only one intrinsic measure, SimLex-999, showing high correlation with extrinsic measures. In concurrent work, we have also observed a similar effect for biomedical domain tasks and word vectors (Chiu et al., 2016). We further considered the differentiation between relatedness (association) and similarity (synonymy) as an explanatory factor, noting that the majority of intrinsic evaluation datasets do not systematically make this distinction.

Our results underline once more the importance of including also extrinsic evaluation when assessing NLP methods and resources. To encourage extrinsic evaluation of vector space representations, we make all of our newly introduced methods available to the community under open licenses from `https://github.com/cambridgeltl/RepEval-2016`.

Acknowledgments

This work has been supported by Medical Research Council grant MR/M013049/1

References

Eneko Agirre, Enrique Alfonseca, Keith Hall, Jana Kravalova, Marius Paşca, and Aitor Soroa. 2009. A study on similarity and relatedness using distributional and wordnet-based approaches. In *Proceedings of NAACL-HLT'09*, pages 19–27.

Steven Bird. 2006. NLTK: the natural language toolkit. In *Proceedings of the COLING/ACL on Interactive presentation sessions*, pages 69–72.

Ondrej Bojar, Christian Buck, Christian Federmann, Barry Haddow, Philipp Koehn, Johannes Leveling, Christof Monz, Pavel Pecina, Matt Post, Herve Saint-Amand, et al. 2014. Findings of the 2014 workshop on statistical machine translation. In *Proceedings of the Ninth Workshop on Statistical Machine Translation*, pages 12–58.

Elia Bruni, Gemma Boleda, Marco Baroni, and Nam-Khanh Tran. 2012. Distributional semantics in technicolor. In *Proceedings of ACL'12*, pages 136–145.

Ciprian Chelba, Tomas Mikolov, Mike Schuster, Qi Ge, Thorsten Brants, Phillipp Koehn, and Tony Robinson. 2014. One billion word benchmark for measuring progress in statistical language modeling. In *Fifteenth Annual Conference of the International Speech Communication Association*.

Yanqing Chen, Bryan Perozzi, Rami Al-Rfou, and Steven Skiena. 2013. The expressive power of word embeddings. *arXiv preprint arXiv:1301.3226*.

Billy Chiu, Gamal Crichton, Sampo Pyysalo, and Anna Korhonen. 2016. How to train good word embeddings for biomedical NLP. In *Proceedings of BioNLP'16*.

Ronan Collobert and Jason Weston. 2008. A unified architecture for natural language processing: Deep neural networks with multitask learning. In *Proceedings of ICML'08*, pages 160–167.

Ronan Collobert, Jason Weston, Léon Bottou, Michael Karlen, Koray Kavukcuoglu, and Pavel Kuksa. 2011. Natural language processing (almost) from scratch. *The Journal of Machine Learning Research*, 12:2493–2537.

Manaal Faruqui and Chris Dyer. 2014. Community evaluation and exchange of word vectors at wordvectors.org. In *Proceedings of ACL'14: System Demonstrations*, June.

Javi Fernández, Yoan Gutiérrez, José M Gómez, and Patricio Martınez-Barco. 2014. Gplsi: Supervised sentiment analysis in twitter using skipgrams. In *Proceedings of SemEval'14*, pages 294–299.

Lev Finkelstein, Evgeniy Gabrilovich, Yossi Matias, Ehud Rivlin, Zach Solan, Gadi Wolfman, and Eytan Ruppin. 2001. Placing search in context: The concept revisited. In *Proceedings of WWW'01*, pages 406–414.

Guy Halawi, Gideon Dror, Evgeniy Gabrilovich, and Yehuda Koren. 2012. Large-scale learning of word relatedness with constraints. In *Proceedings of SIGKDD'12*, pages 1406–1414.

Felix Hill, Roi Reichart, and Anna Korhonen. 2015. Simlex-999: Evaluating semantic models with (genuine) similarity estimation. *Computational Linguistics*.

Diederik Kingma and Jimmy Ba. 2015. Adam: A method for stochastic optimization. In *Proceedings of ICLR'15*.

Omer Levy and Yoav Goldberg. 2014. Dependency-based word embeddings. In *Proceedings of ACL'14*, pages 302–308.

Omer Levy, Yoav Goldberg, and Ido Dagan. 2015. Improving distributional similarity with lessons learned from word embeddings. *Transactions of the Association for Computational Linguistics*, 3:211–225.

Thang Luong, Richard Socher, and Christopher Manning. 2013. Better word representations with recursive neural networks for morphology. In *Proceedings of CoNLL*, pages 104–113.

Mitchell P Marcus, Mary Ann Marcınkıewıcz, and Beatrice Santorini. 1993. Building a large annotated corpus of english: The penn treebank. *Computational linguistics*, 19(2):313–330.

Tomas Mikolov, Kai Chen, Greg Corrado, and Jeffrey Dean. 2013a. Efficient estimation of word representations in vector space. In *Proceedings of Workshop at ICLR*.

Tomas Mikolov, Ilya Sutskever, Kai Chen, Greg S Corrado, and Jeff Dean. 2013b. Distributed representations of words and phrases and their compositionality. In *Proceedings of NIPS'13*, pages 3111–3119.

George A Miller and Walter G Charles. 1991. Contextual correlates of semantic similarity. *Language and cognitive processes*, 6(1):1–28.

Kira Radinsky, Eugene Agichtein, Evgeniy Gabrilovich, and Shaul Markovitch. 2011. A word at a time: computing word relatedness using temporal semantic analysis. In *Proceedings of WWW'11*, pages 337–346.

Tobias Schnabel, Igor Labutov, David Mimno, and Thorsten Joachims. 2015. Evaluation methods for unsupervised word embeddings. In *Proceedings of EMNLP'15*.

Erik F Tjong Kim Sang and Sabine Buchholz. 2000. Introduction to the conll-2000 shared task: Chunking. In *Proceedings of CoNLL'00*, pages 127–132.

Erik F Tjong Kim Sang and Fien De Meulder. 2003. Introduction to the conll-2003 shared task: Language-independent named entity recognition. In *Proceedings of CoNLL'03*, pages 142–147.

Joseph Turian, Lev Ratinov, and Yoshua Bengio. 2010. Word representations: a simple and general method for semi-supervised learning. In *Proceedings of ACL'10*, pages 384–394.

Peter D Turney. 2012. Domain and function: A dual-space model of semantic relations and compositions. *Journal of Artificial Intelligence Research*, pages 533–585.

Wikipedia. 2016. Wikipedia, the free encyclopedia. https://dumps.wikimedia.org/enwiki/latest/.

Dongqiang Yang and David MW Powers. 2006. Verb similarity on the taxonomy of wordnet. In *Proceedings of GWC'06*.

A critique of word similarity as a method for evaluating distributional semantic models

Miroslav Batchkarov, Thomas Kober, Jeremy Reffin, Julie Weeds and **David Weir**
Text Analysis Group, Department of Informatics, University of Sussex
{M.Batchkarov, T.Kober, J.P.Reffin, J.E.Weeds, D.J.Weir}@sussex.ac.uk

Abstract

This paper aims to re-think the role of the word similarity task in distributional semantics research. We argue while it is a valuable tool, it should be used with care because it provides only an approximate measure of the quality of a distributional model. Word similarity evaluations assume there exists a single notion of similarity that is independent of a particular application. Further, the small size and low inter-annotator agreement of existing data sets makes it challenging to find significant differences between models.

1 Introduction

Distributional models of lexical semantics have recently attracted considerable interest in the NLP community. With the increase in popularity, the issue of evaluation is becoming more important. While extrinsic (task-based) evaluations are increasingly common, the most frequently used family of evaluation procedures (intrinsic evaluations) attempt to directly measure the "inherent" quality of a word representation. This often takes the form of computing the extent to which a model agrees with human-provided word or phrase similarity scores.

This paper highlights the theoretical and practical issues with the word similarity task, which make it a poor measure of the quality of a distributional model. We investigate five commonly used word similarity datasets, RG (Rubenstein and Goodenough, 1965), MC (Miller and Charles, 1991), WS353 (Finkelstein et al., 2001), MEN (Bruni et al., 2014) and SimLex (Hill et al., 2015). Our contributions are as follows. We argue that the notion of lexical similarity is difficult to define outside of the context of a task and

without conflating different concepts such as "similarity" or "relatedness". We show inter-annotator agreement at the word similarity task is considerably lower compared to other tasks such as document classification or textual entailment. Furthermore, we demonstrate that the quality of a model, as measured by a given word similarity data set, can vary substantially because of the small size of the data set. Lastly, we introduce a simple sanity check for word similarity data sets that tests whether a data set is able to reliably identify corrupted word vectors. These findings can be adopted as guidelines for designers of evaluation data sets. The code for our experiments is available at github.com/mbatchkarov/repeval2016.

2 Definition of Similarity

The notion of similarity is challenging to define precisely. Existing word similarity data sets typically contain a broad range of semantic relations such as synonymy, antonymy, hypernymy, co-hypernymy, meronymy and topical relatedness. Earlier word similarity work such as WS353 does not attempt to differentiate between those. In contrast, more recent work such as MEN and SimLex distinguishes between "similarity" and "relatedness" and provide human annotators with more specific instructions as to what makes words similar.

However, all data sets considered in this paper assume that there exists a single gold-standard score for each pair of words, which can vary considerably across data sets, depending on what notion of similarity is used. For example, the pair "chicken–rice" has a normalised score of 0.14 in SimLex and 0.68 in MEN, while "man–woman" scores 0.33 and 0.84 respectively.

We argue that every downstream application de-

Proceedings of the 1st Workshop on Evaluating Vector Space Representations for NLP, pages 7–12,
Berlin, Germany, August 12, 2016. ©2016 Association for Computational Linguistics

fines its own kind of similarity. Words are therefore not inherently similar or dissimilar. For example, "good acting" and "cluttered set" are highly dissimilar in terms of the sentiment they express towards a theatrical play. However, they are very similar in the context of detecting news items related to the theatre, as both phrases are highly indicative of theatre-related content. It is often unclear what kind of similarity is useful for a downstream problem in advance. Indeed, it has been shown that being able to learn the notion defined by a particular word similarity task does not necessarily translate to superior extrinsic performance (Schnabel et al., 2015). This argument parallels that of von Luxburg et al. (2012, p 2), who argue that "[d]epending on the use to which a clustering is to be put, the same clustering can either be helpful or useless". The quality of an unsupervised algorithm can therefore only be assessed in the context of an application.

3 Subjectivity and task difficultly

When human judges annotate word pairs for similarity, the distinctions in meaning they are asked to make are often very subtle, especially in the absence of context. For instance, the normalised similarity scores provided by 13 annotators for the pair "tiger–cat" range from 0.5 to 0.9 in WS353. This results in low inter-annotator agreement even between native speakers. This section analyses the variation in similarity scores produced by different annotators, and compares the agreement score for the first 13 annotators of WS353 and the two authors of MEN to typical agreements reported in the NLP literature for tasks such as document classification and textual entailment.

Figure 1 shows a kernel density estimate of the distribution of similarity scores between judges for MEN and WS353[1]. Both data sets exhibit undesirable characteristics. The distribution of scores assigned by both judges in MEN appears to be bimodal, which suggests that the annotators are operating on a three-point scale rather than on a seven-point one. There is also a significant amount of variation—the similarity assigned to a word pair exceeds two points (out of seven) in 313 cases[2] (10.4%) and can vary by as many as six points. WS353 exhibits a strong bias towards

---

[1]The other data sets used in this study do not provide the annotations of each individual subject.

[2]MEN contains a total of 3000 annotated pairs.

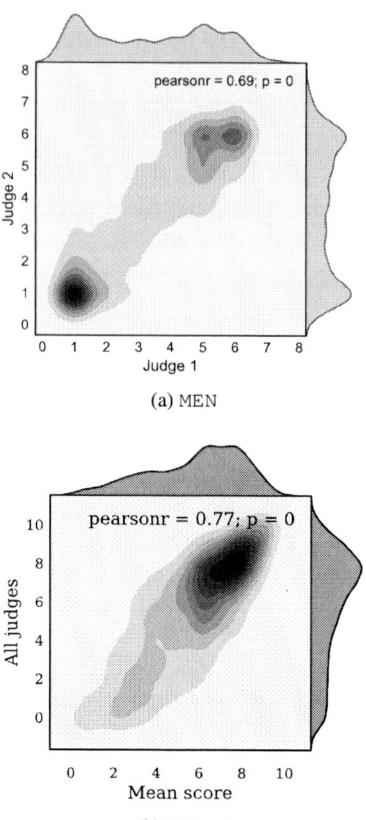

Figure 1: Distribution of similarity scores between annotators

high-similarity word pairs. However, individual judges exhibit a bias towards similarity scores in the middle of the spectrum. Variance is also high — 535 individual annotations (10.3% of all cases) for a given word pair differ by more than two points (out of ten) from the mean score for that pair[3].

It is not possible to compare inter-annotator agreement scores for word similarity and other natural-language labelling tasks directly. Labels in the former are on an ordinal scale, so agreement is measured using Spearman's rho (ρ). In contrast, the labels in other tasks are often categorical; agreement is typically measured using Cohen's kappa (κ). To address this issue, we convert word similarity scores to discrete labels by placing the continuous scores into equally sized bins. For example, the range of similarity scores in WS353

---

[3]WS353 contains 353 unique word pairs annotated by at least 13 judges for a total of 5189 (word pair, annotation) units.

is $[0, 10]$, and the bin boundaries are at $[0, 5, 10]$ when using two bins and at $[0, 3.33, 6.66, 10]$ when using three bins. The three-item continuous labelling $[2.1, 5.8, 7.9]$ is converted to $[A, B, B]$ when using two bins and to $[A, B, C]$ when using three bins.

This conversion process suffers from two drawbacks. First, order information is lost, so misplacing an item in bin A instead of in bin B is considered as severe an error as misplacing an item from bin A into bin F. This is less of an issue when the bin count is small. Second, the number of bins is a free parameter ranging between 1 (all items in the same bin) and 7 or 10 (all items in original bins)[4]. κ is a decreasing function of the number of bins because it becomes harder for annotators to agree when there is a large number of bins to choose from. This analysis is agnostic as to how many bins should be used. We experiment with values between 2 and 5.

The inter-annotator agreement of WS353 and MEN (converted to Cohen's κ) is shown in Figure 2. Because κ is only applicable when there are exactly two annotators, we report an average κ over all pairwise comparisons[5]. A κ score can be computed between each of the 91 pairs of judges ("WS353-P"), or between each judge and the mean across all judges ("WS353-M") (as in Hill et al. (2015, Section 2.3)). Mean agreement ranges from $\kappa = 0.21$ to $\kappa = 0.62$.

For comparison, Kim and Hovy (2004) report $\kappa = 0.91$ for a binary sentiment task. Gamon et al. (2005) report a κ of 0.7–0.8 for a three-way sentiment task. Wilson et al. (2005) report $\kappa = 0.72$ for a four-class short expressions sentiment task, rising to $\kappa = 0.84$ if phrases marked as "unsure" are removed. McCormick et al. (2008) report $\kappa = 0.84$ for a five-way text classification task. Stolcke et al. (2000) report $\kappa = 0.8$ for a 42-label dialogue act tagging task. Toledo et al. (2012) achieve $\kappa = 0.7$ for a textual entailment task, and Sammons et al. (2010) report $\kappa = 0.8$ to $\kappa = 1$ for a domain identification task. All these κ scores are considerably higher than those achieved by WS353 and MEN.

---

[4] WS353 was annotated on a ten-point scale, whereas MEN used a seven-point scale.

[5] Averaging is only needed for WS353, which has been annotated by (at least) 13 judges. MEN only provides full annotations for two judges.

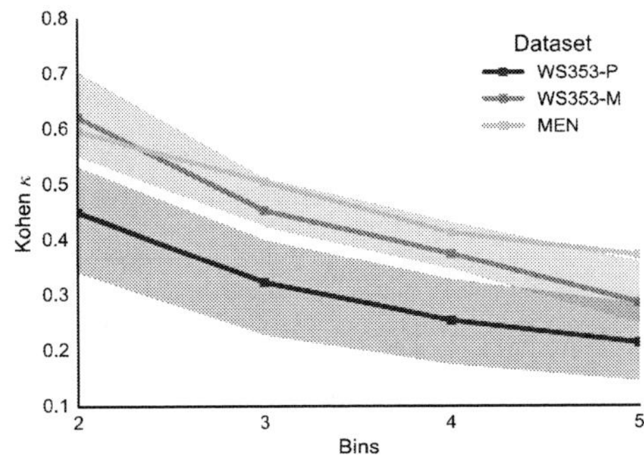

Figure 2: Inter-annotator agreement of WS353, measured in Cohen's κ. Shaded region shows the mean and one standard deviation around it. A standard deviation is not shown for MEN as only the annotation of a single pair of raters are available.

4 Size of data set

Another issue with existing word similarity data sets is their small size. This ranges from 30 to 3000 data points (Miller and Charles, 1991; Rubenstein and Goodenough, 1965; Landauer and Dumais, 1997; Finkelstein et al., 2001; Hill et al., 2015; Huang et al., 2012; Luong et al., 2013; Bruni et al., 2014). Moreover, they only feature a "tidy" subset of all naturally occurring words, free of spelling variation, domain-specific terminology and named entities. The focus is predominantly on relatively high-frequency words, so the quality of the model cannot be quantified fully. In contrast, typical distributional models "in the wild" have a vocabulary of tens or hundreds of thousands of types.

For practical applications, users need to understand the entire distributional model, not just the small fraction of it covered by an intrinsic evaluation. A side effect of using small evaluation data sets is that the measured correlation scores may vary significantly. However, variance is seldom reported in the literature. To quantify it, we train a word2vec model (Mikolov et al., 2013) on a mid-2011 copy of English Wikipedia. We use the CBOW objective with negative sampling and a window size of 5, as implemented in gensim (Řehůřek and Sojka, 2010). The model is evaluated on five word similarity data sets— MC, RG, WS353, SimLex and MEN. We compute the empirical distribution of correlation with human scores by bootstrapping. Each data set is resampled 500 times with replacement. The distributional model is evaluated on each sample (Efron and Tibshirani, 1994). Results are shown in Table 1a. We also evaluate a baseline model that represents words as completely random vectors, sampled from continuous uniform distribution $\mathcal{U}(0, 1)$ (Table 1b).

Dataset	Mean	Std	Min	Max	Size
MC	0.71	0.12	0.29	0.95	30
RG	0.72	0.06	0.50	0.87	65
WS353	0.64	0.04	0.53	0.75	353
SimLex	0.31	0.03	0.23	0.39	999
MEN	0.67	0.01	0.64	0.70	3000

(a) `word2vec` vectors

Dataset	Mean	Std	Min	Max	Size
MC	-0.01	0.19	-0.53	0.55	30
RG	0.08	0.11	-0.28	0.41	65
WS353	-0.08	0.05	-0.24	0.10	353
SimLex	0.01	0.03	-0.09	0.12	999
MEN	-0.02	0.02	-0.08	0.04	3000

(b) Random vectors

Table 1: Distribution of Spearman ρ between model predictions and gold standard data set.

The mean correlation is in line with values reported in the literature. However, standard deviation is strongly dependent on the size of the gold-standard data set. Even for MEN, which is the largest word similarity data set in this study, the measured correlation varies as much as 0.06. However, this fact is not often addressed in the literature. For instance, the difference between the recently proposed `Swivel` (Shazeer et al., 2016) and `word2vec` with negative sampling is less than 0.02 on WS353, SimLex and MEN. Table 1 suggests that these differences may well not be statistically significant.

5 Sensitivity to noise

In this section we propose a simple sanity check for word similarity data sets, which we suggest is used periodically while developing a data set. It is based on the requirement that for a given evaluation method, good word representations should perform measurably better than poor ones. One method of reliably generating poor word vectors is to start with a distributional model and decrease its quality by adding random noise. The evalua-

tion framework should be able to detect the difference between the original and corrupted models. Model performance, as measured by the evaluation method, should be a monotonically decreasing function of the amount of noise added. In the extreme case, a completely random distributional model should achieve a correlation of zero with the human-provided intrinsic similarity scores (Table 1b).

Figure 3 shows an application of our proposal to MC, RG and MEN. We add uniform random noise $\mathcal{U}(-n, n)$ to all elements of all word vectors from Section 4, where $n \in [0, 3]$. This is a considerable perturbation as the word vectors used have have a mean L2 norm of 2.4. RG and MC do not sufficiently capture the degradation of vector quality as noise is added because ρ may increase with n. The variance of the measurements is also very high. Both datasets therefore fail the sanity check. MEN's performance is considerably better, with smaller standard deviation and correlation tending to zero as noise is added. WS353 and SimLex exhibit similar behaviour to MEN, but have higher variance.

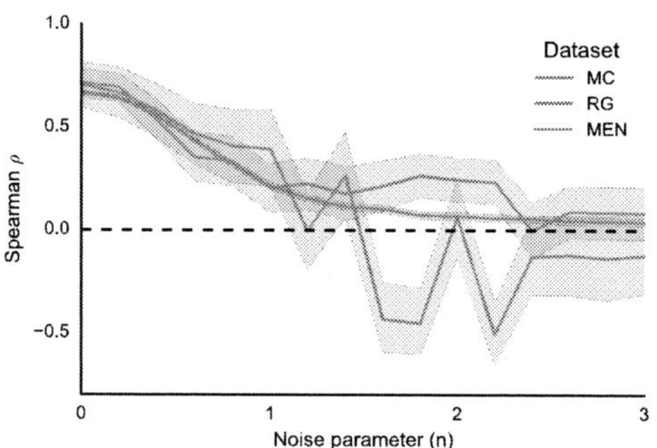

Figure 3: Word similarity noise test. Shaded region shows one standard deviation around the mean, which is estimated via bootstrapping.

6 Conclusion

This paper showed the word similarity task is considerably more challenging for annotators than extrinsic tasks such as document classification. Further, the small size of existing word similarity data sets results in high variance, making it difficult to reliably differentiate between models. More fundamentally, the task assumes there exists a single similarity score between a pair of words which is independent of a particular application. These results challenge the value of intrinsic data sets as a gold standard. We argue that word similarity still has a place in NLP, but researchers should be aware of its limitations. We view the task as a computationally efficient approximate measure of model quality, which can be useful in the early stage of model development. However, research should place less emphasis on word similarity performance and more on extrinsic results such as (Batchkarov, 2015; Huang and Yates, 2009; Milajevs et al., 2014; Schnabel et al., 2015; Turian et al., 2010; Weston et al., 2015).

Acknowledgements

This work was funded by UK EPSRC project EP/IO37458/1 *"A Unified Model of Compositional and Distributional Compositional Semantics: Theory and Applications"*. We would like to thank all members of the TAG lab team and our anonymous reviewers for their helpful comments.

References

Miroslav Batchkarov. 2015. *Evaluating distributional models of compositional semantics*. Ph.D. thesis, University of Sussex.

Elia Bruni, Nam-Khanh Tran, and Marco Baroni. 2014. Multimodal distributional semantics. *Proceedings of JAIR* 49:1–47.

Bradley Efron and Robert Tibshirani. 1994. *An Introduction to the Bootstrap*. CRC press.

Lev Finkelstein, Evgeniy Gabrilovich, Yossi Matias, Ehud Rivlin, Zach Solan, Gadi Wolfman, and Eytan Ruppin. 2001. Placing search in context: The concept revisited. *Proceedings of the 10th international conference on World Wide Web* pages 406–414.

Michael Gamon, Anthony Aue, Simon Corston-Oliver, and Eric Ringger. 2005. Pulse: Mining customer opinions from free text. In *Advances in Intelligent Data Analysis VI*, Springer, pages 121–132.

Felix Hill, Roi Reichart, and Anna Korhonen. 2015. Simlex-999: Evaluating semantic models with (genuine) similarity estimation. *Computational Linguistics* .

Eric Huang, Richard Socher, Christopher Manning, and Andrew Ng. 2012. Improving word representations via global context and multiple word prototypes. *Proceedings of ACL* pages 873–882.

Fei Huang and Alexander Yates. 2009. Distributional representations for handling sparsity in supervised sequence-labeling. *Proceedings of ACL-IJCNLP* pages 495–503.

Soo-Min Kim and Eduard Hovy. 2004. Determining the sentiment of opinions. *Proceedings of ACL* page 1367.

Thomas Landauer and Susan Dumais. 1997. A solution to Plato's problem: The latent semantic analysis theory of acquisition, induction, and representation of knowledge. *Psychological Review* 104(2):211.

Minh-Thang Luong, Richard Socher, and Christopher Manning. 2013. Better word representations with recursive neural networks for morphology. *Proceedings of CoNLL* 104.

Patrick McCormick, Noémie Elhadad, and Peter Stetson. 2008. Use of semantic features to classify patient smoking status. *AMIA Annual Symposium Proceedings* 2008.

Tomas Mikolov, Kai Chen, Greg Corrado, and Jeffrey Dean. 2013. Efficient estimation of word representations in vector space. *arXiv Preprint arXiv:1301.3781* .

Dmitrijs Milajevs, Dimitri Kartsaklis, Mehrnoosh Sadrzadeh, and Matthew Purver. 2014. Evaluating neural word representations in tensor-based compositional settings. *Proceedings of EMNLP* pages 708–719.

George Miller and Walter Charles. 1991. Contextual correlates of semantic similarity. *Language and Cognitive Processes* 6(1):1–28.

Radim Řehůřek and Petr Sojka. 2010. Software framework for topic modelling with large corpora. *Proceedings of the LREC 2010 Workshop on New Challenges for NLP Frameworks* pages 45–50.

Herbert Rubenstein and John Goodenough. 1965. Contextual correlates of synonymy. *Communications of the ACM* 8(10):627–633.

Mark Sammons, V. G. Vinod Vydiswaran, and Dan Roth. 2010. Ask not what textual entailment can do for you... In *Proceedings of the 48th Annual Meeting of the Association for Computational Linguistics*. Association for Computational Linguistics, pages 1199–1208.

Tobias Schnabel, Igor Labutov, David Mimno, and Thorsten Joachims. 2015. Evaluation methods for unsupervised word embeddings .

Noam Shazeer, Ryan Doherty, Colin Evans, and Chris Waterson. 2016. Swivel: Improving embeddings by noticing what's missing. *arXiv preprint arXiv:1602.02215* .

Andreas Stolcke, Noah Coccaro, Rebecca Bates, Paul Taylor, Carol Van Ess-Dykema, Klaus Ries, Elizabeth Shriberg, Daniel Jurafsky, Rachel Martin, and Marie Meteer. 2000. Dialogue act modeling for automatic tagging and recognition of conversational speech. *Computational linguistics* 26(3):339–373.

Assaf Toledo, Sophia Katrenko, Stavroula Alexandropoulou, Heidi Klockmann, Asher Stern, Ido Dagan, and Yoad Winter. 2012. Semantic annotation for textual entailment recognition. In *Advances in Computational Intelligence*, Springer, pages 12–25.

Joseph Turian, Lev Ratinov, and Yoshua Bengio. 2010. Word representations: A simple and general method for semi-supervised learning. *Proceedings of ACL* pages 384–394.

Ulrike von Luxburg, Robert Williamson, and Isabelle Guyon. 2012. Clustering: Science or art? *ICML Unsupervised and Transfer Learning* pages 65–80.

Jason Weston, Antoine Bordes, Sumit Chopra, and Tomas Mikolov. 2015. Towards AI-complete question answering: A set of prerequisite toy tasks. *arXiv Preprint arXiv:1502.05698* .

Theresa Wilson, Janyce Wiebe, and Paul Hoffmann. 2005. Recognizing contextual polarity in phrase-level sentiment analysis. *Proceedings of HLT-EMNLP* pages 347–354.

Issues in evaluating semantic spaces using word analogies

Tal Linzen
LSCP & IJN
École Normale Supérieure
PSL Research University
`tal.linzen@ens.fr`

Abstract

The offset method for solving word analogies has become a standard evaluation tool for vector-space semantic models: it is considered desirable for a space to represent semantic relations as consistent vector offsets. We show that the method's reliance on cosine similarity conflates offset consistency with largely irrelevant neighborhood structure, and propose simple baselines that should be used to improve the utility of the method in vector space evaluation.

1 Introduction

Vector space models of semantics (VSMs) represent words as points in a high-dimensional space (Turney and Pantel, 2010). There is considerable interest in evaluating VSMs without needing to embed them in a complete NLP system. One such intrinsic evaluation strategy that has gained in popularity in recent years uses the offset approach to solving word analogy problems (Levy and Goldberg, 2014; Mikolov et al., 2013c; Mikolov et al., 2013a; Turney, 2012). This method assesses whether a linguistic relation — for example, between the base and gerund form of a verb (*debug* and *debugging*) — is consistently encoded as a particular linear offset in the space. If that is the case, estimating the offset using one pair of words related in a particular way should enable us to go back and forth between other pairs of words that are related in the same way, e.g., *scream* and *screaming* in the base-to-gerund case (Figure 1).

Since VSMs are typically continuous spaces, adding the offset between *debug* and *debugging* to *scream* is unlikely to land us exactly on any particular word. The solution to the analogy problem is therefore taken to be the word closest in

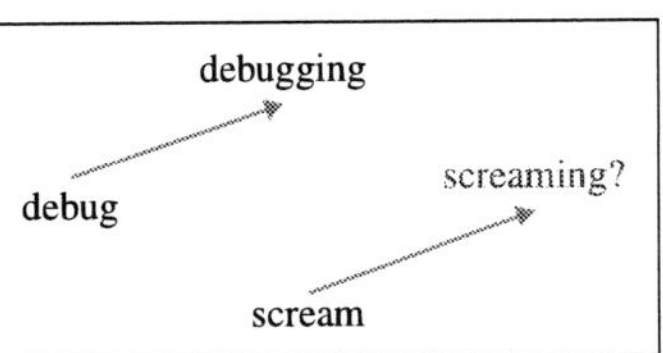

Figure 1: Using the vector offset method to solve the analogy task (Mikolov et al., 2013c).

cosine similarity to the landing point. Formally, if the analogy is given by

$$a : a^* :: b : \underline{\quad} \tag{1}$$

where in our example a is *debug*, a^* is *debugging* and b is *scream*, then the proposed answer to the analogy problem is

$$x^* = \underset{x'}{\operatorname{argmax}} \cos(x', a^* - a + b) \tag{2}$$

where

$$\cos(v, w) = \frac{v \cdot w}{\|v\| \|w\|} \tag{3}$$

The central role of cosine similarity in this method raises the concern that the method does not only evaluate the consistency of the offsets $a^* - a$ and $b^* - b$ but also the neighborhood structure of $x = a^* - a + b$. For instance, if a^* and a are very similar to each other (as *scream* and *screaming* are likely to be) the nearest word to x may simply be the nearest neighbor of b. If in a given set of analogies the nearest neighbor of b tends to be b^*, then, the method may give the correct answer regardless of the consistency of the offsets (Figure 2).

In this note we assess to what extent the performance of the offset method provides evidence for offset consistency despite its potentially problematic reliance on cosine similarity. We use two

Proceedings of the 1st Workshop on Evaluating Vector Space Representations for NLP, pages 13–18,
Berlin, Germany, August 12, 2016. ©2016 Association for Computational Linguistics

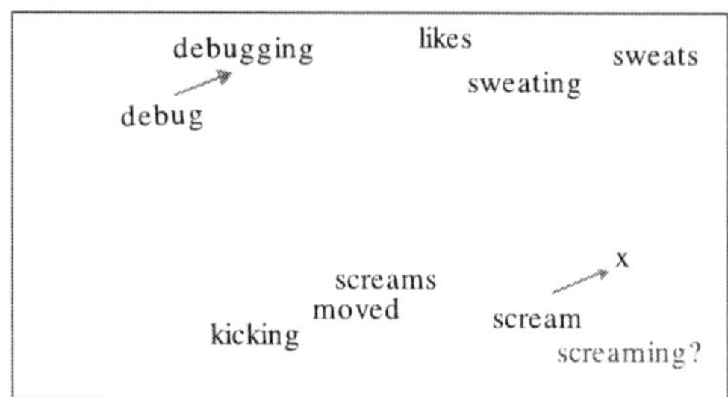

Figure 2: When $a^* - a$ is small and b and b^* are close, the expected answer may be returned even when the offsets are inconsistent (here *screaming* is closest to x).

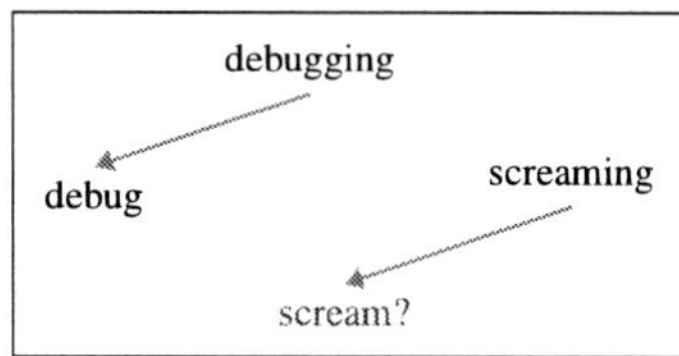

Figure 3: Reversing the direction of the task.

methods. First, we propose new baselines that perform the task without using the offset $a^* - a$ and argue that the performance of the offset method should be compared to those baselines. Second, we measure how the performance of the method is affected by reversing the direction of each analogy problem (Figure 3). If the method truly measures offset consistency, this reversal should not affect its accuracy.

2 Analogy functions

We experiment with the following functions. In all of the methods, every word in the vocabulary can serve as a guess, except when a, a^* or b are explicitly excluded as noted below. Since the size of the vocabulary is typically very large, chance performance, or the probability of a random word in the vocabulary being the correct guess, is extremely low.

VANILLA: This function implements the offset method literally (Equation 2).

ADD: The x^* obtained from Equation 2 is often trivial (typically equal to b). In practice, most studies exclude a, a^* and b from consideration:

$$x^* = \operatorname*{argmax}_{x' \notin \{a,a^*,b\}} \cos(x', a^* - a + b) \qquad (4)$$

ONLY-B: This method ignores both a and a^* and simply returns the nearest neighbor of b:

$$x^* = \operatorname*{argmax}_{x' \notin \{a,a^*,b\}} \cos(x', b) \qquad (5)$$

As shown in Figure 2, this baseline is likely to give a correct answer in cases where $a^* - a$ is small and b^* happens to be the nearest neighbor of b.

IGNORE-A: This baseline ignores a and returns the word that is most similar to both a^* and b:

$$x^* = \operatorname*{argmax}_{x' \notin \{a,a^*,b\}} \cos(x', a^* + b) \qquad (6)$$

A correct answer using this method indicates that b^* is closest to a point y that lies mid-way between a^* and b (i.e. that maximizes the similarity to both words).

ADD-OPPOSITE: This function takes the logic behind the ONLY-B baseline a step further – if the neighborhood of b is sufficiently sparse, we will get the correct answer even if we go in the *opposite* direction from the offset $a^* - a$:

$$x^* = \operatorname*{argmax}_{x' \notin \{a,a^*,b\}} \cos(x', -(a^* - a) + b) \qquad (7)$$

MULTIPLY: Levy and Goldberg (2014) show that Equation 2 is equivalent to adding and subtracting cosine similarities, and propose replacing it with multiplication and division of similarities:

$$x^* = \operatorname*{argmax}_{x' \notin \{a,a^*,b\}} \frac{\cos(x', a^*) \cos(x', b)}{\cos(x', a)} \qquad (8)$$

REVERSE (ADD): This is simply ADD applied to the reverse analogy problem: if the original problem is *debug : debugging :: scream : ___*, the reverse problem is *debugging : debug :: screaming : ___*. A substantial difference in accuracy between the two directions in a particular type of analogy problem (e.g., base-to-gerund compared to gerund-to-base) would indicate that the neighborhoods of one of the word categories (e.g., gerund) tend to be sparser than the neighborhoods of the other type (e.g., base).

REVERSE (ONLY-B): This baseline is equivalent to ONLY-B, but applied to the reverse problem: it returns b^*, in the notation of the original analogy problem.

	a	a^*	n
Common capitals:	*athens*	*greece*	506
All capitals:	*abuja*	*nigeria*	4524
US cities:	*chicago*	*illinois*	2467
Currencies:	*algeria*	*dinar*	866
Nationalities:	*albania*	*albanian*	1599
Gender:	*boy*	*girl*	506
Plurals:	*banana*	*bananas*	1332
Base to gerund:	*code*	*coding*	1056
Gerund to past:	*dancing*	*danced*	1560
Base to third person:	*decrease*	*decreases*	870
Adj. to adverb:	*amazing*	*amazingly*	992
Adj. to comparative:	*bad*	*worse*	1332
Adj. to superlative:	*bad*	*worst*	1122
Adj. un- prefixation:	*acceptable*	*unacceptable*	812

Table 1: The analogy categories of Mikolov et al. (2013a) and the number of problems per category.

3 Experimental setup

Analogy problems: We use the analogy dataset proposed by Mikolov et al. (2013a). This dataset, which has become a standard VSM evaluation set (Baroni et al., 2014; Faruqui et al., 2015; Schnabel et al., 2015; Zhai et al., 2016), contains 14 categories; see Table 1 for a full list. A number of these categories, sometimes referred to as "syntactic", test whether the structure of the space captures simple morphological relations, such as the relation between the base and gerund form of a verb (*scream : screaming*). Others evaluate the knowledge that the space encodes about the world, e.g., the relation between a country and its currency (*latvia : lats*). A final category that doesn't fit neatly into either of those groups is the relation between masculine and feminine versions of the same concept (*groom : bride*). We follow Levy and Goldberg (2014) in calculating separate accuracy measures for each category.

Semantic spaces: In addition to comparing the performance of the analogy functions within a single VSM, we seek to understand to what extent this performance can differ across VSMs. To this end, we selected three VSMs out of the set of spaces evaluated by Linzen et al. (2016). All three spaces were produced by the skip-gram with negative sampling algorithm implemented in word2vec (Mikolov et al., 2013b), and were trained on the concatenation of ukWaC (Baroni et al., 2009) and a 2013 dump of the English Wikipedia.

The spaces, which we refer to as s_2, s_5 and s_{10}, differed only in their context window parameters. In s_2, the window consisted of two words on ei-

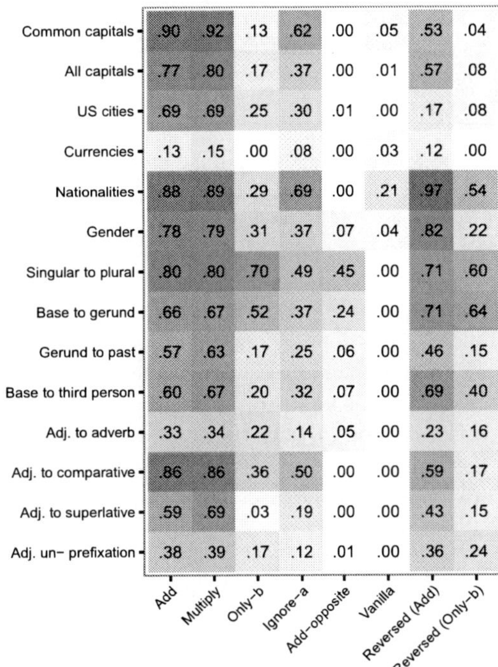

	Add	Multiply	Only-b	Ignore-a	Add-opposite	Vanilla	Reversed (Add)	Reversed (Only-b)
Common capitals	.90	.92	.13	.62	.00	.05	.53	.04
All capitals	.77	.80	.17	.37	.00	.01	.57	.08
US cities	.69	.69	.25	.30	.01	.00	.17	.08
Currencies	.13	.15	.00	.08	.00	.03	.12	.00
Nationalities	.88	.89	.29	.69	.00	.21	.97	.54
Gender	.78	.79	.31	.37	.07	.04	.82	.22
Singular to plural	.80	.80	.70	.49	.45	.00	.71	.60
Base to gerund	.66	.67	.52	.37	.24	.00	.71	.64
Gerund to past	.57	.63	.17	.25	.06	.00	.46	.15
Base to third person	.60	.67	.20	.32	.07	.00	.69	.40
Adj. to adverb	.33	.34	.22	.14	.05	.00	.23	.16
Adj. to comparative	.86	.86	.36	.50	.00	.00	.59	.17
Adj. to superlative	.59	.69	.03	.19	.00	.00	.43	.15
Adj. un- prefixation	.38	.39	.17	.12	.01	.00	.36	.24

Figure 4: Accuracy of all functions on space s_5.

ther side of the focus word. In s_5 it included five words on either side of the focus word, and was "dynamic" – that is, it was expanded if any of the context words were excluded for low or high frequency (for details, see Levy et al. (2015)). Finally, the context in s_{10} was a dynamic window of ten words on either side. All other hyperparameters were set to standard values.

4 Results

Baselines: Figure 4 shows the success of all of the analogy functions in recovering the intended analogy target b^* in space s_5. In line with Levy and Goldberg (2014), there was a slight advantage for MULTIPLY over ADD (mean difference in accuracy: .03), as well as dramatic variability across categories (ranging from .13 to .90 in ADD). This variability cuts across the distinction between the world-knowledge and morphological categories; performance on currencies and adjectives-to-adverbs was poor, while performance on capitals and comparatives was high.

Although ADD and MULTIPLY always outperformed the baselines, the margin varied widely across categories. The most striking case is the plurals category, where the accuracy of ONLY-B reached .70, and even ADD-OPPOSITE achieved

Space	ADD	ADD - IGNORE-A	ADD - ONLY-B
s_2	.53	.41	.42
s_5	.6	.29	.36
s_{10}	.58	.26	.33

Table 2: Overall scores and the advantage of ADD over two of the baselines across spaces.

a decent accuracy (.45). Taking a^* but not a into account (IGNORE-A) outperformed ONLY-B in ten out of 14 categories. Finally, the poor performance of VANILLA confirms that a, a^* and b must be excluded from the pool of potential answers for the offset method to work. When these words were not excluded, the nearest neighbor of $a^* - a + b$ was b in 93% of the cases and a^* in 5% of the cases (it was never a).

Reversed analogies: Accuracy decreased in most categories when the direction of the analogy was reversed (mean difference -0.11). The changes in the accuracy of ADD between the original and reversed problems were correlated across categories with the changes in the performance of the ONLY-B baseline before and after reversal (Pearson's $r = .72$). The fact that the performance of the baseline that ignores the offset was a reliable predictor of the performance of the offset method again suggests that the offset method when applied to the Mikolov et al. (2013a) sets jointly evaluates the consistency of the offsets and the probability that b^* is the nearest neighbor of b.

The most dramatic decrease was in the US cities category (.69 to .17). This is plausibly due to the fact that the city-to-state relation is a many-to-one mapping; as such, the offsets derived from two specific city-states pairs — e.g., *Sacramento:California* and *Chicago:Illinois* — are unlikely to be exactly the same. Another sharp decrease was observed in the common capitals category (.9 to .53), even though that category is presumably a one-to-one mapping.

Comparison across spaces: The overall accuracy of ADD was similar across spaces, with a small advantage for s_5 (Table 2). Yet the breakdown of the results by category (Figure 5) shows that the similarity in average performance across the spaces obscures differences across categories: s_2 performed much better than s_{10} in some of the morphological inflection categories (e.g., .7 compared to .44 for the base-to-third-person relation),

	Add			Add - Ignore-a			Add - Only-b		
Adj. un- prefixation	.34	.38	.31	.30	.26	.12	.28	.21	.17
Adj. to superlative	.72	.59	.51	.51	.40	.40	.72	.56	.48
Adj. to comparative	.89	.86	.77	.39	.36	.36	.51	.50	.31
Adj. to adverb	.19	.33	.37	.15	.18	.23	.16	.11	.03
Base to third person	.70	.60	.44	.46	.28	.21	.49	.40	.30
Gerund to past	.60	.57	.55	.47	.31	.31	.47	.39	.38
Base to gerund	.57	.66	.62	.45	.29	.31	.24	.14	.07
Singular to plural	.78	.80	.81	.49	.31	.25	.13	.10	.08
Gender	.76	.78	.69	.44	.41	.37	.54	.47	.47
Nationalities	.84	.88	.86	.51	.19	.23	.84	.59	.59
Currencies	.12	.13	.12	.05	.05	.06	.12	.13	.12
US cities	.42	.69	.68	.41	.39	.24	.40	.44	.45
All capitals	.61	.77	.81	.59	.40	.32	.61	.60	.60
Common capitals	.92	.90	.91	.69	.28	.23	.92	.77	.69
	s_2	s_5	s_{10}	s_2	s_5	s_{10}	s_2	s_5	s_{10}

Figure 5: Comparison across spaces. The leftmost panel shows the accuracy of ADD, and the next two panels show the improvement in accuracy of ADD over the baselines.

whereas s_{10} had a large advantage in some of the world-knowledge categories (e.g., .68 compared to .42 in the US cities category). The advantage of smaller window sizes in capturing "syntactic" information is consistent with previous studies (Redington et al., 1998; Sahlgren, 2006). Note also that overall accuracy figures are potentially misleading in light of the considerable variability in the number of analogies in each category (see Table 1): the "all capitals" category has a much greater effect on overall accuracy than gender, for example.

Spaces also differed in how much ADD improved over the baselines. The overall advantage over the baselines was highest for s_2 and lowest for s_{10} (Table 2). In particular, although accuracy was similar across spaces in the nationalities and common capitals categories, much more of this accuracy was already captured by the IGNORE-A baseline in s_{10} than in s_2 (Figure 5)

5 Discussion

The success of the offset method in solving word analogy problems has been taken to indicate that systematic relations between words are represented in the space as consistent vector offsets

(Mikolov et al., 2013c). The present note has examined potential difficulties with this interpretation. A literal ("vanilla") implementation of the method failed to perform the task: the nearest neighbor of $a^* - a + b$ was almost always b or a^*.[1] Even when those candidates were excluded, some of the success of the method on the analogy sets that we considered could also be obtained by baselines that ignored a or even both a and a^*. Finally, reversing the direction of the analogy affected accuracy substantially, even though the same offset was involved in both directions.

The performance of the baselines varied widely across analogy categories. Baseline performance was poor in the adjective-to-superlative relation, and was very high in the plurals category (even when both a and a^* were ignored). This suggests that analogy problems in the plural category category may not measure whether the space encodes the single-to-plural relation as a vector offset, but rather whether the plural form of a noun tends to be close in the vector space to its singular form. Baseline performance varied across spaces as well; in fact, the space with the weakest overall performance (s_2) showed the largest increases over the baselines, and therefore the most evidence for consistent offsets.

We suggest that future studies employing the analogy task report the performance of the simple baselines we have suggested, in particular ONLY-B and possibly also IGNORE-A. Other methods for evaluating the consistency of vector offsets may be less vulnerable to trivial responses and neighborhood structure, and should be considered instead of the offset method (Dunbar et al., 2015).

Our results also highlight the difficulty in comparing spaces based on accuracy measures averaged across heterogeneous and unbalanced analogy sets (Gladkova et al., 2016). Spaces with similar overall accuracy can vary in their success on particular categories of analogies; effective representations of "world-knowledge" information are likely to be useful for different downstream tasks than effective representations of formal linguistic properties. Greater attention to the fine-grained strengths of particular spaces may lead to the development of new spaces that combine these strengths.

Acknowledgments

I thank Ewan Dunbar, Emmanuel Dupoux, Omer Levy and Benjamin Spector for comments and discussion. This research was supported by the European Research Council (grant ERC-2011-AdG 295810 BOOTPHON) and the Agence Nationale pour la Recherche (grants ANR-10-IDEX-0001-02 PSL and ANR-10-LABX-0087 IEC).

References

Marco Baroni, Silvia Bernardini, Adriano Ferraresi, and Eros Zanchetta. 2009. The WaCky wide web: a collection of very large linguistically processed web-crawled corpora. *Language Resources and Evaluation*, 43(3):209–226.

Marco Baroni, Georgiana Dinu, and Germán Kruszewski. 2014. Don't count, predict! A systematic comparison of context-counting vs. context-predicting semantic vectors. In *Proceedings of the 52nd Annual Meeting of the Association for Computational Linguistics*, pages 238–247.

Ewan Dunbar, Gabriel Synnaeve, and Emmanuel Dupoux. 2015. Quantitative methods for comparing featural representations. In *Proceedings of the 18th International Congress of Phonetic Sciences*.

Manaal Faruqui, Jesse Dodge, Sujay Kumar Jauhar, Chris Dyer, Eduard Hovy, and Noah A. Smith. 2015. Retrofitting word vectors to semantic lexicons. In *Proceedings of the 2015 Conference of the North American Chapter of the Association for Computational Linguistics: Human Language Technologies*, pages 1606–1615, Denver, Colorado, May–June. Association for Computational Linguistics.

Anna Gladkova, Aleksandr Drozd, and Satoshi Matsuoka. 2016. Analogy-based detection of morphological and semantic relations with word embeddings: what works and what doesn't. In *Proceedings of the NAACL Student Research Workshop*, pages 8–15, San Diego, California, June. Association for Computational Linguistics.

Omer Levy and Yoav Goldberg. 2014. Linguistic regularities in sparse and explicit word representations. In *Proceedings of the Eighteenth Conference on Computational Language Learning*, pages 171–180.

Omer Levy, Yoav Goldberg, and Ido Dagan. 2015. Improving distributional similarity with lessons learned from word embeddings. *Transactions of the Association for Computational Linguistics*, 3:211–225.

---

[1] A human with any reasonable understanding of the analogy task is likely to also exclude a, a^* and b as possible responses, of course. However, such heuristics that are baked into an analogy solver, while likely to improve its performance, call into question the interpretation of the success of the analogy solver as evidence for the geometric organization of the underlying semantic space.

Tal Linzen, Emmanuel Dupoux, and Benjamin Spector. 2016. Quantificational features in distributional word representations. In *Proceedings of the Fifth Joint Conference on Lexical and Computational Semantics (*SEM 2016)*.

Tomas Mikolov, Kai Chen, Greg Corrado, and Jeffrey Dean. 2013a. Efficient estimation of word representations in vector space. *Proceedings of ICLR*.

Tomas Mikolov, Ilya Sutskever, Kai Chen, Greg Corrado, and Jeff Dean. 2013b. Distributed representations of words and phrases and their compositionality. In *Advances in Neural Information Processing Systems*, pages 3111–3119.

Tomas Mikolov, Wen-tau Yih, and Geoffrey Zweig. 2013c. Linguistic regularities in continuous space word representations. In *Proceedings of NAACL-HLT*, pages 746–751.

Martin Redington, Nick Chater, and Steven Finch. 1998. Distributional information: A powerful cue for acquiring syntactic categories. *Cognitive Science*, 22(4):425–469.

Magnus Sahlgren. 2006. *The Word-Space Model: Using distributional analysis to represent syntagmatic and paradigmatic relations between words in high-dimensional vector spaces*. Ph.D. thesis, Stockholm University.

Tobias Schnabel, Igor Labutov, David Mimno, and Thorsten Joachims. 2015. Evaluation methods for unsupervised word embeddings. In *Proceedings of EMNLP*.

Peter D. Turney and Patrick Pantel. 2010. From frequency to meaning: Vector space models of semantics. *Journal of Artificial Intelligence Research*, 37(1):141–188.

Peter D Turney. 2012. Domain and function: A dual-space model of semantic relations and compositions. *Journal of Artificial Intelligence Research*, pages 533–585.

Michael Zhai, Johnny Tan, and Jinho D Choi. 2016. Intrinsic and extrinsic evaluations of word embeddings. In *Thirtieth AAAI Conference on Artificial Intelligence*.

Evaluating Word Embeddings Using a Representative Suite of Practical Tasks

Neha Nayak
Stanford University
Stanford, CA 94305

Gabor Angeli
Stanford University
Stanford, CA 94305

Christopher D. Manning
Stanford University
Stanford, CA 94305

{nayakne, angeli, manning}@cs.stanford.edu

Abstract

Word embeddings are increasingly used in natural language understanding tasks requiring sophisticated semantic information. However, the quality of new embedding methods is usually evaluated based on simple word similarity benchmarks. We propose evaluating word embeddings *in vivo* by evaluating them on a suite of popular downstream tasks. To ensure the ease of use of the evaluation, we take care to find a good point in the tradeoff space between (1) creating a thorough evaluation – i.e., we evaluate on a diverse set of tasks; and (2) ensuring an easy and fast evaluation – by using simple models with few tuned hyperparameters. This allows us to release this evaluation as a standardized script and online evaluation, available at http://veceval.com/.

1 Introduction

Many modern NLP systems, especially those employing deep learning techniques, benefit from word representations in the form of low-dimensional word embeddings. This has led to a burgeoning body of work focusing on improving these representations. These word representations are used either as features for a conventional statistical classifier, or in a deep learning setup, where they are tuned to a particular task through back-propagation.

However, the quality of these unsupervised embeddings is often asserted on the basis of restricted lexical semantics tasks, such as scoring word similarity or linear relationships for analogies. These intrinsic evaluations are carried out with little attention paid to how performance correlates with downstream tasks. We propose instead evaluat-

ing word embeddings using a standardized suite of characteristic downstream tasks.

This has two advantages, which constitute the main contributions of the paper. First, an improvement in performance on these representative tasks is more likely to generalize to real-world applications of the embedding, as compared to improvements in performance on current word similarity benchmarks. Therefore, this evaluation offers a better metric to hill-climb on than current lexical semantics tasks.

Second, this evaluation allows for higher fidelity qualitative assessment on the strengths and weaknesses of an embedding method. For instance, certain embeddings may excel at syntactic tasks, or on sequence modeling tasks, whereas others may capture the semantics of a word better, or work better for classification tasks. We believe this evaluation can facilitate consolidating and formalizing such insights, currently latent in the collective consciousness of the NLP community.

2 Related work

Existing work on creating evaluations for word embeddings has focused on lexical semantics tasks. An example of such tasks is WordSim-353 (Finkelstein et al., 2001), in which a series of word pairs are assigned similarity judgments by human annotators, and these are compared to the similarity scores obtained from word embeddings.

A thorough such lexical semantics evaluation was created by Faruqui and Dyer (2014)[1]. This website allows a user to upload a set of embeddings, and evaluates these embeddings on a series of word similarity benchmarks. We follow the model presented in Faruqui and Dyer (2014), but extend to a series of more realistic downstream tasks.

---

[1]http://www.wordvectors.org

Proceedings of the 1st Workshop on Evaluating Vector Space Representations for NLP, pages 19–23,
Berlin, Germany, August 12, 2016. ©2016 Association for Computational Linguistics

Schnabel et al. (2015) carried out both a thorough intrinsic evaluation of word vectors, and a limited extrinsic evaluation showing that an embedding's intrinsic performance did not necessarily correlate with its real-world performance. This finding is a key motivation for this work – we aim to create a metric which does correlate with downstream performance.

3   Motivation

While extensive research has gone into the development of meaningful intrinsic evaluation methods, extrinsic evaluation remains the de-facto proving ground for novel word embedding methods (Pennington et al., 2014; Dhillon et al., 2012). We aim to create an evaluation methodology which is representative of real-world performance, but nonetheless fast and easy to evaluate against. These two criteria are somewhat at odds with each other, which necessitates finding a good point in a number of key tradeoffs:

Choice of Tasks   Optimally, new embeddings would be evaluated on as large a number of tasks as possible. However, such an evaluation would become prohibitively slow and impractical. Therefore, we limit our evaluation to 6 tasks of moderate size, allowing models to be trained and evaluated quickly while nonetheless covering a range of NLP phenomena.

Choice of Models   Optimally, new embeddings would be evaluated as components of a range of different models. However, the addition of more models – and in particular more sophisticated models – slows down the evaluation. Therefore, we opt to use uncontroversial off-the-shelf neural models for each task. Although none of the models achieve state-of-the-art results, we only care about *relative* scores between embeddings. Simple models are equally, if not more suitable for this criterion.

Choice of hyperparameters   The performance of neural models often vary greatly depending on the choice of hyperparameters. To be fair to everyone, we must either cross-validate for each embedding, or aggressively minimize the number of hyperparameters. For the sake of efficiency, we opt for the latter.

Reproducibility   To ensure reproducibility, we release our evaluation script, and host a public website where users can upload their embeddings to be evaluated.

4   Tasks

The following are a selection of tasks to be included in the benchmark suite. These were chosen to be a representative – though certainly not exhaustive – sampling of relevant downstream tasks.

Two tasks are included to test syntactic properties of the word embeddings – part-of-speech tagging and chunking. Part-of-speech tagging is carried out on the WSJ dataset described in Toutanova et al. (2003). In order to simplify the task and avoid hand-coded features, we evaluate against the universal part-of-speech tags proposed in Petrov et al. (2012). For chunking, we use the dataset from the CoNLL 2000 shared task (Tjong Kim Sang and Buchholz, 2000), derived from the Wall Street Journal.

Four tasks test the semantic properties of the word embeddings. At the word level, we include named entity recognition. We evaluate on a 4-class Named Entity Recognition task: PERSON, LOCATION, ORGANIZATION, and MISC, using the CoNLL 2003 dataset (Tjong Kim Sang and De Meulder, 2003), and an IOB tagging scheme. At the sentence level, we include two tasks – sentiment classification and question classification. We implement binary sentiment classification using the Stanford Sentiment Treebank dataset, and the coarse-grained question classification task described in Li and Roth (2006).

Finally, above the word level, we test the ability of word embeddings to propagate the lexical relation information they contain into representations of larger units of text. This involves the task of phrase-level natural language inference, derived from a dataset presented in Ganitkevitch et al. (2013).

These tasks were selected so as to cover both syntactic and semantic capabilities, but also as they are fast to train, fulfilling another of the characteristics put forward in Section 3.

5   Models

Our goal is to select the simplest possible models for each task, while maintaining respectable performance. We therefore train straightforward models using standard neural net layers.

For tasks with word-level labeling, we use a window-based model akin to that in Collobert et al. (2011). Features for each token in a sequence are constructed by concatenating the word embeddings of a window of words centered on the token. This is passed through a two-layer neural network, followed by a softmax classifier.

For tasks with sentence-level labeling, sentence representations are constructed using a basic LSTM. Classification is then carried out by passing through a one-layer neural network, followed by a softmax classifier.

Finally, the NLI task requires representations for both the premise and hypothesis sequences. Embeddings for each sequence are constructed as described in the sentence embedding tasks, using two separate LSTMs. These embeddings are concatenated, and similarly passed through a one-layer neural network and softmax classifier. Our implementations of these simple models are able to train with a new set of embeddings and evaluate the resulting model in a few hours.

Although these simplistic models do not achieve state-of-the-art performance on any of the tasks, they are faster and in many ways more robust to variations in training methodology than more sophisticated models, maintaining a reduced hyperparameter set. Furthermore, a valid comparison between word vectors requires only that the model is *fair* to each representation, not necessarily that the models achieve state-of-the-art performance, fulfilling our requirements from Section 3.

This evaluation aims solely to test the properties of word embeddings, and not phrase or sentence embeddings. For the tasks that demand phrase and sentence representations, we elect to construct these from the word embeddings using an LSTM, rather than to extend the evaluation to other types of embeddings.

6 Evaluation metrics

Our goal is to distill performance on extrinsic tasks into a short but comprehensive "report" that indicates the strengths and weaknesses of a particular set of embeddings on a variety of downstream tasks. For each set of embeddings tested, we report results based on the metric most appropriate for the task – F_1 score for NER, and accuracy for the rest of the tasks.

We use SVD as a baseline embedding method. Using the hyperwords software of Levy et al. (2015), we apply SVD to a PMI-transformed co-occurrence matrix derived from the same pre-

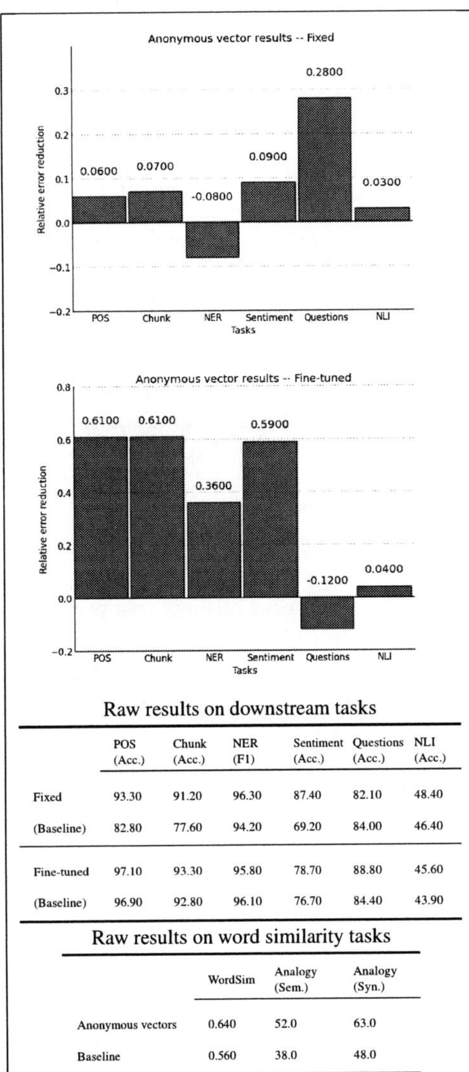

Raw results on downstream tasks

	POS (Acc.)	Chunk (Acc.)	NER (F1)	Sentiment (Acc.)	Questions (Acc.)	NLI (Acc.)
Fixed	93.30	91.20	96.30	87.40	82.10	48.40
(Baseline)	82.80	77.60	94.20	69.20	84.00	46.40
Fine-tuned	97.10	93.30	95.80	78.70	88.80	45.60
(Baseline)	96.90	92.80	96.10	76.70	84.40	43.90

Raw results on word similarity tasks

	WordSim	Analogy (Sem.)	Analogy (Syn.)
Anonymous vectors	0.640	52.0	63.0
Baseline	0.560	38.0	48.0

Figure 1: An example of the type of result report created by our evaluation. The first chart shows the relative error reduction of the embedding method compared to the SVD baseline, *disallowing* backpropagation into the vectors. This measures the extent to which the original vectors capture linguistic phenomena. Values above 0 perform better than SVD on the task; the magnitude of the improvement are on comparable scales between tasks. The second chart is identical to the first chart, but allowing backpropagation into the vectors. This measures how good the vectors are as an initialization for neural network methods. The first table shows the raw accuracy numbers for each task. The second table shows the vectors' result on the WordSim and Analogy tasks.

scribed corpus, resulting in a set of SVD vectors. We present a baseline for each task, which is the F_1 score or accuracy attained by the SVD vectors.

Due to the diversity of the tasks, it is difficult to compare the raw values or differences over the baseline. These measures, especially when aggregated, tend to implicitly reward large improvements over low-baseline tasks more than small improvements over high-baseline tasks. To illustrate, whereas a 1% improvement on POS tagging should be considered significant, the same 1% improvement on a task with a 80% baseline is less impressive. As such, the primary metric we report is not accuracy or F_1, but rather the *relative error reduction* as compared to the SVD baseline. This allows us to calculate a meaningful aggregate, averaging relative error reduction over tasks. For backwards compatibility with prior work, we also report correlations on WordSim-353, as well as precision at 1 for the analogy task presented in Mikolov et al. (2013).

The figure shows an example report generated by our evaluation, using arbitrary but realistic values. It can be seen that the relative error reduction depicted in the charts enables a clearer representation of the relative performance on different tasks, as compared to the raw values provided in the table.

7 Experimental methodology

7.1 Training hyperparameters

Following Schnabel et al. (2015), we prescribe the use of a fixed snapshot of Wikipedia (dated 2008-03-01) for training the embeddings to be evaluated. This corpus was selected to be as close in time as possible to the corpus Collobert et al. (2011)'s embeddings were trained on. It was preprocessed by applying the Stanford tokenizer (Manning et al., 2014), and replacing all digits with zeros.

7.2 Avoiding bias

Since this method of evaluation involves training a number of neural network models, there is a significant danger of overfitting to the embeddings used to find the hyperparameters. We attempt to mitigate this in two ways.

First, we use simple models with standard neural net layers to limit the number of hyperparameters tuned. We tune only the optimizer type, the l2 coefficient for regularization, and the learning rate. We set any additional hyperparameters to fast yet reasonable defaults, which also facilitate short training times. For example, in an LSTM layer, we use a hidden layer size equal to the input vector size. Second, rather than optimizing for each individual task, we select only two hyperparameter settings – one for the sequence labelling tasks (POS tagging, chunking and NER), and a separate setting for the other tasks. This is necessitated by the difference in model structure.

7.3 Fine-tuning

Most deep learning-based models backpropagate into the word embeddings used so as to fine tune them to the task at hand. This is a realistic setting in which to examine the performance of word embeddings, in their capacity as an initialization for the various tasks. In contrast, disallowing backpropagation into the embeddings allows us to determine the amount of syntactic or semantic information inherently present in the embeddings. As such, we propose reporting accuracies attained in both these settings.

8 Practical details

Evaluation takes place on the web site `http://www.veceval.com`. It is assumed that the user will train word embeddings to be evaluated, using the corpus provided on the website. The sentence and phrase embeddings used in the evaluation are produced by composing these given word embeddings. The user is required to prepare a gzipped text file, containing the word embeddings to be evaluated, in a simple format specified on the website. When the file is uploaded to the website, evaluation will begin. Once the evaluation is complete, a link to a report of the embeddings' performance appears on the homepage.

It is expected that the evaluation will take a few hours. For example, the best performing hyperparameters on the baseline embeddings result in a running time of 4 hours and 24 minutes.

9 Conclusion

We have presented a proposal for a fair and replicable evaluation for word embeddings. We plan to make this evaluation available as a script, allowing it to be run on new embeddings. It is our hope that this benchmark will enable extrinsic evaluations to be compared in a more interpretable way.

References

Ronan Collobert, Jason Weston, Léon Bottou, Michael Karlen, Koray Kavukcuoglu, and Pavel Kuksa. 2011. Natural language processing (almost) from scratch. *The Journal of Machine Learning Research*, 12:2493–2537.

Paramveer Dhillon, Jordan Rodu, Dean Foster, and Lyle Ungar. 2012. Two step cca: A new spectral method for estimating vector models of words. *arXiv preprint arXiv:1206.6403*.

Manaal Faruqui and Chris Dyer. 2014. Community evaluation and exchange of word vectors at wordvectors. org. In *Proceedings of the 52nd Annual Meeting of the Association for Computational Linguistics: System Demonstrations. Association for Computational Linguistics*.

Lev Finkelstein, Evgeniy Gabrilovich, Yossi Matias, Ehud Rivlin, Zach Solan, Gadi Wolfman, and Eytan Ruppin. 2001. Placing search in context: The concept revisited. In *Proceedings of the 10th international conference on World Wide Web*, pages 406–414. ACM.

Juri Ganitkevitch, Benjamin Van Durme, and Chris Callison-Burch. 2013. PPDB: The paraphrase database. In *HLT-NAACL*.

Omer Levy, Yoav Goldberg, and Ido Dagan. 2015. Improving distributional similarity with lessons learned from word embeddings. *Transactions of the Association for Computational Linguistics*, 3:211–225.

Xin Li and Dan Roth. 2006. Learning question classifiers: the role of semantic information. *Natural Language Engineering*, 12(03):229–249.

Christopher D Manning, Mihai Surdeanu, John Bauer, Jenny Finkel, Steven J Bethard, and David McClosky. 2014. The stanford corenlp natural language processing toolkit. In *Proceedings of 52nd Annual Meeting of the Association for Computational Linguistics: System Demonstrations*, pages 55–60.

Tomas Mikolov, Kai Chen, Greg Corrado, and Jeffrey Dean. 2013. Efficient estimation of word representations in vector space. *arXiv preprint arXiv:1301.3781*.

Jeffrey Pennington, Richard Socher, and Christopher D Manning. 2014. Glove: Global vectors for word representation. *Proceedings of the Empiricial Methods in Natural Language Processing (EMNLP 2014)*, 12:1532–1543.

Slav Petrov, Dipanjan Das, and Ryan McDonald. 2012. A universal part-of-speech tagset. In *Proceedings of LREC*, May.

Tobias Schnabel, Igor Labutov, David Mimno, and Thorsten Joachims. 2015. Evaluation methods for unsupervised word embeddings. In *Proceedings of the Conference on Empirical Methods in Natural Language Processing (EMNLP)*.

Erik F Tjong Kim Sang and Sabine Buchholz. 2000. Introduction to the CoNLL-2000 shared task: Chunking. In *CoNLL*.

Erik F Tjong Kim Sang and Fien De Meulder. 2003. Introduction to the CoNLL-2003 shared task: Language-independent named entity recognition. In *HLT-NAACL*.

Kristina Toutanova, Dan Klein, Christopher D Manning, and Yoram Singer. 2003. Feature-rich part-of-speech tagging with a cyclic dependency network. In *Proceedings of the 2003 Conference of the North American Chapter of the Association for Computational Linguistics on Human Language Technology-Volume 1*, pages 173–180.

Story Cloze Evaluator: Vector Space Representation Evaluation by Predicting What Happens Next

Nasrin Mostafazadeh[1], Lucy Vanderwende[2], Wen-tau Yih[2], Pushmeet Kohli[2], James Allen[1,3]

1 University of Rochester, 2 Microsoft Research, 3 The Institute for Human & Machine Cognition

`{nasrinm, james}@cs.rochester.edu`, `{lucyv, scottyih, pkohli}@microsoft.com`

Abstract

The main intrinsic evaluation for vector space representation has been focused on textual similarity, where the task is to predict how semantically similar two words or sentences are. We propose a novel framework, Story Cloze Evaluator, for evaluating vector representations which goes beyond textual similarity and captures the notion of predicting what should happen next given a context. This evaluation methodology is *simple to run, scalable, reproducible by the community, non-subjective, 100% agreeable by human, and challenging to the state-of-the-art models*, which makes it a promising new framework for further investment of the representation learning community.

1 Introduction

There has been a surge of work in the vector representation research in the past few years. While one could evaluate a given vector representation (embedding) on various down-stream applications, it is time-consuming at both implementation and runtime, which gives rise to focusing on an intrinsic evaluation. The intrinsic evaluation has been mostly focused on textual similarity where the task is to predict how semantically similar two words/sentences are, which is evaluated against the gold human similarity scores.

It has been shown that semantic similarity tasks do not accurately measure the effectiveness of an embedding in the other down-stream tasks (Schnabel et al., 2015; Tsvetkov et al., 2015). Furthermore, human annotation of similarity at sentence-level without any underlying context can be subjective, resulting in lower inter-annotator agreement and hence a less reliable evaluation method.

There has not been any standardized intrinsic evaluation for the quality of sentence and document-level vector representations beyond textual similarity[1]. There is therefore a crucial need for new ways of evaluating semantic representations of language which capture other linguistic phenomena.

In this paper we propose a new proxy task, Story Cloze Test, for measuring the quality of vector space representations for generic language understanding and commonsense reasoning. In this task, given a four-sentence story (called the context) and two alternative endings to the story, the system is tasked with choosing the right ending. We propose the following Story Cloze Evaluator modules: (1) Given an embedding of a four-sentence story (the context) and two alternative ending sentences, this module rewards the system if the embedding of the context is closer to the right ending than the wrong ending. (2) Given the embedding for each of the four sentences and each of the two alternatives, this module uses the trajectory of the four vectors to predict the embedding of the fifth sentence. Then the system is rewarded if the predicted vector is closer to the right ending than the wrong ending.

A vector representation that achieves a high score according to the Story Cloze Evaluator is demonstrating some level of language and narrative understanding. We describe the Story Cloze Test in Section 2, where we show that this test is scalable, non-subjective and 100% agreeable by human. We further describe our evaluation methodology in Section 3. As with any evaluation framework, we expect the setup to be modified over time, the updates of which can be followed through `http://`

---

[1] Examples of this include the semantic relatedness (SICK) dataset (Marelli et al., 2014), where given two sentences, the task is to produce a score of how semantically related these sentences are

Proceedings of the 1st Workshop on Evaluating Vector Space Representations for NLP, pages 24–29,
Berlin, Germany, August 12, 2016. ©2016 Association for Computational Linguistics

2 Story Cloze Test: Predicting What Happens Next

Representation and learning of commonsense knowledge is one of the foundational problems for enabling deep language understanding. This issue is the most challenging for understanding casual and correlational relationships between events, and predicting what happens next. A recent framework for evaluating story and script[2] understanding (Schank and Abelson, 1977) is the 'Story Cloze Test' (Mostafazadeh et al., 2016), where given two alternative endings to a four-sentence story (the context), a system is tasked with choosing the right ending. Table 1 shows a few example instances of the Story Cloze Test[3].

Although the Story Cloze Test was initially proposed to evaluate story understanding and script learning capabilities of a system, we see it as a perfect fit for intrinsic evaluation of vector space representation at sentence and paragraph level. The Story Cloze Test is unique in requiring a system to demonstrate generic commonsense understanding about stereotypical causal and temporal relations between daily events, making it a unique proxy task for vector space representation at sentence and paragraph level.

Story Cloze Test looks similar to language modeling at sentence level. However, predicting an ending to a story is less subjective and more deterministic than only predicting the next sentence. Experimental evaluation has shown (Mostafazadeh et al., 2016) that huamn performs 100% on this task, which makes it a very reliable test framework. Moreover, evaluation results have shown that a host of state-of-the-art models struggle to achieve a high score on this test [4], which makes the task even more compelling for the representation learning community to focus on.

2.1 Crowdsourcing Story Cloze Test

Story Cloze Test dataset can be easily scaled to hundreds of thousands of instances by crowdsourcing. The crowdsourcing starts from sampling complete five-sentence stories from the ROCStories corpus. This corpus is a collection of ∼50,000 crowdsourced short commonsense everyday stories [5], each of which has the following major characterisics: (1) is realistic and non-fictional, (2) has a clear beginning and ending where something happens in between, (3) does not include anything irrelevant to the core story. These stories are full of stereotypical causal and temporal relations between events, making them a great resource for commonsense reasoning and generic language understanding.

The crowdsourcing process continues as follows: given a complete five-sentence story, the fifth sentence is dropped and only the first four sentences (the context) are shown to the crowd workers. For each context, a worker was asked to write a 'right ending' and a 'wrong ending'. The workers were prompted to write 'wrong ending' which satisfies two conditions: (1) The sentence should follow up the story by sharing at least one of the characters of the story, and (2) The sentence should be entirely realistic and sensible when read in isolation. These conditions make sure that the Story Cloze Test cases are not trivial.

Quality Control. The accuracy of the Story Cloze test set plays a crucial role in propelling the research community towards the right direction. A two-step quality control step makes sure that there are no vague or boundary cases in the test set. First, the initially collected Story Cloze Test cases are compiled into two sets of full five-sentence stories. Then for each five-sentence story, independently, three crowd workers are tasked to verify whether or not the given sequence of five sentences makes sense as a meaningful and coherent story, rating within $\{-1, 0, 1\}$. Then, only the initial test cases which get three ratings of 1 for their 'right ending' compilation and three ratings of -1 for their 'wrong ending' compilation are included in the final dataset. This process ensures that there are no boundary case of vague, incoherent, or hard to follow stories, making human performance of 100% accuracy possible.

Data Split. Any collection of Story Cloze Test instances will be split into validation and test sets[6], where the test set will be blind and not accessible by the systems under evaluation. There is cur-

---

[2]Scripts represent structured knowledge about stereotypical event sequences together with their participants, e.g., {X kills Y, Y dies, X gets detained}.

[3]More examples can be found here: http://cs.rochester.edu/nlp/rocstories/

[4]The best performing system based on Deep Structured Semantic Model (DSSM) (Huang et al., 2013) performs with the accuracy of 58%, where a random baseline achieves 50%.

[5]These stories can be found via http://cs.rochester.edu/nlp/rocstories

[6]We also consider providing a designated training set, however, different models can choose to use any resources for training.

Context	Right Ending	Wrong Ending
Karen was assigned a roommate her first year of college. Her roommate asked her to go to a nearby city for a concert. Karen agreed happily. The show was absolutely exhilarating.	Karen became good friends with her roommate.	Karen hated her roommate.
Sarah had been dreaming of visiting Europe for years. She had finally saved enough for the trip. She landed in Spain and traveled east across the continent. She didn't like how different everything was.	Sarah decided that she preferred her home over Europe.	Sarah then decided to move to Europe.
Jim got his first credit card in college. He didn't have a job so he bought everything on his card. After he graduated he amounted a $10,000 debt. Jim realized that he was foolish to spend so much money.	Jim decided to devise a plan for repayment.	Jim decided to open another credit card.
Gina misplaced her phone at her grandparents. It wasn't anywhere in the living room. She realized she was in the car before. She grabbed her dad's keys and ran outside.	She didn't want her phone anymore.	She found her phone in the car.
When I first moved into my house, I didn't know my neighbors. While mowing one day, I found a kickball in my yard. I felt this was the perfect opportunity to meet my neighbors. I grabbed the ball and went next door to return it.	They were very friendly and appreciated it.	I threw the kickball through their closed window.
Amber had a lot of things to do this Sunday. She made a list of all the places she needed to go. She hurried to get ready. She was worried that she would not have enough time.	Amber was so hurried that she left the list at home.	Amber enjoyed a relaxing two hour brunch.
Tim was entering a baking contest. He decided to make his famous donuts. He made a big batch and entered them into the contest. The judges thought they were delicious.	Tim won the baking contest.	The judges vomited from the taste of the donuts.

Table 1: Example Story Cloze Test instances.

rently 3,744 instances of Story Cloze Test[7] that showcase our desired quality for the larger dataset.

3 Story Cloze Evaluator

There are various ways we can use Story Cloze Test for evaluating an embedding model at paragraph and sentence level. We propose the following alternatives.

3.1 Joint Paragraph and Sentence Level Evaluator

For this evaluator, a system should have two different modules for embedding either an alternative (a sentence) or a context (a paragraph), which ideally should be trained jointly. The evaluator works as follows: given the vector representations of the two alternative endings and the four-sentence context as a whole (Figure 1), it rewards the embedding model if the context's embedding is closer to the right ending embedding than the wrong ending. The closeness can be measured via cosine similarity of the embeddings.

This method evaluates joint paragraph-level and sentence-level vector representations, where all the representations are projected into the same vector space. Representing semantics of a paragraph as a vector is a major unresolved issue in the field, requiring its own detailed discussions.

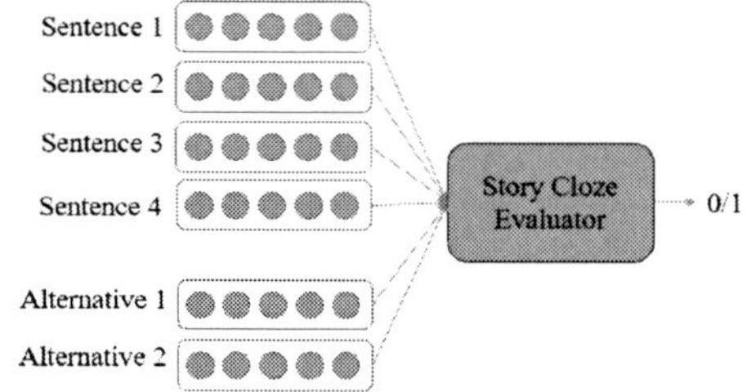

Figure 1: Sentence-level stroy cloze evaluator.

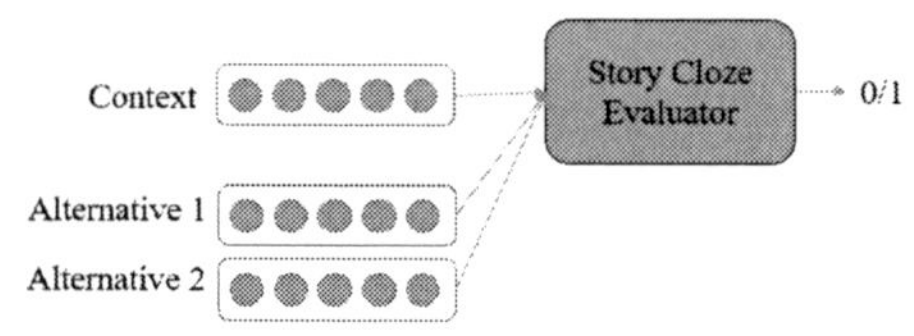

Figure 2: Joint paragraph and sentence level story cloze evaluator.

Here, we represent a paragraph according to what should happen next, which can be beneficial for various generic language comprehension frameworks. Deferring the representation of the context paragraph to the system under evaluation, makes it possible to use various sequence modeling techniques, among others, for representing the context.

---

[7]Accessible through http://cs.rochester.edu/nlp/rocstories/.

3.2 Sentence-level Evaluator

For this evaluator, the embedding should be at sentence-level. The evaluator works as follows: given the vector representations for each of the four sentences and the two alternative endings (Figure 2), the evaluator component uses the trajectory of the four sentences to predict the embedding of the ending sentences. Then the embedding model is rewarded if the predicted embedding is closer to the right ending than the wrong ending.

Given that the evaluator module should be simple and deterministic, we do not want to use any learning components inside the evaluator. Hence, we need a simple and deterministic procedure for predicting the ending embedding. There are different vector operations that can be used for this purpose. Addition operation is one option, however, addition is commutative whereas the relative temporal ordering of the sentences in a story is not. Taking into account the temporal progression of a story, we propose to use the distance vector between adjacent sentences: for a given context of sentences a, b, c, d, we need to predict the distance vector $e - d$ which then predicts the ending vector e. This can be achieved using a basic multivariable curve fitting among the distance vectors of adjacent sentences, e.g., using linear least squares error. Of course the validity of this technique, or any other ones trying to compose the sentence vectors into one vector, requires large scale testing and a comprehensive analysis. As with the other vector space evaluations such as word analogy, further details about this evaluation setup should be finalized after future experiments.

3.3 Baselines

We present preliminary results on evaluating basic embedding models on Story Cloze Test. Here we use the test set split of the available Story Cloze Test dataset, comprising of 1,872 instances. We experiment with the following models:

1. Word2Vec: Encodes a given sentence or paragraph with its average per-word word2vec (Mikolov et al., 2013) embedding.

6. Skip-thoughts Model: A Sentence2Vec embedding (Kiros et al., 2015) which models the semantic space of novels. This model is trained on the 'BookCorpus' (Zhu et al., 2015) (containing 16 different genres) of over 11,000 books. We retrieve the skip-thoughts embedding for the two alternatives and the four sentences, representing the context as the average embedding of the four sentences.

9. Deep Structured Semantic Model (DSSM): This model (Huang et al., 2013) learns to project two different inputs into the same vector space, consisting of two separate embedding modules. It is trained on ROCStories corpus, consisting of 49,255 stories. We retrieve the DSSM embedding for the two alternatives and the context of four-sentences.

For this evaluation we use the joint paragraph and sentence level evaluator module (Section 3.1). Table 2 shows the results, where 'constant' model simply chooses the first alternative constantly. As the results show, there is a wide-gap between human performance and the best performing baseline, making this test a challenging new framework for the community.

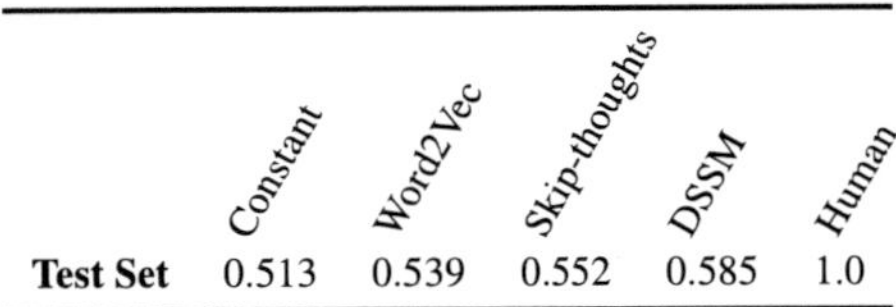

Test Set	Constant	Word2Vec	Skip-thoughts	DSSM	Human
	0.513	0.539	0.552	0.585	1.0

Table 2: The preliminary results on Story Cloze Test.

4 Major Characteristics

Our proposed method for representation learning captures the linguistic and semantic property of scripts, which has not been captured by any of the other many existing intrinsic benchmarks. Our method goes beyond capturing human ratings of the similarity of two words or sentences, and towards a more interesting linguistic phenomena of capturing 'what is next', which can potentially affect many other downstream applications.

Our evaluation method is very simple to implement and is based on a high quality resource for accurate evaluation. The human agreement on choosing the right ending of the Story Cloze Test is 100%, making the evaluation schema reliable for making further meaningful progress in the field. Story Cloze evaluation together with the dataset are accurately reproducible by the community. Furthermore, hundreds of thousands of Story Cloze instances can be crowdsourced to non-expert workers in the crowd, making the evaluation scalable.

Although the embeddings models will be trained for the specific application of predicting the ending to a given short story, their impact is not isolated to narrative understanding since they capture the generic characteristics of a sequence of logically related sentences. Hence, we can hypothesize that the context vector representations which perform well on our method can be used as features in other language understanding and commonsense reasoning tasks, e.g., reading comprehension tests (Hermann et al., 2015; Weston et al., 2015; Richardson et al., 2013) which often require a system to infer additional events given a premise paragraph. Of course, demonstrating that this knowledge is indeed transferable well among different language tasks will be the next step. However, given that the Story Cloze Test is designed as a test of a model's ability to understand and reason with language in a fairly general sense, it does seem plausible that success on Story Cloze Test can translate into success in other downstream language understanding tasks.

5 Conclusion

In this paper we propose a new method for vector representation evaluation which captures a model's capability in predicting what happens next given a context. Our evaluation methodology and the dataset are simple, easily replicable and scalable by crowdsourcing for quickly expanding the resource. Human performs with an accuracy of 100% on this task, which further promises the validity of benchmarking the progress in the field using this evaluation method.

Representation learning community's focus on commonsense reasoning and inferential frameworks can help the research community to make further progress in this crucial area of NLP and AI. We expect the embedding models which somehow leverage commonsense knowledge, perhaps in the form of narrative structures or other knowledge resources, to perform better on our evaluation framework. We believe that a vector representation that achieves a high score according to the Story Cloze Evaluator is demonstrating some level of commonsense reasoning and deeper language understanding.

Acknowledgments

We would like to thank the anonymous reviewers for their helpful comments. This work was supported in part by Grant W911NF-15-1-0542 with the US Defense Advanced Research Projects Agency (DARPA), the Army Research Office (ARO) and the Office of Naval Research (ONR).

References

Karl Moritz Hermann, Tomas Kocisky, Edward Grefenstette, Lasse Espeholt, Will Kay, Mustafa Suleyman, and Phil Blunsom. 2015. Teaching machines to read and comprehend. In C. Cortes, N. D. Lawrence, D. D. Lee, M. Sugiyama, and R. Garnett, editors, *Advances in Neural Information Processing Systems 28*, pages 1693–1701. Curran Associates, Inc.

Po-Sen Huang, Xiaodong He, Jianfeng Gao, Li Deng, Alex Acero, and Larry Heck. 2013. Learning deep structured semantic models for web search using clickthrough data. In *Proceedings of the 22Nd ACM International Conference on Information & Knowledge Management*, CIKM '13, pages 2333–2338, New York, NY, USA. ACM.

Ryan Kiros, Yukun Zhu, Ruslan Salakhutdinov, Richard S Zemel, Antonio Torralba, Raquel Urtasun, and Sanja Fidler. 2015. Skip-thought vectors. *NIPS*.

Marco Marelli, Stefano Menini, Marco Baroni, Luisa Bentivogli, Raffaella Bernardi, and Roberto Zamparelli. 2014. A sick cure for the evaluation of compositional distributional semantic models. In Nicoletta Calzolari (Conference Chair), Khalid Choukri, Thierry Declerck, Hrafn Loftsson, Bente Maegaard, Joseph Mariani, Asuncion Moreno, Jan Odijk, and Stelios Piperidis, editors, *Proceedings of the Ninth International Conference on Language Resources and Evaluation (LREC'14)*, Reykjavik, Iceland, may. European Language Resources Association (ELRA).

Tomas Mikolov, Ilya Sutskever, Kai Chen, Gregory S. Corrado, and Jeffrey Dean. 2013. Distributed representations of words and phrases and their compositionality. In *Advances in Neural Information Processing Systems 26: 27th Annual Conference on Neural Information Processing Systems 2013. Proceedings of a meeting held December 5-8, 2013, Lake Tahoe, Nevada, United States.*, pages 3111–3119.

Nasrin Mostafazadeh, Nathanael Chambers, Xiaodong He, Devi Parikh, Dhruv Batra, Lucy Vanderwende, Pushmeet Kohli, and James Allen. 2016. A corpus and cloze evaluation for deeper understanding of commonsense stories. In *Proceedings of NAACL HLT*, San Diego, California. Association for Computational Linguistics.

Matthew Richardson, Christopher J. C. Burges, and Erin Renshaw. 2013. Mctest: A challenge dataset for the open-domain machine comprehension of text. In *EMNLP*, pages 193–203. ACL.

Roger C. Schank and Robert P. Abelson. 1977. *Scripts, Plans, Goals and Understanding: an Inquiry into Human Knowledge Structures*. L. Erlbaum, Hillsdale, NJ.

Tobias Schnabel, Igor Labutov, David Mimno, and Thorsten Joachims. 2015. Evaluation methods for unsupervised word embeddings. In *Proceedings of the Conference on Empirical Methods in Natural Language Processing (EMNLP)*, pages 298–307.

Yulia Tsvetkov, Manaal Faruqui, Wang Ling, Guillaume Lample, and Chris Dyer. 2015. Evaluation of word vector representations by subspace alignment. In *Proceedings of EMNLP*.

Jason Weston, Antoine Bordes, Sumit Chopra, and Tomas Mikolov. 2015. Towards ai-complete question answering: A set of prerequisite toy tasks. *CoRR*, abs/1502.05698.

Yukun Zhu, Ryan Kiros, Richard Zemel, Ruslan Salakhutdinov, Raquel Urtasun, Antonio Torralba, and Sanja Fidler. 2015. Aligning books and movies: Towards story-like visual explanations by watching movies and reading books. In *arXiv preprint arXiv:1506.06724*.

Problems With Evaluation of Word Embeddings Using Word Similarity Tasks

Manaal Faruqui[1] **Yulia Tsvetkov**[1] **Pushpendre Rastogi**[2] **Chris Dyer**[1]
[1]Language Technologies Institute, Carnegie Mellon University
[2]Department of Computer Science, Johns Hopkins University
{mfaruqui,ytsvetko,cdyer}@cs.cmu.edu, pushpendre@jhu.edu

Abstract

Lacking standardized extrinsic evaluation methods for vector representations of words, the NLP community has relied heavily on *word similarity* tasks as a proxy for intrinsic evaluation of word vectors. Word similarity evaluation, which correlates the distance between vectors and human judgments of "semantic similarity" is attractive, because it is computationally inexpensive and fast. In this paper we present several problems associated with the evaluation of word vectors on word similarity datasets, and summarize existing solutions. Our study suggests that the use of word similarity tasks for evaluation of word vectors is not sustainable and calls for further research on evaluation methods.

1 Introduction

Despite the ubiquity of word vector representations in NLP, there is no consensus in the community on what is the best way for evaluating word vectors. The most popular intrinsic evaluation task is the *word similarity* evaluation. In word similarity evaluation, a list of pairs of words along with their similarity rating (as judged by human annotators) is provided. The task is to measure how well the notion of word similarity according to humans is captured by the word vector representations. Table 1 shows some word pairs along with their similarity judgments from WS-353 (Finkelstein et al., 2002), a popular word similarity dataset.

Let a, b be two words, and $\mathbf{a}, \mathbf{b} \in \mathbb{R}^D$ be their corresponding word vectors in a D-dimensional vector space. Word similarity in the vector-space can be obtained by computing the cosine similar-

Word$_1$	Word$_2$	Similarity score [0,10]
love	sex	6.77
stock	jaguar	0.92
money	cash	9.15
development	issue	3.97
lad	brother	4.46

Table 1: Sample word pairs along with their human similarity judgment from WS-353.

ity between the word vectors of a pair of words:

$$\mathrm{cosine}(\mathbf{a}, \mathbf{b}) = \frac{\mathbf{a} \cdot \mathbf{b}}{\|\mathbf{a}\| \, \|\mathbf{b}\|} \qquad (1)$$

where, $\|\mathbf{a}\|$ is the ℓ_2-norm of the vector, and $\mathbf{a} \cdot \mathbf{b}$ is the dot product of the two vectors. Once the vector-space similarity between the words is computed, we obtain the lists of pairs of words sorted according to vector-space similarity, and human similarity. Computing Spearman's correlation (Myers and Well, 1995) between these ranked lists provides some insight into how well the learned word vectors capture intuitive notions of word similarity.

Word similarity evaluation is attractive, because it is computationally inexpensive and fast, leading to faster prototyping and development of word vector models. The origin of word similarity tasks can be tracked back to Rubenstein and Goodenough (1965) who constructed a list of 65 word pairs with annotations of human similarity judgment. They created this dataset to validate the veracity of the distributional hypothesis (Harris, 1954) according to which the meaning of words is evidenced by the context they occur in. They found a positive correlation between contextual similarity and human-annotated similarity of word pairs. Since then, the lack of a standard evaluation method for word vectors has led to the creation of several *ad hoc* word similarity datasets. Table 2 provides a list of such benchmarks obtained from wordvectors.org (Faruqui and Dyer, 2014a).

30

Proceedings of the 1st Workshop on Evaluating Vector Space Representations for NLP, pages 30–35,
Berlin, Germany, August 12, 2016. ©2016 Association for Computational Linguistics

Dataset	Word pairs	Reference
RG	65	Rubenstein and Goodenough (1965)
MC	30	Miller and Charles (1991)
WS-353	353	Finkelstein et al. (2002)
YP-130	130	Yang and Powers (2006)
MTurk-287	287	Radinsky et al. (2011)
MTurk-771	771	Halawi et al. (2012)
MEN	3000	Bruni et al. (2012)
RW	2034	Luong et al. (2013)
Verb	144	Baker et al. (2014)
SimLex	999	Hill et al. (2014)

Table 2: Word similarity datasets.

In this paper, we give a comprehensive analysis of the problems that are associated with the evaluation of word vector representations using word similarity tasks.[1] We survey existing literature to construct a list of such problems and also summarize existing solutions to some of the problems. Our findings suggest that word similarity tasks are not appropriate for evaluating word vector representations, and call for further research on better evaluation methods

2 Problems

We now discuss the major issues with evaluation of word vectors using word similarity tasks, and present existing solutions (if available) to address them.

2.1 Subjectivity of the task

The notion of word similarity is subjective and is often confused with relatedness. For example, *cup*, and *coffee* are related to each other, but not similar. *Coffee* refers to a plant (a living organism) or a hot brown drink, whereas *cup* is a man-made object, which contains liquids, often coffee. Nevertheless, *cup* and *coffee* are rated more similar than pairs such as *car* and *train* in WS-353 (Finkelstein et al., 2002). Such anomalies are also found in recently constructed datasets like MEN (Bruni et al., 2012). Thus, such datasets unfairly penalize word vector models that capture the fact that *cup* and *coffee* are dissimilar.

In an attempt to address this limitation, Agirre et al. (2009) divided WS-353 into two sets containing word pairs exhibiting only either similarity or relatedness. Recently, Hill et al. (2014) constructed a new word similarity dataset (SimLex), which captures the degree of similarity between words, and related words are considered dissimilar. Even though it is useful to separate the concept of similarity and relatedness, it is not clear as to which one should the word vector models be expected to capture.

2.2 Semantic or task-specific similarity?

Distributional word vector models capture some aspect of word co-occurrence statistics of the words in a language (Levy and Goldberg, 2014b; Levy et al., 2015). Therefore, to the extent these models produce semantically coherent representations, it can be seen as evidence of the distributional hypothesis of Harris (1954). Thus, word embeddings like Skip-gram, CBOW, Glove, LSA (Turney and Pantel, 2010; Mikolov et al., 2013a; Pennington et al., 2014) which are trained on word co-occurrence counts can be expected to capture semantic word similarity, and hence can be evaluated on word similarity tasks.

Word vector representations which are trained as part of a neural network to solve a particular task (apart from word co-occurrence prediction) are called distributed word embeddings (Collobert and Weston, 2008), and they are task-specific in nature. These embeddings capture task-specific word similarity, for example, if the task is of POS tagging, two nouns *cat* and *man* might be considered similar by the model, even though they are not semantically similar. Thus, evaluating such task-specific word embeddings on word similarity can unfairly penalize them. This raises the question: what kind of word similarity should be captured by the model?

2.3 No standardized splits & overfitting

To obtain generalizable machine learning models, it is necessary to make sure that they do not overfit to a given dataset. Thus, the datasets are usually partitioned into a training, development and test set on which the model is trained, tuned and finally evaluated, respectively (Manning and Schütze, 1999). Existing word similarity datasets are not partitioned into training, development and test sets. Therefore, optimizing the word vectors to perform better at a word similarity task implic-

---

[1] An alternative to correlation-based word similarity evaluation is the *word analogy* task, where the task is to find the missing word b^* in the relation: a is to a^* as b is to b^*, where a, a^* are related by the same relation as a, a^*. For example, $king : man :: queen : woman$. Mikolov et al. (2013b) showed that this problem can be solved using the vector offset method: $b^* \approx b - a + a^*$. Levy and Goldberg (2014a) show that solving this equation is equivalent to computing a linear combination of word similarities between the query word b^*, with the given words a, b, and b^*. Thus, the results we present in this paper naturally extend to the word analogy tasks.

itly *tunes on the test set* and overfits the vectors to the task. On the other hand, if researchers decide to perform their own splits of the data, the results obtained across different studies can be incomparable. Furthermore, the average number of word pairs in the word similarity datasets is small (≈ 781, cf. Table 2), and partitioning them further into smaller subsets may produce unstable results.

We now present some of the solutions suggested by previous work to avoid overfitting of word vectors to word similarity tasks. Faruqui and Dyer (2014b), and Lu et al. (2015) evaluate the word embeddings exclusively on word similarity and word analogy tasks. Faruqui and Dyer (2014b) tune their embedding on one word similarity task and evaluate them on all other tasks. This ensures that their vectors are being evaluated on held-out datasets. Lu et al. (2015) propose to directly evaluate the generalization of a model by measuring the performance of a single model on a large gamut of tasks. This evaluation can be performed in two different ways: (1) choose the hyperparameters with best average performance across all tasks, (2) choose the hyperparameters that beat the baseline vectors on most tasks.[2] By selecting the hyperparameters that perform well across a range of tasks, these methods ensure that the obtained vectors are generalizable. Stratos et al. (2015) divided each word similarity dataset individually into tuning and test set and reported results on the test set.

2.4 Low correlation with extrinsic evaluation

Word similarity evaluation measures how well the notion of word similarity according to humans is captured in the vector-space word representations. Word vectors that can capture word similarity might be expected to perform well on tasks that require a notion of explicit semantic similarity between words like paraphrasing, entailment. However, it has been shown that no strong correlation is found between the performance of word vectors on word similarity and extrinsic evaluation NLP tasks like text classification, parsing, sentiment analysis (Tsvetkov et al., 2015; Schnabel et al., 2015).[3] An absence of strong correlation between the word similarity evaluation and downstream tasks calls for alternative approaches to evaluation.

2.5 Absence of statistical significance

There has been a consistent omission of statistical significance for measuring the difference in performance of two vector models on word similarity tasks. Statistical significance testing is important for validating metric gains in NLP (Berg-Kirkpatrick et al., 2012; Søgaard et al., 2014), specifically while solving non-convex objectives where results obtained due to optimizer instability can often lead to incorrect inferences (Clark et al., 2011). The problem of statistical significance in word similarity evaluation was first systematically addressed by Shalaby and Zadrozny (2015), who used Steiger's test (Steiger, 1980)[4] to compute how significant the difference between rankings produced by two different models is against the gold ranking. However, their method needs explicit ranked list of words produced by the models and cannot work when provided only with the correlation ratio of each model with the gold ranking. This problem was solved by Rastogi et al. (2015), which we describe next.

Rastogi et al. (2015) observed that the improvements shown on small word similarity task datasets by previous work were insignificant. We now briefly describe the method presented by them to compute statistical significance for word similarity evaluation. Let A and B be the rankings produced by two word vector models over a list of words pairs, and T be the human annotated ranking. Let r_{AT}, r_{BT} and r_{AB} denote the Spearman's correlation between $A : T$, $B : T$ and $A : B$ resp. and $\hat{r}_{AT}$, $\hat{r}_{BT}$ and $\hat{r}_{AB}$ be their empirical estimates. Rastogi et al. (2015) introduce $\sigma_{p_0}^r$ as the minimum required difference for significance (MRDS) which satisfies the following:

$$(r_{AB} < r) \wedge (|\hat{r}_{BT} - \hat{r}_{AT}| < \sigma_{p_0}^r) \implies pval > p_0 \tag{2}$$

Here $pval$ is the probability of the test statistic under the null hypothesis that $r_{AT} = r_{BT}$ found using the Steiger's test. The above conditional ensures that if the empirical difference between the rank correlations of the scores of the competing methods to the gold ratings is less than $\sigma_{p_0}^r$ then either the true correlation between the competing methods is greater than r, or the null hypothesis of no difference has p-value greater than p_0. $\sigma_{p_0}^r$

---

[2] Baseline vectors can be any off-the-shelf vector models.

[3] In these studies, extrinsic evaluation tasks are those tasks that use the dimensions of word vectors as features in a machine learning model. The model learns weights for how important these features are for the extrinsic task.

[4] A quick tutorial on Steiger's test & scripts: `http://www.philippsinger.info/?p=347`

depends on the size of the dataset, p_0 and r and Rastogi et al. (2015) present its values for common word similarity datasets. Reporting statistical significance in this way would help estimate the differences between word vector models.

2.6 Frequency effects in cosine similarity

The most common method of measuring the similarity between two words in the vector-space is to compute the cosine similarity between the corresponding word vectors. Cosine similarity implicitly measures the similarity between two unit-length vectors (eq. 1). This prevents any biases in favor of frequent words which are longer as they are updated more often during training (Turian et al., 2010).

Ideally, if the geometry of embedding space is primarily driven by semantics, the relatively small number of frequent words should be evenly distributed through the space, while large number of rare words should cluster around related, but more frequent words. However, it has been shown that vector-spaces contain *hubs*, which are vectors that are close to a large number of other vectors in the space (Radovanović et al., 2010). This problem manifests in word vector-spaces in the form of words that have high cosine similarity with a large number of other words (Dinu et al., 2014). Schnabel et al. (2015) further refine this *hubness* problem to show that there exists a power-law relationship between the frequency-rank[5] of a word and the frequency-rank of its neighbors. Specifically, they showed that the average rank of the 1000 nearest neighbors of a word follows:

$$\text{nn-rank} \approx 1000 \cdot \text{word-rank}^{0.17} \qquad (3)$$

This shows that pairs of words which have similar frequency will be closer in the vector-space, thus showing higher word similarity than they should according to their word meaning. Even though newer datasets of word similarity sample words from different frequency bins (Luong et al., 2013; Hill et al., 2014), this still does not solve the problem that cosine similarity in the vector-space gets polluted by frequency-based effects. Different distance normalization schemes have been proposed to downplay the frequency/hubness effect when computing nearest neighbors in the vector space (Dinu et al., 2014; Tomašev et al., 2011),

---

[5]The rank of a word in vocabulary of the corpus sorted in decreasing order of frequency.

but their applicability as an absolute measure of distance for word similarity tasks still needs to investigated.

2.7 Inability to account for polysemy

Many words have more than one meaning in a language. For example, the word *bank* can either correspond to a financial institution or to the land near a river. However in WS-353, *bank* is given a similarity score of $8.5/10$ to *money*, signifying that *bank* is a financial institution. Such an assumption of one sense per word is prevalent in many of the existing word similarity tasks, and it can incorrectly penalize a word vector model for capturing a specific sense of the word absent in the word similarity task.

To account for sense-specific word similarity, Huang et al. (2012) introduced the Stanford contextual word similarity dataset (SCWS), in which the task is to compute similarity between two words given the contexts they occur in. For example, the words *bank* and *money* should have a low similarity score given the contexts: *"along the east <u>bank</u> of the river"*, and *"the basis of all <u>money</u> laundering"*. Using cues from the word's context, the correct word-sense can be identified and the appropriate word vector can be used. Unfortunately, word senses are also ignored by majority of the frequently used word vector models like Skip-gram and Glove. However, there has been progress on obtaining multiple vectors per word-type to account for different word-senses (Reisinger and Mooney, 2010; Huang et al., 2012; Neelakantan et al., 2014; Jauhar et al., 2015; Rothe and Schütze, 2015).

3 Conclusion

In this paper we have identified problems associated with word similarity evaluation of word vector models, and reviewed existing solutions wherever possible. Our study suggests that the use of word similarity tasks for evaluation of word vectors can lead to incorrect inferences and calls for further research on evaluation methods.

Until a better solution is found for intrinsic evaluation of word vectors, we suggest task-specific evaluation: word vector models should be compared on how well they can perform on a downstream NLP task. Although task-specific evaluation produces different rankings of word vector models for different tasks (Schnabel et al., 2015), this is not necessarily a problem because different vector models capture different types of information which can be more or less useful for a particular task.

References

Eneko Agirre, Enrique Alfonseca, Keith Hall, Jana Kravalova, Marius Paşca, and Aitor Soroa. 2009. A study on similarity and relatedness using distributional and wordnet-based approaches. In *Proc. of NAACL*.

Simon Baker, Roi Reichart, and Anna Korhonen. 2014. An unsupervised model for instance level subcategorization acquisition. In *Proc. of EMNLP*.

Taylor Berg-Kirkpatrick, David Burkett, and Dan Klein. 2012. An empirical investigation of statistical significance in nlp. In *Proc. of EMNLP*.

Elia Bruni, Gemma Boleda, Marco Baroni, and Nam-Khanh Tran. 2012. Distributional semantics in technicolor. In *Proc. of ACL*.

Jonathan H Clark, Chris Dyer, Alon Lavie, and Noah A Smith. 2011. Better hypothesis testing for statistical machine translation: Controlling for optimizer instability. In *Proc. of ACL*.

Ronan Collobert and Jason Weston. 2008. A unified architecture for natural language processing: deep neural networks with multitask learning. In *Proc. of ICML*.

Georgiana Dinu, Angeliki Lazaridou, and Marco Baroni. 2014. Improving zero-shot learning by mitigating the hubness problem. *arXiv preprint arXiv:1412.6568*.

Manaal Faruqui and Chris Dyer. 2014a. Community evaluation and exchange of word vectors at wordvectors.org. In *Proc. of ACL: System Demo*.

Manaal Faruqui and Chris Dyer. 2014b. Improving vector space word representations using multilingual correlation. In *Proc. of EACL*.

Lev Finkelstein, Evgeniy Gabrilovich, Yossi Matias, Ehud Rivlin, Zach Solan, Gadi Wolfman, and Eytan Ruppin. 2002. Placing search in context: The concept revisited. *ACM Transactions on Information Systems*, 20(1).

Guy Halawi, Gideon Dror, Evgeniy Gabrilovich, and Yehuda Koren. 2012. Large-scale learning of word relatedness with constraints. In *Proc. of SIGKDD*.

Zellig Harris. 1954. Distributional structure. *Word*, 10(23):146–162.

Felix Hill, Roi Reichart, and Anna Korhonen. 2014. Simlex-999: Evaluating semantic models with (genuine) similarity estimation. *CoRR*, abs/1408.3456.

Eric H Huang, Richard Socher, Christopher D Manning, and Andrew Y Ng. 2012. Improving word representations via global context and multiple word prototypes. In *Proc. of ACL*.

Sujay Kumar Jauhar, Chris Dyer, and Eduard Hovy. 2015. Ontologically grounded multi-sense representation learning for semantic vector space models. In *Proc. NAACL*.

Omer Levy and Yoav Goldberg. 2014a. Linguistic regularities in sparse and explicit word representations. In *Proc. of CoNLL*.

Omer Levy and Yoav Goldberg. 2014b. Neural word embedding as implicit matrix factorization. In *Proc. of NIPS*.

Omer Levy, Yoav Goldberg, and Ido Dagan. 2015. Improving distributional similarity with lessons learned from word embeddings. *TACL*, 3:211–225.

Ang Lu, Weiran Wang, Mohit Bansal, Kevin Gimpel, and Karen Livescu. 2015. Deep multilingual correlation for improved word embeddings. In *Proc. of NAACL*.

Minh-Thang Luong, Richard Socher, and Christopher D. Manning. 2013. Better word representations with recursive neural networks for morphology. In *Proc. of CoNLL*.

Christopher D. Manning and Hinrich Schütze. 1999. *Foundations of statistical natural language processing*. MIT Press, Cambridge, MA, USA.

Tomas Mikolov, Kai Chen, Greg Corrado, and Jeffrey Dean. 2013a. Efficient estimation of word representations in vector space. *arXiv preprint arXiv:1301.3781*.

Tomas Mikolov, Wen-tau Yih, and Geoffrey Zweig. 2013b. Linguistic regularities in continuous space word representations. In *Proc. of NAACL*.

George Miller and Walter Charles. 1991. Contextual correlates of semantic similarity. In *Language and Cognitive Processes*, pages 1–28.

Jerome L. Myers and Arnold D. Well. 1995. *Research Design & Statistical Analysis*. Routledge.

Arvind Neelakantan, Jeevan Shankar, Alexandre Passos, and Andrew McCallum. 2014. Efficient nonparametric estimation of multiple embeddings per word in vector space. In *Proc. of EMNLP*.

Jeffrey Pennington, Richard Socher, and Christopher D. Manning. 2014. Glove: Global vectors for word representation. In *Proc. of EMNLP*.

Kira Radinsky, Eugene Agichtein, Evgeniy Gabrilovich, and Shaul Markovitch. 2011. A word at a time: computing word relatedness using temporal semantic analysis. In *Proc. of WWW*.

Miloš Radovanović, Alexandros Nanopoulos, and Mirjana Ivanović. 2010. Hubs in space: Popular nearest neighbors in high-dimensional data. *The Journal of Machine Learning Research*, 11:2487–2531.

Pushpendre Rastogi, Benjamin Van Durme, and Raman Arora. 2015. Multiview lsa: Representation learning via generalized cca. In *Proc. of NAACL*.

Joseph Reisinger and Raymond J. Mooney. 2010. Multi-prototype vector-space models of word meaning. In *Proc. of NAACL*.

Sascha Rothe and Hinrich Schütze. 2015. Autoextend: Extending word embeddings to embeddings for synsets and lexemes. In *Proc. of ACL*.

Herbert Rubenstein and John B. Goodenough. 1965. Contextual correlates of synonymy. *Commun. ACM*, 8(10).

Tobias Schnabel, Igor Labutov, David Mimno, and Thorsten Joachims. 2015. Evaluation methods for unsupervised word embeddings. In *Proc. of EMNLP*.

Walid Shalaby and Wlodek Zadrozny. 2015. Measuring semantic relatedness using mined semantic analysis. *CoRR*, abs/1512.03465.

Anders Søgaard, Anders Johannsen, Barbara Plank, Dirk Hovy, and Héctor Martínez Alonso. 2014. What's in a p-value in nlp? In *Proc. of CoNLL*.

James H Steiger. 1980. Tests for comparing elements of a correlation matrix. *Psychological bulletin*, 87(2):245.

Karl Stratos, Michael Collins, and Daniel Hsu. 2015. Model-based word embeddings from decompositions of count matrices. In *Proc. of ACL*.

Nenad Tomašev, Miloš Radovanovic, Dunja Mladenic, and Mirjana Ivanovic. 2011. A probabilistic approach to nearest-neighbor classification: Naive hubness bayesian knn. In *Proc. of CIKM*.

Yulia Tsvetkov, Manaal Faruqui, Wang Ling, Guillaume Lample, and Chris Dyer. 2015. Evaluation of word vector representations by subspace alignment. In *Proc. of EMNLP*.

Joseph Turian, Lev Ratinov, and Yoshua Bengio. 2010. Word representations: a simple and general method for semi-supervised learning. In *Proc. of ACL*.

Peter D. Turney and Patrick Pantel. 2010. From frequency to meaning : Vector space models of semantics. *JAIR*, pages 141–188.

Dongqiang Yang and David M. W. Powers. 2006. Verb similarity on the taxonomy of wordnet. In *3rd International WordNet Conference*.

Intrinsic Evaluations of Word Embeddings: What Can We Do Better?

Anna Gladkova
Department of Language
and Information Sciences
The University of Tokyo
Tokyo, Japan

gladkova@phiz.c.u-tokyo.ac.jp

Aleksandr Drozd
Global Scientific Information
and Computing Center
Tokyo Institute of Technology
Tokyo, Japan

alex@smg.is.titech.ac.jp

Abstract

This paper presents an analysis of existing methods for the intrinsic evaluation of word embeddings. We show that the main methodological premise of such evaluations is "interpretability" of word embeddings: a "good" embedding produces results that make sense in terms of traditional linguistic categories. This approach is not only of limited practical use, but also fails to do justice to the strengths of distributional meaning representations. We argue for a shift from abstract ratings of word embedding "quality" to exploration of their strengths and weaknesses.

1 Introduction

The number of word embeddings is growing every year. A new model is typically evaluated across several tasks, and is considered an improvement if it achieves better accuracy than its predecessors. There are numerous real-use applications that can be used for this purpose, including named entity recognition (Guo et al., 2014), semantic role labeling (Chen et al., 2014), and syntactic parsing (Chen and Manning, 2014).

However, different applications rely on different aspects of word embeddings, and good performance in one application does not necessarily imply equally good performance on another. To avoid laborious evaluation across multiple extrinsic tests a number of intrinsic tasks are used. Ideally they would predict how a model performs in downstream applications. However, it has been shown that intrinsic and extrinsic scores do not always correlate (Tsvetkov et al., 2015; Schnabel et al., 2015).

This study discusses the methodology behind several existing intrinsic evaluations for word em-

beddings, showing that their chief premise is "interpretability" of a model as a measure of its quality. This approach has methodological issues, and it also ignores the unique feature of word embeddings - their ability to represent fluidity and fuzziness of meaning that is unattainable by traditional linguistic analysis. We argue for a shift from absolute ratings of word embeddings towards more exploratory evaluations that would aim not for generic scores, but for identification of strengths and weaknesses of embeddings, thus providing better predictions about their performance in downstream tasks.

2 Existing Intrinsic Evaluations

2.1 Word Similarity and Relatedness Tests

The term "semantic relatedness" is used to refer to any kind of semantic relation between words. The degree of semantic relatedness reflects the degree to which two words share attributes (Turney et al., 2010, p. 149). Similarity is defined by Turney as co-hyponymy (e.g. *car* and *bicycle*), whereas Hill et al. (2015) define it as "the similarity relation is exemplified by pairs of synonyms; words with identical referents" (e.g. *mug* and *cup*).

The widely used relatedness test sets include WordSim-353 (Finkelstein et al., 2002) and MEN (Bruni et al., 2014)[1]. The former contains 353 word pairs, and the latter - 3,000 word pairs with their relatedness ratings by human annotators. On the other hand, SimLex999 (Hill et al., 2015) specializes on semantic similarity.

The task in cases of both semantic relatedness and semantic similarity is to rate the semantic proximity of two words, usually with the cosine similarity metric. The "best" model is the one

---

[1]Note that both of these sets also include semantically similar words as a subset of semantic relatedness, e.g. "*cathedral, church*" in MEN and "*football, soccer*" in WordSim.

Proceedings of the 1st Workshop on Evaluating Vector Space Representations for NLP, pages 36–42,
Berlin, Germany, August 12, 2016. ©2016 Association for Computational Linguistics

that comes closest to the ratings of human annotators. Therefore these tests directly assesses interpretability of the model's output - to what extent it mimics human judgments of semantic relations.

The immediate problem with the similarity and relatedness tests is that distributional similarity conflates not only semantic similarity and relatedness, but also morphological relations and simply collocations, and it is not clear whether a model should generally score higher for preferring either of them. Specializing on one of these relations (Kiela et al., 2015) is certainly useful for specific downstream applications, but it would not make a word embedding either generally "good" or universally applicable.

Another concern is, traditionally, the (un)reliability of human linguistic judgements, which are subject to over 50 potential linguistic, psychological, and social confounds (Schutze, 1996). With Amazon Mechanical Turk, typically used to collect ratings, it is impossible to ensure that the participants are native speakers, to get accurate timing, or to control the environment in which they provide responses. Inter-annotator agreement provides an estimate of uniformity of the data, but, if there is a general problem, we would not detect it.

Semantic relatedness is particularly confusing to rate. Consider WordSim scores for hyponymy and hypernymy: *"money, dollar"* (8.42) vs *"tiger, mammal"* (6.85). There is no theoretical ground for rating either semantic relation higher; subjects are likely to rank based on frequency, prototypicality, and speed of association, and not "semantic relatedness" *per se*.

It is also worth mentioning that word embeddings vary in the amount of frequency information that they encode, and frequency can confound estimates of relatedness (Schnabel et al., 2015; Wilson and Schakel, 2015). Thus, depending on the embedding, results of tests such as WordSim need to be considered in the context of the corpus.

2.2 Comparative Intrinsic Evaluation

The comparative intrinsic evaluation for word embeddings was introduced by Schnabel et al. (2015). Several models are trained on the same corpus, and polled for the nearest neighbors of words from a test set. For each word, human raters choose the most "similar" answer, and the model that gets the most votes is deemed the best.

The advantage of this method is the possibility to compare first, second, etc. nearest neighbors in different models. However, it inherits the problem with human interpretation of distributional similarity, which we discussed above. Consider the examples[2] in table 1:

	Target word	GloVe	SVD
1	phone	telephone	mobile
2	coffee	tea	drinks
3	grammar	vocabulary	grammatical
4	cohesiveness	cohesion	inclusiveness

Table 1: Examples of nearest neighbors in GloVe and SVD

Subjects asked to choose the most "similar" word would presumably prefer synonyms (word 1 in table 1), if any were present (thus the "best" model would be the one favoring similarity over relatedness). They would easily exclude the clearly unrelated words (word 4 for SVD model). But they would provide less reliable feedback on "related" options, where the choice would be between different semantic relations (words 2,3). Many answers would be subjective, if not random, and likely to reflect frequency, speed of association, and possibly the order of presentation of words - rather than purely semantic factors that we are trying to evaluate.

2.3 "Coherence" of Semantic Space

Schnabel et al. (2015) also suggested that a "good" word embedding should have coherent neighborhoods for each word vector. The test they proposed consists in choosing two nearest neighbors of a test word, and adding a random word. A human rater should be able to identify the "intruder". For example, in our GloVe the nearest neighbors of *true* are *indeed* and *fact*; they are more semantically related to each other than to a random word *taxi*.

This test still relies on human interpretation, but it is more likely to produce reliable results than the methods discussed above. However, to apply it on

---

[2] Unless specified otherwise, the examples cited in this study are derived from 2 word embeddings: GloVe (Pennington et al., 2014) and SVD, trained at 300 dimensions, window size 10. GloVe parameters: 100 iterations, x_{max}= 100, a = 3/4. The SVD (Singular Vector Decomposition) model was built with Pointwise Mutual Information (PMI), a = 1, using the co-occurrence extraction kernel by Drozd et al. (2015). The 5B web-corpus combines Wikipedia (1.8B tokens), Araneum Anglicum Maius (1.2B) (Benko, 2014) and ukWaC (2B) (Baroni et al., 2009).

a large scale we would need to establish the size of neighborhoods that should be coherent. This number differs between words (see examples in table 2), and a "better" model should recognize that *beautiful* has more "good" neighbors than *knob*. But it is hard to tell the exact number a priori, and independently of a particular corpus.

beautiful	write	knob
lovely, 0.81	writing, 0.75	knobs, 0.60
gorgeous, 0.77	read, 0.72	gearshift, 0.48
wonderful, 0.64	written, 0.65	toggle, 0.41
magnificent, 0.63	want, 0.64	dials, 0.40
elegant, 0.61	wish, 0.62	dashboard, 0.38

Table 2: Nearest neighbors of *beautiful, write* and *knob* in GloVe

2.4 Alignment with Linguistic Features

Tsvetkov et al. (2015) proposed the QVec system that evaluates how well the dimensions of a word embedding can be aligned with dimensions of "linguistic" vectors (constructed from a semantically annotated corpus)[3]. This system does not involve human raters, but it still focuses on the "interpretability", as any linguistic categories are themselves a product of a certain theoretical interpretation of the language system.

The core assumption of QVec is that dimensions of word embeddings correspond to linguistic features (in this case, 41 supersenses of WordNet (Miller and Fellbaum, 1998) such as *food* or *motion*). Each linguistic feature can be mapped onto several dimensions of the word embedding, but each dimension of the word embedding can be mapped onto at most one linguistic feature. This assumption could be challenged: it is not clear why one dimension could not encode several linguistic features, or even that a certain cluster or pattern of dimensions could not correspond to one or several linguistic features.

Crucially, the authors report that the correlation of QVec with performance on different tasks varies with vector dimensionality (0.32 for 50 dimensions, 0.78 for 300 and 0.60 for 1000 on the sentiment analysis task). Such variation could be explained by the intuition that in smaller word embeddings dimensions have to be multi-functional,

and in larger embeddings more complex patterns of correspondence could be expected to occur. And increasingly complex patterns are likely to make decreasing amount of sense to humans.

3 General Methodological Concerns

3.1 Do Dimensions Have to Be Interpretable?

Although both people and word embeddings acquire the meanings of words from context, there are many important differences between human semantic knowledge and what can be expected from word embeddings. The latter depend on corpora that are static, noisy, and small. Co-occurrence frequencies do not mirror the frequencies of events that give rise to natural language semantics (e.g. *"dog bites man"* is less likely to be mentioned than *"man bites dog"*) (Erk, 2016).

Thus even the most perfect word embedding is unlikely to have exactly the same "concepts" as us, or that their structure would mirror the categories of some linguistic theory. QVec proves that to some extent the dimensions of the vector space are indeed interpretable, but the point we would like to make is this: by focusing on the structures that we expect the word embeddings to have, we might be missing the structures that they actually have.

Figure 1 compares the overlap of dimensions for 10 random words and 10 co-hyponyms in 300-dimensional GloVe vectors (darker dimensions indicate overlap between more words in the sample). It is clear that there are hundreds of features relevant for felines. We could hypothesize about them ("animal"? "nounhood"? "catness"?), but clearly this embedding has more "feline" features thanwhat we could find in dictionaries or elicit from human subjects. Some of such features might not even be in our conceptual inventory. Perhaps there is a dimension or a group of dimensions created by the co-occurrences with words like *jump, stretch, hunt,* and *purr* - some "feline behavior" category that we would not find in any linguistic resource.

Distributional models are gradient by nature. This makes them less interpretable, but also more similar to connectionist cognitive models (Lenci, 2008). We do not know to what extent word embeddings are cognitively plausible, but they do offer a new way to represent meaning that goes beyond symbolic approaches. We would be missing the point if we were only seeking features that we

---

[3] See also (Faruqui et al., 2015) for decomposition of word embeddings into sparse vectors to increase their correspondence to linguistic features. Such vectors are reported to be more "interpretable" to human annotators in the word intrusion task.

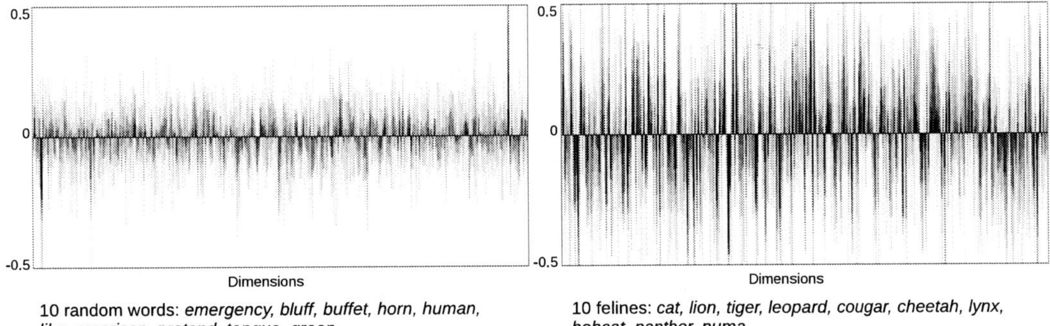

10 random words: *emergency, bluff, buffet, horn, human, like, american, pretend, tongue, green*

10 felines: *cat, lion, tiger, leopard, cougar, cheetah, lynx, bobcat, panther, puma*

Figure 1: Heatmap histogram of 10 random words and 10 co-hyponyms in GloVe

know from traditional linguistics.

3.2 Polysemy: the Elephant in the Room

Another general problem with all evaluations discussed above stems from the (lack of) treatment of polysemy in word-level word embeddings. Do we expect the vector for *apple* to be closer to *computer* or to *pear*? The cosine similarity-based tests choose only the "strongest" sense of a word in a given corpus. Therefore the accuracy of the current intrinsic evaluation methods also depends on whether the relations in the test word pairs match the distribution of senses of these words in a particular corpus. *"Apple, pear"* could be rated low, and *"apple, computer"* - high, but preference for either pair would say nothing about quality of the word embedding itself.

One way to deal with this problem is to exclude ambiguous words from tests, as it is done in BLESS; but this would be hard to guarantee for all corpora, it would significantly limit the tests (as more frequent words tend to be more polysemous), and it would avoid the issue rather than deal with it. Alternatively, we could attempt word sense disambiguation (Neelakantan et al., 2014; Bartunov et al., 2015); but the accuracy would be hard to guarantee, and we would need to provide the mapping from the word senses in the test to the word senses in the corpus.

The alternative is to embrace ambiguity as an intrinsic characteristic of word embeddings. We are looking for interpretable dimensions because we are used to discrete linguistic features, and similarly we are trying to bring meaning representations in word embeddings down to neat lists of word senses in dictionaries that we are used to. But anyone who has done lexicographic work knows that dictionaries are only an abstraction, never complete or free of inconsistencies and subjectivity. The distributional approach offers us a novel way to capture the full continuum of meaning (Erk, 2009). From this perspective, the problem with polysemy in tests for word embeddings is not the polysemy itself, but the fact that we are ignoring it with out-of-context test words and cosine similarity.

4 Back to the Drawing Board

4.1 What We Should Start Thinking About

To sum up, all intrinsic evaluations of word embeddings discussed above are based on the idea of interpretability by humans, and suffer from the problem of word ambiguity. We argue that both problems stem from the underlying methodological principle - the attempt to transfer the traditional lexicographic model of discrete word senses and linguistic features onto the continuous semantic space.

The reason that this methodology is so widespread is that linguistics does not yet offer an alternative, and finding one would require a lot of (collaborative) work by both theoretical and computational linguists. We will need to think of answers to some very basic questions. For example, how granular do we want our semantics to be? (individual word senses? lexical groups?) Should embeddings aim at separating word groups as neatly as possible, or rather at blending them by giving more weight to cases that would puzzle human annotators? The former would be easier to work with from the point of view of downstream applications; the latter would arguably provide a truer model of language for the linguists.

With respect to "interpretability" of word embeddings, the biggest question is the nature of those potentially non-interpretable dimensions. We can continue ignoring them and work only with the ones we can understand (which could prove to be enough for certain applications). The alternative is to accept that from now on we will not really understand our semantics, and delegate the interpretation to machine learning algorithms.

4.2 What Can We Do Right Now?

The above discussion does not yet offer any alternatives to current evaluations of word embeddings, but it does offer some insights about their interpretation. Things that we can learn from existing tests include:

- the degree to which a word embedding encodes frequency information, and is likely to be biased by it (Schnabel et al., 2015; Wilson and Schakel, 2015);

- the richness of representations for rare words (Wartena, 2014);

- performance on different size of corpora (while more data is mostly better, we also need "good" word embeddings for low-resource languages);

- specialization for a particular type of relation in distributional similarity, if any.

The last option is explored in such test sets as BLESS (Baroni and Lenci, 2011) and EVALution (Santus et al., 2015). They include pairs of words with different kinds of relations, such as synonymy and meronymy, but no annotator ratings. The word embeddings are queried on similarity between these pairs of words. The distribution of similarity ratings across different relations shows what linguistic relations are "favored" by the given embedding. This approach can be fruitfully extended to other types of linguistic relations, such as derivational morphology and frame relations.

Ideally, evaluations of a new model would also include publishing results of systematic tests for different parameters (Levy et al., 2015; Lai et al., 2015) and types of context (Melamud et al., 2016), as well as different types of linguistic relations (Gladkova et al., 2016). This kind of data is often viewed as something simply to be used for choosing a model for a particular task - but it does

also offer insights into its nature, and could help us understand the deeper properties of word embeddings, which could eventually lead to new types of tests.

None of these above-mentioned characteristics of word embeddings provides a one-number answer about how "good" a model is. But we can take a more exploratory approach, identifying the properties of a model rather than aiming to establish its superiority to others.

Lastly, when evaluating word embeddings we should not forget that the result of any evaluation is down to not only the embedding itself, but also the test, the corpus, and the method of identifying particular relations. Thus we cannot interpret, e.g., a low score on analogy test as evidence that a given model does not *contain* some linguistic feature: all it means is that we could not *detect* it with a given method, and perhaps a different method would work better (Drozd and Matsuoka, 2016).

5 Conclusion

This paper discusses the current methods of intrinsic evaluation of word embeddings. We show that they rely on "interpretability" of the model's output or structure, and we argue that this might not be the best approach, as it ignores the key features of distributional semantics, and does not always yield good predictions for how a word embedding would perform on a downstream application. We suggest focusing not on absolute ratings of abstract "quality" of embeddings, but on exploration of their characteristics.

We hope to draw attention of both computational and theoretical linguists to the need of working together on new models of language that would help us make better sense, and better use, of word embeddings.

References

Marco Baroni and Alessandro Lenci. 2011. How we BLESSed distributional semantic evaluation. In *Proceedings of the GEMS 2011 Workshop on GEometrical Models of Natural Language Semantics*, GEMS '11, pages 1–10. Association for Computational Linguistics.

Marco Baroni, Silvia Bernardini, Adriano Ferraresi, and Eros Zanchetta. 2009. The wacky wide web: a collection of very large linguistically processed web-crawled corpora. *Language Resources and Evaluation*, 43(3):209–226.

Sergey Bartunov, Dmitry Kondrashkin, Anton Osokin, and Dmitry Vetrov. 2015. Breaking sticks and ambiguities with adaptive skip-gram. *arXiv:1502.07257*.

Vladimír Benko. 2014. Aranea: Yet another family of (comparable) web corpora. In Petr Sojka, Aleš Horák, Ivan Kopeček, and Karel Pala, editors, *Text, speech, and dialogue: 17th international conference, TSD 2014, Brno, Czech Republic, September 8-12, 2014. Proceedings*, LNCS 8655, pages 257–264. Springer.

Elia Bruni, Nam-Khanh Tran, and Marco Baroni. 2014. Multimodal Distributional Semantics. *JAIR*, 49(1-47).

Danqi Chen and Christopher D. Manning. 2014. A fast and accurate dependency parser using neural networks. In *Proceedings of the Empiricial Methods in Natural Language Processing (EMNLP) 2014*, pages 740–750.

Yun-Nung Chen, William Yang Wang, and Alexander I. Rudnicky. 2014. Leveraging frame semantics and distributional semantics for unsupervised semantic slot induction in spoken dialogue systems. In *Spoken Language Technology Workshop (SLT), 2014 IEEE*, pages 584–589. IEEE.

Aleksandr Drozd and Satoshi Matsuoka. 2016. Linguistic regularities from multiple samples. Technical Report C-283, Department of Mathematical and Computing Sciences, Tokyo Institute of Technology.

Aleksandr Drozd, Anna Gladkova, and Satoshi Matsuoka. 2015. Python, performance, and natural language processing. In *Proceedings of the 5th Workshop on Python for High-Performance and Scientific Computing*, PyHPC '15, pages 1:1–1:10, New York, NY, USA. ACM.

Katrin Erk. 2009. Supporting inferences in semantic space: representing words as regions. In *Proceedings of the Eighth International Conference on Computational Semantics*, IWCS-8 '09, pages 104–115. Association for Computational Linguistics.

Katrin Erk. 2016. What do you know about an alligator when you know the company it keeps? *Semantics and Pragmatics*, 9(17):1–63, April.

Manaal Faruqui, Yulia Tsvetkov, Dani Yogatama, Chris Dyer, and Noah Smith. 2015. Sparse overcomplete word vector representations. *arXiv:1506.02004*.

Lev Finkelstein, Evgeniy Gabrilovich, Yossi Matias, Ehud Rivlin, Zach Solan, Gadi Wolfman, and Eytan Ruppin. 2002. Placing search in context: The concept revisited. In *ACM Transactions on Information Systems,*, volume 20(1), pages 116–131. ACM.

Anna Gladkova, Aleksandr Drozd, and Satoshi Matsuoka. 2016. Analogy-based detection of morphological and semantic relations with word embeddings: what works and what doesn't. In *Proceedings*

of NAACL-HLT 2016, pages 47–54. Association for Computational Linguistics.

Jiang Guo, Wanxiang Che, Haifeng Wang, and Ting Liu. 2014. Revisiting embedding features for simple semi-supervised learning. In *Proceedings of the Empiricial Methods in Natural Language Processing (EMNLP) 2014*, pages 110–120.

Felix Hill, Roi Reichart, and Anna Korhonen. 2015. Simlex-999: Evaluating semantic models with (genuine) similarity estimation. *Computational Linguistics*, 41(4):665–695.

Douwe Kiela, Felix Hill, and Stephen Clark. 2015. Specializing word embeddings for similarity or relatedness. In *Proceedings of the 2015 Conference on Empirical Methods in Natural Language Processing (EMNLP))*, pages 2044–2048. Association for Computational Linguistics.

Siwei Lai, Kang Liu, Liheng Xu, and Jun Zhao. 2015. How to generate a good word embedding? *arXiv:1507.05523*.

Alessandro Lenci. 2008. Distributional semantics in linguistic and cognitive research. *From context to meaning: Distributional models of the lexicon in linguistics and cognitive science, special issue of the Italian Journal of Linguistics*, 20(1):1–31.

Omer Levy, Yoav Goldberg, and Ido Dagan. 2015. Improving distributional similarity with lessons learned from word embeddings. In *Transactions of the Association for Computational Linguistics*, volume 3, pages 211–225.

Oren Melamud, David McClosky, Siddharth Patwardhan, and Mohit Bansal. 2016. The role of context types and dimensionality in learning word embeddings. *arXiv:1601.00893*.

George Miller and Christiane Fellbaum. 1998. *Wordnet: An electronic lexical database*. MIT Press: Cambridge.

Arvind Neelakantan, Jeevan Shankar, Alexandre Passos, and Andrew McCallum. 2014. Efficient non-parametric estimation of multiple embeddings per word in vector space. In *Proceedings of the Empiricial Methods in Natural Language Processing (EMNLP 2014)*, pages 1059–1069. Association for Computational Linguistics.

Jeffrey Pennington, Richard Socher, and Christopher D. Manning. 2014. Glove: Global vectors for word representation. In *Proceedings of the Empiricial Methods in Natural Language Processing (EMNLP 2014)*, volume 12, pages 1532–1543.

Enrico Santus, Frances Yung, Alessandro Lenci, and Chu-Ren Huang. 2015. EVALution 1.0: an evolving semantic dataset for training and evaluation of distributional semantic models. In *Proceedings of the 4th Workshop on Linked Data in Linguistics (LDL-2015)*, pages 64–69. Association for Computational Linguistics.

Tobias Schnabel, Igor Labutov, David Mimno, and Thorsten Joachims. 2015. Evaluation methods for unsupervised word embeddings. In *Proceedings of the 2015 Conference on Empirical Methods in Natural Language Processing (EMNLP 2015), Lisbon, Portugal*, pages 298–307. Association for Computational Linguistics.

Carson T. Schutze. 1996. *The Empirical Base of Linguistics: Grammaticality Judgments and Linguistic Methodology*. University of Chicago Press.

Yulia Tsvetkov, Manaal Faruqui, Wang Ling, Guillaume Lample, and Chris Dyer. 2015. Evaluation of word vector representations by subspace alignment. In *Proceedings of the 2015 Conference on Empirical Methods in Natural Language Processing*, pages 2049–2054. Association for Computational Linguistics.

Peter D. Turney, Patrick Pantel, and others. 2010. From frequency to meaning: Vector space models of semantics. *JAIR*, 37(1):141–188.

Christian Wartena. 2014. On the effect of word frequency on distributional similarity. In *Proceedings of the 12th edition of the KONVENS conference - Hildesheim*, volume 1, pages 1–10.

Benjamin J. Wilson and Adriaan MJ Schakel. 2015. Controlled experiments for word embeddings. *arXiv:1510.02675*.

Find the word that does not belong:
A Framework for an Intrinsic Evaluation of Word Vector Representations

José Camacho-Collados and **Roberto Navigli**
Department of Computer Science
Sapienza University of Rome
`{collados,navigli}@di.uniroma1.it`

Abstract

We present a new framework for an intrinsic evaluation of word vector representations based on the *outlier detection* task. This task is intended to test the capability of vector space models to create semantic clusters in the space. We carried out a pilot study building a gold standard dataset and the results revealed two important features: human performance on the task is extremely high compared to the standard word similarity task, and state-of-the-art word embedding models, whose current shortcomings were highlighted as part of the evaluation, still have considerable room for improvement.

1 Introduction

Vector Space Models have been successfully used on many NLP tasks (Turney and Pantel, 2010) such as automatic thesaurus generation (Crouch, 1988; Curran and Moens, 2002), word similarity (Deerwester et al., 1990; Turney et al., 2003; Radinsky et al., 2011) and clustering (Pantel and Lin, 2002), query expansion (Xu and Croft, 1996), information extraction (Laender et al., 2002), semantic role labeling (Erk, 2007; Pennacchiotti et al., 2008), spelling correction (Jones and Martin, 1997), and Word Sense Disambiguation (Navigli, 2012). These models are in the main based on the distributional hypothesis of Harris (1954) claiming that words that occur in the same contexts tend to have similar meanings. Recently, more complex models based on neural networks going beyond simple co-occurrence statistics have been developed (Mikolov et al., 2013; Pennington et al., 2014) and have proved beneficial on key NLP applications such as syntactic parsing (Weiss et al., 2015), Machine Translation (Zou et al., 2013), and

Question Answering (Bordes et al., 2014).

Word similarity, which numerically measures the extent to which two words are similar, is generally viewed as the most direct intrinsic evaluation of these word vector representations (Baroni et al., 2014; Levy et al., 2015). Given a gold standard of human-assigned scores, the usual evaluation procedure consists of calculating the correlation between these human similarity scores and scores calculated by the system. While word similarity has been shown to be an interesting task for measuring the semantic coherence of a vector space model, it suffers from various problems. First, the human inter-annotator agreement of standard datasets has been shown to be relatively too low for it to be considered a reliable evaluation benchmark (Batchkarov et al., 2016). In fact, many systems have already surpassed the human inter-annotator agreement upper bound in most of the standard word similarity datasets (Hill et al., 2015). Another drawback of the word similarity evaluation benchmark is its simplicity, as words are simply viewed as points in the vector space. Other interesting properties of vector space models are not directly addressed in the task.

As an alternative we propose the *outlier detection* task, which tests the capability of vector space models to create semantic clusters (i.e. clusters of semantically similar items). As is the case with word similarity, this task aims at evaluating the semantic coherence of vector space models, but providing two main advantages: (1) it provides a clear gold standard, thanks to the high human performance on the task, and (2) it tests an interesting language understanding property of vector space models not fully addressed to date, and this is their ability to create semantic clusters in the vector space, with potential applications to various NLP tasks.

43

Proceedings of the 1st Workshop on Evaluating Vector Space Representations for NLP, pages 43–50,
Berlin, Germany, August 12, 2016. ©2016 Association for Computational Linguistics

2 Outlier Detection Task

The proposed task, referred to as *outlier detection* henceforth, is based on a standard vocabulary question of language exams (Richards, 1976). Given a group of words, the goal is to identify the word that does not belong in the group. This question is intended to test the student's vocabulary understanding and knowledge of the world. For example, *book* would be an outlier for the set of words *apple, banana, lemon, book, orange*, as it is not a fruit like the others. A similar task has already been explored as an *ad-hoc* evaluation of the interpretability of topic models (Chang et al., 2009) and word vector dimensions (Murphy et al., 2012; Fyshe et al., 2015; Faruqui et al., 2015).

In order to deal with the outlier detection task, vector space models should be able to create semantic clusters (i.e. fruits in the example) compact enough to detect all possible outliers. A formalization of the task and its evaluation is presented in Section 2.1 and some potential applications are discussed in Section 2.2.

2.1 Formalization

Formally, given a set of words $W = \{w_1, w_2, \ldots, w_n, w_{n+1}\}$, the task consists of identifying the word (*outlier*) that does not belong to the same group as the remaining words. For notational simplicity, we will assume that $w_1, \ldots, w_n$ belong to the same cluster and w_{n+1} is the outlier. In what follows we explain a procedure for detecting outliers based on semantic similarity.

We define the *compactness score* $c(w)$ of a word $w \in W$ as the compactness of the cluster $W \setminus \{w\}$, calculated by averaging all pair-wise semantic similarities of the words in $W \setminus \{w\}$:

$$c(w) = \frac{1}{k} \sum_{w_i \in W \setminus \{w\}} \sum_{\substack{w_j \in W \setminus \{w\} \\ w_j \neq w_i}} sim(w_i, w_j) \quad (1)$$

where $k = n(n-1)$. We propose two measures for computing the reliability of a system in detecting an outlier given a set of words: Outlier Position (OP) and Outlier Detection (OD). Given a set W of $n+1$ words, OP is defined as the position of the outlier w_{n+1} according to the compactness score, which ranges from 0 to n (position 0 indicates the lowest overall score among all words in W, and position n indicates the highest overall score). OD is, instead, defined as 1 if the outlier is correctly detected (i.e. $OP(w_{n+1}) = n$) and 0 otherwise. To estimate the overall performance on a dataset D (composed of $|D|$ sets of words), we define the Outlier Position Percentage (OPP) and Accuracy measures:

$$OPP = \frac{\sum_{W \in D} \frac{OP(W)}{|W|-1}}{|D|} \times 100 \quad (2)$$

$$Accuracy = \frac{\sum_{W \in D} OD(W)}{|D|} \times 100 \quad (3)$$

The *compactness score* of a word may be expensive to calculate if the number of elements in the cluster is large. In fact, the complexity of calculating OP and OD measures given a cluster and an outlier is $(n+1) \times n \times (n-1) = O(n^3)$. However, this complexity can be effectively reduced to $(n+1) \times 2n = O(n^2)$. Our proposed calculations and the proof are included in Appendix A.

2.2 Potential applications

In this work we focus on the intrinsic semantic properties of vector space models which can be inferred from the outlier detection task. In addition, since it is a task based partially on semantic similarity, high-performing models in the outlier detection task are expected to contribute to applications in which semantic similarity has already shown its potential: Information Retrieval (Hliaoutakis et al., 2006), Machine Translation (Lavie and Denkowski, 2009), Lexical Substitution (McCarthy and Navigli, 2009), Question Answering (Mohler et al., 2011), Text Summarization (Mohammad and Hirst, 2012), and Word Sense Disambiguation (Patwardhan et al., 2003), to name a few. Furthermore, there are other NLP applications directly connected with the semantic clustering proposed in the outlier detection task. Ontology Learning is probably the most straightforward application, as a meaningful cluster of items is expected to share a common hypernym, a property that has already been exploited in recent studies using embeddings (Fu et al., 2014; Espinosa-Anke et al., 2016). In fact, building ontologies is a time-consuming task and generally relies on automatic or semi-automatic steps (Velardi et al., 2013; Alfarone and Davis, 2015). Ontologies are one of the basic components of the Semantic Web (Berners-Lee et al., 2000) and have already proved their importance in downstream applications like Question Answering (Mann, 2002),

	Big cats	European football teams	Solar System planets	Months
Cluster elements	tiger	FC Barcelona	Mercury	January
	lion	Bayern Munich	Venus	March
	cougar	Real Madrid	Earth	May
	jaguar	AC Milan	Mars	July
	leopard	Juventus	Jupiter	September
	cheetah	Atletico Madrid	Saturn	November
	wildcat	Chelsea	Uranus	February
	lynx	Borussia Dortmund	Neptune	June
1st Outlier	dog	Miami Dolphins	Sun	Wednesday
2nd Outlier	mouse	McLaren	Moon	winter
3rd Outlier	dolphin	Los Angeles Lakers	Triton	date
4th Outlier	shark	Bundesliga	Comet Halley	year
5th Outlier	savanna	football	eclipse	astrology
6th Outlier	jungle	goal	astronaut	birthday
7th Outlier	day	couch	lunch	ball
8th Outlier	car	fridge	window	paper

Table 1: First four clusters (including outliers) of the *8-8-8* outlier detection dataset.

which in the main rely on large structured knowledge bases (Bordes et al., 2014).

In this paper we do not perform any quantitative evaluation to measure the correlation between the performance of word vectors on the outlier detection task and downstream applications. We argue that the conclusions drawn by recent works (Tsvetkov et al., 2015; Chiu et al., 2016) as a result of measuring the correlation between standard intrinsic evaluation benchmarks (e.g. word similarity datasets) and downstream task performances are hampered by a serious methodological issue: in both cases, the sample set of word vectors used for measuring the correlation is not representative enough, which is essential for this type of statistical study (Patton, 2005). All sample vectors came from corpus-based models[1] trained on the same corpus and all perform *well* on the considered intrinsic tasks, which constitute a highly homogeneous and not representative sample set. Moreover, using only a reduced selected set of applications does not seem sufficient to draw general conclusions about the quality of an intrinsic task, but rather about its potential on those specific applications. Further work should focus on these issues before using downstream applications to measure the impact of intrinsic tasks for evaluating the quality of word vectors. However, this is out of the scope of this paper.

3 Pilot Study

We carried out a pilot study on the outlier detection task. To this end, we developed a new dataset, *8-8-8* henceforth. The dataset consisted of eight different topics each made up of a cluster of eight words and eight possible outliers. Four annotators were used for the creation of the dataset. Each annotator was asked to first identify two topics, and for each topic to provide a set of eight words belonging to the chosen topic (*elements in the cluster*), and a set of eight heterogeneous *outliers*, selected varying their similarity to and relatedness with the elements of the cluster[2]. In total, the dataset included sixty-four sets of $8 + 1$ words for the evaluation. Tables 1 and 2 show the eight clusters and their respective outliers of the *8-8-8* outlier detection dataset.

When we consider the time annotators had to spend creating the relatively small dataset for this pilot study, the indications are that building a large-scale dataset may not need to be very time-consuming. In our study, the annotators spent most of their time reading and understanding the guidelines, and then thinking about suitable topics. In fact, with a view to constructing a large-scale dataset, this topic selection step may be carried out prior to giving the assignments to the annotators, providing topics to annotators according to their

---

[1]In the case of Chiu et al. (2016) all word vectors in the sample come from the Skip-Gram model of Word2Vec (Mikolov et al., 2013).

[2]We release the full dataset and guidelines for the creation of the topics at `http://lcl.uniroma1.it/outlier-detection`

	IT companies	German car manufacturers	Apostles of Jesus Christ	South American countries
Cluster elements	Apple	Mercedes Benz	Peter	Brazil
	Foxconn	BMW	Andrew	Colombia
	Amazon	Audi	James	Argentina
	HP	Opel	John	Peru
	Microsoft	Volkswagen	Thaddaeus	Venezuela
	IBM	Porsche	Bartholomew	Chile
	Google	Alpina	Thomas	Ecuador
	Sony	Smart	Matthew	Bolivia
1st Outlier	Opel	Michelin	Noah	Bogotá
2nd Outlier	Boeing	Bridgestone	Mary	Rio de Janeiro
3rd Outlier	Nestlé	Boeing	Pope Benedict XVI	New York
4th Outlier	Adidas	Samsung	Ambrose	Madrid
5th Outlier	computer	Michael Schumacher	crucifixion	town
6th Outlier	software	Angela Merkel	church	government
7th Outlier	chair	Capri	airplane	bottle
8th Outlier	plant	pineapple	Microsoft	telephone

Table 2: Last four clusters (including outliers) from the *8-8-8* outlier detection dataset.

expertise. The time spent for the actual creation of a cluster (including outliers) was in all cases less than ten minutes.

3.1 Human performance

We assessed the human performance of eight annotators in the task via accuracy. To this end, each annotator was given eight different groups of words, one for each of the topics of the *8-8-8* dataset. Each group of words was made up of the set of eight words comprising the cluster, plus one additional outlier. All the words were shuffled and given to the annotator without any additional information (e.g. annotators did not know the topic of the cluster). The task for the annotators consisted of detecting the outlier in each set of nine words. To this end, each annotator was asked to provide two different answers: one without any external help, and a second one in which the annotator could use the Web as external help for three minutes before giving his answer. This human performance in the outlier detection task may be viewed as equivalent to the inter-annotator agreement in word similarity, which is used to measure the human performance in the task.

The results of the experiment were the following: an accuracy of 98.4% for the first task in which annotators did not use any external help, and an accuracy of 100% for the second task in which annotators were allowed to use external help. This contrasts with the evaluation performed in word similarity, which is based on human-assigned scores with a relatively low inter-annotator agreement. For example, the inter-annotator agreements in the standard WordSim-353 (Finkelstein et al., 2002) and SimLex-999 (Hill et al., 2015) word similarity datasets were, respectively, 0.61 and 0.67 according to average pair-wise Spearman correlation. In fact, both upper-bound values have already been surpassed by automatic models (Huang et al., 2012; Wieting et al., 2015).

3.2 Word embeddings performance

We tested the performance of three standard word embedding models in the outlier detection task: the CBOW and Skip-Gram models of Word2Vec (Mikolov et al., 2013) and GloVe (Pennington et al., 2014). We report the results of each of the models trained on the 3B-words UMBC webbase corpus [3] (Han et al., 2013), and the 1.7B-words English Wikipedia[4] with standard hyperparameters[5]. For each of the models, we used as multiword expressions the phrases contained in the pretrained Word2Vec word embeddings trained on the Google News corpus. The evaluation was performed as explained in Section 2.1, using cosine

---

[3] `http://ebiquity.umbc. edu/blogger/2013/05/01/ umbc-webbase-corpus-of-3b-english-words/`

[4] We used the Wikipedia dump of November 2014.

[5] The dimensionality of the vectors was set to 300 for the three models. Context-size 5 for CBOW and 10 for Skip-Gram and GloVe; hierarchichal softmax for CBOW and negative sampling for Skip-Gram and GloVe.

Model	Corpus	OPP	Acc.
CBOW	UMBC	93.8	**73.4**
	Wikipedia	**95.3**	**73.4**
Skip-Gram	UMBC	92.6	64.1
	Wikipedia	93.8	70.3
	Google News	94.7	70.3
GloVe	UMBC	81.6	40.6
	Wikipedia	91.8	56.3

Table 3: Outlier Position Percentage (OPP) and Accuracy (Acc.) of different word embedding models on the *8-8-8* outlier detection dataset.

as similarity measure (*sim* in Equation 1).

Table 3 shows the results of all the word embedding models on the *8-8-8* outlier detection dataset. Outliers, which were detected in over 40% of cases by all models, were consistently given high compactness scores. This was reflected in the OPP results (above 80% in all cases), which proves the potential and the capability of word embeddings to create compact clusters. All the models performed particularly well in the *Months* and *South American countries* clusters. However, the best model in terms of accuracy, i.e. CBOW, achieved 73.4%, which is far below the human performance, estimated in the 98.4%-100% range.

In fact, taking a deeper look at the output we find common errors committed by these models. First, the lack of meaningful occurrences for a given word, which is crucial for obtaining an accurate word vector representation, seems to have been causing problems in the cases of the *wildcat* and *lynx* instances of the *Big cats* cluster, and of *Alpina* from the *German car manufacturers* cluster. Second, the models produced some errors on outliers closely related to the words of the clusters, incorrectly considering them as part of the cluster. Examples of this phenomenon are found in the outliers *Bundesliga* from the *European football teams* cluster, and *software* from the *IT companies* cluster. Third, the ambiguity, highlighted in the word *Smart* from the *German car manufacturers* cluster and in the *Apostles of Jesus Christ* cluster, is an inherent problem of all these word-based models. Finally, we encountered the issue of having more than one lexicalization (i.e. synonyms) for a given instance (e.g. *Real, Madrid, Real Madrid,* or *Real Madrid CF*), which causes the representations of a given lexicalization to be ambiguous or not so accurate and, in some cases,

to miss a representation for a given lexicalization if that lexicalization is not found enough times in the corpus[6]. In order to overcome these ambiguity and synonymy issues, it might be interesting for future work to leverage vector representations constructed from large lexical resources such, as FreeBase (Bordes et al., 2011; Bordes et al., 2014), Wikipedia (Camacho-Collados et al., 2015a), or BabelNet (Iacobacci et al., 2015; Camacho-Collados et al., 2015b).

4 Conclusion

In this paper we presented the *outlier detection* task and a framework for an intrinsic evaluation of word vector space models. The task is intended to test interesting semantic properties of vector space models not fully addressed to date. As shown in our pilot study, state-of-the-art word embeddings perform reasonably well in the task but are still far from human performance. As opposed to the word similarity task, the outlier detection task achieves a very high human performance, proving the reliability of the gold standard. Finally, we release the *8-8-8* outlier detection dataset and the guidelines given to the annotators as part of the pilot study, and an easy-to-use Python code for evaluating the performance of word vector representations given a gold standard dataset at `http://lcl.uniroma1.it/ outlier-detection`.

Acknowledgments

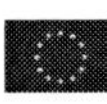 The authors gratefully acknowledge the support of the ERC Starting Grant MultiJEDI No. 259234.

We would like to thank Claudio Delli Bovi, Ilenia Giambruno, Ignacio Iacobacci, Massimiliano Mancini, Tommaso Pasini, Taher Pilehvar, and Alessandro Raganato for their help in the construction and evaluation of the outlier detection dataset. We would also like to thank Jim McManus for his comments on the manuscript.

References

Daniele Alfarone and Jesse Davis. 2015. Unsupervised learning of an is-a taxonomy from a limited domain-specific corpus. In *Proceedings of IJCAI*.

---

[6]This last issue was not present in this evaluation as for the multiword instances we carefully selected the lexicalizations which were covered by the pre-trained Word2Vec vectors, which ensured a full coverage of all models.

Marco Baroni, Georgiana Dinu, and Germán Kruszewski. 2014. Don't count, predict! a systematic comparison of context-counting vs. context-predicting semantic vectors. In *Proceedings of ACL*, pages 238–247.

Miroslav Batchkarov, Thomas Kober, Jeremy Reffin, Julie Weeds, and David Weir. 2016. A critique of word similarity as a method for evaluating distributional semantic models. In *Proceedings of the ACL Workshop on Evaluating Vector Space Representations for NLP*, Berlin, Germany.

Tim Berners-Lee, Mark Fischetti, and Michael L Foreword By-Dertouzos. 2000. *Weaving the Web: The original design and ultimate destiny of the World Wide Web by its inventor*. HarperCollins.

Antoine Bordes, Jason Weston, Ronan Collobert, and Yoshua Bengio. 2011. Learning structured embeddings of knowledge bases. In *Twenty-Fifth AAAI Conference on Artificial Intelligence*.

Antoine Bordes, Sumit Chopra, and Jason Weston. 2014. Question answering with subgraph embeddings. In *EMNLP*.

José Camacho-Collados, Mohammad Taher Pilehvar, and Roberto Navigli. 2015a. NASARI: a Novel Approach to a Semantically-Aware Representation of Items. In *Proceedings of NAACL*, pages 567–577.

José Camacho-Collados, Mohammad Taher Pilehvar, and Roberto Navigli. 2015b. A Unified Multilingual Semantic Representation of Concepts. In *Proceedings of ACL*, pages 741–751.

Jonathan Chang, Sean Gerrish, Chong Wang, Jordan L Boyd-Graber, and David M Blei. 2009. Reading tea leaves: How humans interpret topic models. In *Advances in neural information processing systems*, pages 288–296.

Billy Chiu, Anna Korhonen, and Sampo Pyysalo. 2016. Intrinsic evaluation of word vectors fails to predict extrinsic performance. In *Proceedings of the ACL Workshop on Evaluating Vector Space Representations for NLP*, Berlin, Germany.

C. J. Crouch. 1988. A cluster-based approach to thesaurus construction. In *Proceedings of the 11th Annual International ACM SIGIR Conference on Research and Development in Information Retrieval*, SIGIR '88, pages 309–320.

James R. Curran and Marc Moens. 2002. Improvements in automatic thesaurus extraction. In *Proceedings of the ACL-02 Workshop on Unsupervised Lexical Acquisition - Volume 9*, ULA '02, pages 59–66.

Scott C. Deerwester, Susan T. Dumais, Thomas K. Landauer, George W. Furnas, and Richard A. Harshman. 1990. Indexing by latent semantic analysis. *Journal of American Society for Information Science*, 41(6):391–407.

Katrin Erk. 2007. A simple, similarity-based model for selectional preferences. In *Proceedings of ACL*, Prague, Czech Republic.

Luis Espinosa-Anke, Horacio Saggion, Francesco Ronzano, and Roberto Navigli. 2016. ExTaSem! Extending, Taxonomizing and Semantifying Domain Terminologies. In *Proceedings of the 30th Conference on Artificial Intelligence (AAAI'16)*.

Manaal Faruqui, Yulia Tsvetkov, Dani Yogatama, Chris Dyer, and Noah Smith. 2015. Sparse overcomplete word vector representations. In *Proceedings of ACL*, Beijing, China.

Lev Finkelstein, Gabrilovich Evgeniy, Matias Yossi, Rivlin Ehud, Solan Zach, Wolfman Gadi, and Ruppin Eytan. 2002. Placing search in context: The concept revisited. *ACM Transactions on Information Systems*, 20(1):116–131.

Ruiji Fu, Jiang Guo, Bing Qin, Wanxiang Che, Haifeng Wang, and Ting Liu. 2014. Learning semantic hierarchies via word embeddings. In *ACL (1)*, pages 1199–1209.

Alona Fyshe, Leila Wehbe, Partha P Talukdar, Brian Murphy, and Tom M Mitchell. 2015. A compositional and interpretable semantic space. In *Proc. of NAACL*.

Lushan Han, Abhay Kashyap, Tim Finin, James Mayfield, and Jonathan Weese. 2013. UMBC EBIQUITY-CORE: Semantic textual similarity systems. In *Proceedings of the Second Joint Conference on Lexical and Computational Semantics*, volume 1, pages 44–52.

Zellig Harris. 1954. Distributional structure. *Word*, 10:146–162.

Felix Hill, Roi Reichart, and Anna Korhonen. 2015. Simlex-999: Evaluating semantic models with (genuine) similarity estimation. *Computational Linguistics*.

Angelos Hliaoutakis, Giannis Varelas, Epimenidis Voutsakis, Euripides GM Petrakis, and Evangelos Milios. 2006. Information retrieval by semantic similarity. *International Journal on Semantic Web and Information Systems*, 2(3):55–73.

Eric H. Huang, Richard Socher, Christopher D. Manning, and Andrew Y. Ng. 2012. Improving word representations via global context and multiple word prototypes. In *Proceedings of ACL*, pages 873–882, Jeju Island, Korea.

Ignacio Iacobacci, Mohammad Taher Pilehvar, and Roberto Navigli. 2015. Sensembed: Learning sense embeddings for word and relational similarity. In *Proceedings of ACL*, pages 95–105, Beijing, China.

Michael P. Jones and James H. Martin. 1997. Contextual spelling correction using latent semantic analysis. In *Proceedings of the Fifth Conference on*

Applied Natural Language Processing, ANLC '97, pages 166–173.

Alberto H. F. Laender, Berthier A. Ribeiro-Neto, Altigran S. da Silva, and Juliana S. Teixeira. 2002. A brief survey of web data extraction tools. *SIGMOD Rec.*, 31(2):84–93.

Alon Lavie and Michael J. Denkowski. 2009. The Meteor metric for automatic evaluation of Machine Translation. *Machine Translation*, 23(2-3):105–115.

Omer Levy, Yoav Goldberg, and Ido Dagan. 2015. Improving distributional similarity with lessons learned from word embeddings. *Transactions of the Association for Computational Linguistics*, 3:211–225.

Gideon S Mann. 2002. Fine-grained proper noun ontologies for question answering. In *Proceedings of the 2002 workshop on Building and using semantic networks-Volume 11*, pages 1–7. Association for Computational Linguistics.

Diana McCarthy and Roberto Navigli. 2009. The english lexical substitution task. *Language resources and evaluation*, 43(2):139–159.

Tomas Mikolov, Kai Chen, Greg Corrado, and Jeffrey Dean. 2013. Efficient estimation of word representations in vector space. *CoRR*, abs/1301.3781.

Saif Mohammad and Graeme Hirst. 2012. Distributional measures of semantic distance: A survey. *CoRR*, abs/1203.1858.

Michael Mohler, Razvan Bunescu, and Rada Mihalcea. 2011. Learning to grade short answer questions using semantic similarity measures and dependency graph alignments. In *Proceedings of ACL*, pages 752–762, Portland, Oregon.

Brian Murphy, Partha Pratim Talukdar, and Tom M Mitchell. 2012. Learning effective and interpretable semantic models using non-negative sparse embedding. In *COLING*, pages 1933–1950.

Roberto Navigli. 2012. A quick tour of word sense disambiguation, induction and related approaches. In *SOFSEM 2012: Theory and practice of computer science*, pages 115–129. Springer.

Patrick Pantel and Dekang Lin. 2002. Document clustering with committees. In *Proceedings of SIGIR 2002*, pages 199–206, Tampere, Finland.

Michael Quinn Patton. 2005. *Qualitative research*. Wiley Online Library.

Siddharth Patwardhan, Satanjeev Banerjee, and Ted Pedersen. 2003. Using measures of semantic relatedness for word sense disambiguation. In *Computational linguistics and intelligent text processing*, pages 241–257. Springer.

Marco Pennacchiotti, Diego De Cao, Roberto Basili, Danilo Croce, and Michael Roth. 2008. Automatic induction of FrameNet lexical units. In *Proceedings of EMNLP*, pages 457–465.

Jeffrey Pennington, Richard Socher, and Christopher D Manning. 2014. GloVe: Global vectors for word representation. In *Proceedings of EMNLP*, pages 1532–1543.

Kira Radinsky, Eugene Agichtein, Evgeniy Gabrilovich, and Shaul Markovitch. 2011. A word at a time: computing word relatedness using temporal semantic analysis. In *Proceedings of WWW*, pages 337–346, Hyderabad, India.

Jack C Richards. 1976. The role of vocabulary teaching. *TESOl Quarterly*, pages 77–89.

Yulia Tsvetkov, Manaal Faruqui, Wang Ling, Guillaume Lample, and Chris Dyer. 2015. Evaluation of word vector representations by subspace alignment. In *Proceedings of EMNLP (2)*, pages 2049–2054, Lisbon, Portugal.

Peter D. Turney and Patrick Pantel. 2010. From frequency to meaning: Vector space models of semantics. *Journal of Artificial Intelligence Research*, 37:141–188.

Peter D. Turney, Michael L. Littman, Jeffrey Bigham, and Victor Shnayder. 2003. Combining independent modules to solve multiple-choice synonym and analogy problems. In *Proceedings of Recent Advances in Natural Language Processing*, pages 482–489, Borovets, Bulgaria.

Paola Velardi, Stefano Faralli, and Roberto Navigli. 2013. Ontolearn reloaded: A graph-based algorithm for taxonomy induction. *Computational Linguistics*, 39(3):665–707.

David Weiss, Chris Alberti, Michael Collins, and Slav Petrov. 2015. Structured training for neural network transition-based parsing. In *Proceedings of ACL*, Beijing, China.

John Wieting, Mohit Bansal, Kevin Gimpel, Karen Livescu, and Dan Roth. 2015. From paraphrase database to compositional paraphrase model and back. *TACL*.

Jinxi Xu and W. Bruce Croft. 1996. Query expansion using local and global document analysis. In *Proceedings of the 19th Annual International ACM SIGIR Conference on Research and Development in Information Retrieval*, SIGIR '96, pages 4–11.

Will Y Zou, Richard Socher, Daniel M Cer, and Christopher D Manning. 2013. Bilingual word embeddings for phrase-based machine translation. In *Proceedings of EMNLP*, pages 1393–1398.

A Proposition 1

The complexity for calculating $OP(w)$ can be reduced to $2n$ by calculating the following *pseudo-inverted compactness score*[7] $p(w)$ instead of the *compactness score* $c(w)$ of Equation 1, and defining $OP_p(w)$ as the position of the outlier in W according to the inverted *pseudo-inverted compactness score*:

$$p(w) = \frac{1}{k'}\left(\sum_{\substack{w_i \in W \\ w_i \neq w}} sim(w_i, w) + \sum_{\substack{w_i \in W \\ w_i \neq w}} sim(w, w_i) \right)$$

(4)

where $k' = 2(|W| - 1)$.

Proof. Since $OP(w)$ is given by the position of $c(w)$ with respect to the remaining words in W and $\leq$ represents a relation of total order, we only have to prove the following statement:

$$c(w) \leq c(w') \Leftrightarrow p(w') \leq p(w), \forall w, w' \in W$$

(5)

Given any $w \in W$, we can calculate the sum of all pair-wise similarities of the words in W (i.e. μ) as follows:

$$\mu = \sum_{w_i \in W \setminus \{w\}} \sum_{\substack{w_j \in W \setminus \{w\} \\ w_j \neq w_i}} sim(w_i, w_j) +$$

$$+ \sum_{w_i \in W \setminus \{w\}} sim(w_i, w) + \sum_{w_i \in W \setminus \{w\}} sim(w, w_i)$$

$$= k \cdot c(w) + k' \cdot p(w)$$

(6)

where $k = (|W| - 1)(|W| - 2)$. Therefore,

$$\mu = k \cdot c(w) + k' \cdot p(w), \forall w \in W \qquad (7)$$

Since k, k' (being both k and k' positive values) and μ are all fixed values only depending on W, we can trivially infer the following statement from Equation 7 given any $w, w' \in W$:

$$c(w) \leq c(w') \Leftrightarrow p(w') \leq p(w) \qquad (8)$$

Hence, we have proved the proposition.

$\square$

---

[7]In this proposition we do not assume any special property to the function $sim(.,.)$ for generalization. If $sim(.,.)$ were symmetrical (e.g. cosine similarity is symmetrical), we could simply define the *pseudo-inverted compactness score* as $p(w) = \sum_{w_i \in W} sim(w_i, w)$, which would lead to a complexity of n.

Capturing Discriminative Attributes in a Distributional Space:
Task Proposal

Alicia Krebs and **Denis Paperno**
`a.m.krebs@student.rug.nl` | `denis.paperno@unitn.it`
Center for Mind and Brain Sciences (CIMeC), University of Trento, Rovereto, Italy

Abstract

If lexical similarity is not enough to reliably assess how word vectors would perform on various specific tasks, we need other ways of evaluating semantic representations. We propose a new task, which consists in extracting semantic *differences* using distributional models: given two words, what is the difference between their meanings? We present two proof of concept datasets for this task and outline how it may be performed.

1 Introduction

All similar pairs of words are similar in the same way: they share a substantial number of semantic properties (although properties themselves may belong to different groups, i.e. visual, functional, etc.). Cosine of two feature vectors in a distributional semantic space is a formalization of this idea, standardly used as a measure of semantic similarity for the evaluation of distributional models (Baroni et al., 2014a; Landauer and Dumais, 1997). While similarity tasks have become the standard in the evaluation of distributional models, the validity of those tasks has been put into question: inter-annotator agreement tends to be low, the small size of some of the most popular datasets is a concern, and subjective similarity scores have limitations when it comes to task-specific applications (Faruqui et al., 2016; Batchkarov et al., 2016). In contrast to similarity, the nature of semantic *difference* between two (related) words can vary greatly. Modeling difference can help capture individual aspects of meaning; similarity alone may be too simple a task to assess semantic representations in all their complexity, and therefore insufficient for driving the progress of computational models. Our project is related to previous

work that attempts to predict the discriminative features of referents, using natural images to represent the input objects (Lazaridou et al., 2016). Attributes have also been used to simulate similarity judgements and concept categorization (Silberer and Lapata, 2014). On a more abstract level, our work is related to previous attempts at using offset vectors to capture lexical relations without explicit supervision (Mikolov et al., 2013), which have been shown to be able to generalise well to a range of relations (Vylomova et al., 2015).

We created two proof of concept datasets for the difference task: a small dataset of differences as feature oppositions and a bigger one with differences as presence vs. absence of a feature.

2 The Small Dataset

We used a random sample of seed words from the BLESS dataset (Baroni and Lenci, 2011) along with their semantic neighbors to create word pairs that were in some ways similar and denoted concrete objects. For each word pair, one or more pair(s) of discriminating attributes were assigned manually. For example, the word pair `[scooter, moped]` received two pairs of attributes: `[big, small]` and `[fast, slow]`. Some word pairs were also added manually to further exemplify specific differences, such as `[horse, foal]` for the age properties. The resulting dataset contains 91 items. To get a simple unsupervised baseline on the detection of difference direction, we calculated a similarity score for each item, using the cooccurrence counts of the best count-based configuration presented in Baroni et al. (2014b), which were extracted from the concatenation of the web-crawled ukWack corpus (Baroni et al., 2009), Wikipedia, and the BNC, for a total of 2.8 billion tokens. This similarity score calculates whether the attribute is closer to the first

Proceedings of the 1st Workshop on Evaluating Vector Space Representations for NLP, pages 51–54,
Berlin, Germany, August 12, 2016. ©2016 Association for Computational Linguistics

or second word. We found that 67% of items had positive scores. The most successful types of attributes were *color* (34 out 51), *age* (9 out of 9) and *diet* (4 out of 5).

$$Score = (CosSim(w_1, a_1) \cdot CosSim(w_1, a_2))$$
$$-(CosSim(w_2, a_2) \cdot CosSim(w_2, a_1))$$

The dataset is too small for training supervised models; our attempts (logistic regression on pairwise cosines with cross-validation) showed negligibly low results.

3 Feature Norms Dataset

Only some differences can be expressed in the format assumed above, i.e. as the opposition of two attributes, such as *yellow* vs. *red* being the difference between bananas and apples. Other differences are better expressed as the presence or absence of a feature. For instance, the difference between a narwhal and a dolphin is the presence of a horn. For natural salient features of word concepts, we turned to property norms.

We used the set of feature norms collected by McRae et al. (2005), which includes features for 541 concepts (living and non-living entities), collected by asking 725 participants to produce features they found important for each concept. Production frequencies of these features indicate how salient they are. Feature norms of concepts are able to encode semantic knowledge because they tap into the representations that the participants have acquired through repeated exposure to those concepts. McRae et al. divided disjunctive features, so that if a participant produced the feature is_green_or_red the concept will be associated with both the feature is_green and the feature is_red. Concepts that have different meanings had been disambiguated before being shown to participants. For example, there are two entries for *bow*, bow_(weapon) and bow_(ribbon). Because the word vector for *bow* encodes the properties of both senses, we did not differentiate between entries that have multiple senses. In our dataset, the concept bow has the features of both the weapon and the ribbon.

The McRae dataset uses the brain region taxonomy (Cree and McRae, 2003) to classify features into different types, such as *function*, *sound* or *taxonomic*. We decided to only work with visual features, which exist for all concrete concepts,

while features such as *sound* or *taste* are only relevant for some concepts. This classification distinguishes between three types of visual features: *motion, color* and *form and surface*. We first selected words that had at least one visual feature of any type. We then created word pairs by selecting the 50 closest neighbours of every word in the dataset.

For each word pair, if there was a feature that the first word had but the second didn't, that word pair and feature item was added to our dataset. The set was built in such a way that the feature of each item always refers to an attribute of the first word. For example, in Table 2, *wings* is an attribute of *airplane*. The word pair [airplane,helicopter] will only be included in the order [helicopter,airplane] if *helicopter* has a feature that *airplane* doesn't have. The relations are thus asymmetric and have fixed directionality. For simplicity, multi-word features were processed so that only the final word is taken into account (e.g. has_wings becomes wings). In total, our dataset contains 528 concepts, 24 963 word pairs, and 128 515 items.

$word_1$	$word_2$	$feature$
airplane	helicopter	wings
bagpipe	accordion	pipes
canoe	sailboat	fibreglass
dolphin	seal	fins
gorilla	crocodile	bananas
oak	pine	leaves
octopus	lobster	tentacles
pajamas	necklace	silk
skirt	jacket	pleats
subway	train	dirty

Table 2: Examples of word pairs and their features

We computed a simple unsupervised baseline for direction of difference (e.g. is *subway* or *train* dirty?), choosing the first word iff $\cos(w_1 w_f) > \cos(w_2, w_f)$, and achieved 69% accuracy. Ultimately, this dataset could be used to build a model that can predict an exhaustive list of distinctive attributes for any pair of words. This could be done in a binary set-up where the dataset has been supplemented with negative examples: for a given triple, predict whether the attribute is a difference between $word_1$ and $word_2$.

type	w_1	w_2	a_1	a_2
color	tomato	spinach	red	green
color	banana	carrot	yellow	orange
color	tiger	panther	orange	black
age	cat	kitten	old	young
age	dog	pup	old	young
age	horse	foal	old	young
diet	deer	fox	herbivorous	carnivorous
diet	cow	lion	herbivorous	carnivorous
sex	pig	sow	male	female
sex	tiger	tigress	male	female

Table 1: Small Dataset: Examples of distinctive attribute pairs.

4 Conclusion

A system for basic language understanding should be able to detect when concepts are similar to each other, but also in what way concepts differ from each other. We've demonstrated how an evaluation set that captures differences between concepts can be built.

The baselines we computed show that the difference task we propose is a non-trivial semantic task. Even with the simplest evaluation setting where the difference was given and only the direction of the difference was to be established (e.g. where the task was to establish if tomato is red and spinach green or vice versa), the baseline methods achieved less than 70% accuracy. A more realistic evaluation setup would challenge models to produce a set of differences between two given concepts.

The dataset versions described in this paper are proof of concept realizations, and we keep working on improving the test sets. For instance, to counter the inherent noise of feature norms, we plan on using human annotation to confirm the validity of the test partition of the dataset.

In the future, solving the difference task could help in various applications, for example automatized lexicography (automatically generating features to include in dictionary definitions), conversational agents (choosing lexical items with contextually relevant differential features can help create more pragmatically appropriate, human-like dialogs), machine translation (where explicitly taking into account semantic differences between translation variants can improve the quality of the output), etc.

References

Marco Baroni and Alessandro Lenci. 2011. How we blessed distributional semantic evaluation. In *Proceedings of the GEMS 2011 Workshop on GEometrical Models of Natural Language Semantics*, pages 1–10. Association for Computational Linguistics.

Marco Baroni, Silvia Bernardini, Adriano Ferraresi, and Eros Zanchetta. 2009. The wacky wide web: a collection of very large linguistically processed web-crawled corpora. *Language resources and evaluation*, 43(3):209–226.

Marco Baroni, Raffaela Bernardi, and Roberto Zamparelli. 2014a. Frege in space: A program of compositional distributional semantics. *Linguistic Issues in Language Technology*, 9.

Marco Baroni, Georgiana Dinu, and Germán Kruszewski. 2014b. Don't count, predict! a systematic comparison of context-counting vs. context-predicting semantic vectors. In *ACL (1)*, pages 238–247.

Miroslav Batchkarov, Thomas Kober, Jeremy Reffin, Julie Weeds, and David Weir. 2016. A critique of word similarity as a method for evaluating distributional semantic models. In *First Workshop on Evaluating Vector Space Representations for NLP (RepEval 2016)*.

George S Cree and Ken McRae. 2003. Analyzing the factors underlying the structure and computation of the meaning of chipmunk, cherry, chisel, cheese, and cello (and many other such concrete nouns). *Journal of Experimental Psychology: General*, 132(2):163.

Manaal Faruqui, Yulia Tsvetkov, Pushpendre Rastogi, and Chris Dyer. 2016. Problems with evaluation of word embeddings using word similarity tasks. In *First Workshop on Evaluating Vector Space Representations for NLP (RepEval 2016)*.

Thomas K Landauer and Susan T Dumais. 1997. A solution to plato's problem: The latent semantic analysis theory of acquisition, induction, and representation of knowledge. *Psychological review*, 104(2):211.

Angeliki Lazaridou, Nghia The Pham, and Marco Baroni. 2016. The red one!: On learning to refer to things based on their discriminative properties. *arXiv preprint arXiv:1603.02618*.

Ken McRae, George S Cree, Mark S Seidenberg, and Chris McNorgan. 2005. Semantic feature production norms for a large set of living and nonliving things. *Behavior research methods*, 37(4):547–559.

Tomas Mikolov, Wen-tau Yih, and Geoffrey Zweig. 2013. Linguistic regularities in continuous space word representations. In *HLT-NAACL*, volume 13, pages 746–751.

Carina Silberer and Mirella Lapata. 2014. Learning grounded meaning representations with autoencoders. In *ACL (1)*, pages 721–732.

Ekaterina Vylomova, Laura Rimmel, Trevor Cohn, and Timothy Baldwin. 2015. Take and took, gaggle and goose, book and read: Evaluating the utility of vector differences for lexical relation learning. *arXiv preprint arXiv:1509.01692*.

An Improved Crowdsourcing Based Evaluation Technique for Word Embedding Methods

Farhana Ferdousi Liza
School of Computing
University of Kent
Canterbury, CT2 7NY, UK
fl207@kent.ac.uk

Marek Grześ
School of Computing
University of Kent
Canterbury, CT2 7NY, UK
m.grzes@kent.ac.uk

Abstract

In this proposal track paper, we have presented a crowdsourcing-based word embedding evaluation technique that will be more reliable and linguistically justified. The method is designed for intrinsic evaluation and extends the approach proposed in (Schnabel et al., 2015). Our improved evaluation technique captures word relatedness based on the word context.

1 Introduction

The semantic relatedness between words can be ambiguous if the context of the word is not known (Patwardhan et al., 2003), and word sense disambiguation is the process of assigning a meaning to a polysemous word based on its context. The context defines linguistic and corresponding factual real world knowledge which provides a difference between word's sense and its reference. The sense of a word concerns one of the meanings of a word in a particular language. Reference is used to deal with the relationship between a language and the real world knowledge about an object or entity. The context of a word can be understood through a sentence, and thus understanding a word in a sentential context works as ambiguity resolution (Faust and Chiarello, 1998).

The vector space representation of words (embeddings) keeps related words nearby in the vector space. The word relatedness is usually measured through synonyms, but synonyms can differ in at least one semantic feature. The feature can be 'denotative', referring to some actual, real world difference in the object the language is dealing with, such as, walk, lumber, stroll, meander, lurch, stagger. The feature can be 'connotative', referring to how the user feels about the object rather than any real difference in the object itself,

such as, die, pass away, give up the ghost, kick the bucket, croak. Absolute synonyms are usually rare in a language. For example: sofa and couch are nearly absolute synonyms, however based on the context, they have different meaning in at least one way, such as, couch potato, because there is no word sense available for sofa potato (Vajda, 2001).

Crowdsourcing (Ambati et al., 2010; Callison-Burch, 2009), which allows employing people worldwide to perform short tasks via online platforms, can be an effective tool for performing evaluation in a time and cost-effective way (Ambati, 2012). In (Schnabel et al., 2015), crowdsourcing-based evaluation was proposed for synonyms or a word relatedness task where six word embedding techniques were evaluated. The crowdsourcing-based intrinsic evaluation which tests embeddings for semantic relationship between words focuses on a direct comparison of word embeddings with respect to individual queries. Although the method is promising for evaluating different word embeddings, it has some shortcomings. Specifically, it does not explicitly consider word context. As the approach relies on human interpretation of words, it is important to take into account how humans interpret or understand the meaning of a word. Humans usually understand semantic relatedness between words based on the context. Thus, if the approach is based only on the word without its context, it will be difficult for humans to understand the meaning of a particular word, and it could result in word sense ambiguity (WSA).

In this paper, we show what are the consequences of the lack of the word context in (Schnabel et al., 2015), and we discuss how to address the resulting challenge. Specifically, we add a sentential context to mitigate word sense ambiguity, and this extension leads to an improved evaluation technique that explicitly accounts for multiple senses of a word.

55

Proceedings of the 1st Workshop on Evaluating Vector Space Representations for NLP, pages 55–61,
Berlin, Germany, August 12, 2016. ©2016 Association for Computational Linguistics

2   Crowdsourcing Evaluation

2.1   Details of the Method

The method in (Schnabel et al., 2015) started by creating a *query inventory* which is a pre-selected set of query terms and semantically related target words. The query inventory consists of 100 query terms that balance frequency, part of speech (POS), and concreteness. The query terms were selected from 10 out of 45 broad categories from WordNet (Miller, 1995). Then, 10 random words with one adjective, one adverb, four nouns, and four verbs were selected based on concrete concepts from each category. Among the 10 words, 3 words were rare with the property that the number of their occurrences in the training corpus— Wikipedia dump (2008-03-01)—is smaller than 2500.

For each of those 100 query terms in the inventory, the nearest neighbours at ranks $k \in \{1, 5, 50\}$ for the six embeddings from CBOW (Mikolov et al., 2013), Glove (Pennington et al., 2014), TSCCA (Dhillon et al., 2012), C&W (Collobert et al., 2011), H-PCA (Lebret and Lebret, 2013), and Random Projection (Li et al., 2006) were retrieved. Then, for each k, the query word along with the six words corresponding to the embeddings described above were presented to human testers (Turkers) from Amazon Mechanical Turk (MTurk) for evaluation. Each Turker was requested to evaluate between 20 and 50 items per task, where an item corresponds to the query term and a set of 6 retrieved nearest neighbour words from each of the six embeddings. The Turkers' were then asked to select one of the six words that is the closest synonym to the query word according to their perception. For the selected 100 query words and 3 ranks (k), there were a total of 300 terms on which Turkers' perception-based choices were used for evaluating the embedding techniques. The comparison of embeddings was done by averaging the win ratio, where the win ratio was how many times the Turker chose a particular embedding divided by the number of total ratings for the corresponding query word.

2.2   Shortcomings of the Method

A word relatedness evaluation task for word embeddings is challenging due to ambiguity inherent in word sense and corresponding reference. Although the experiments in (Schnabel et al., 2015) incorporated participants with adequate knowledge of English, the ambiguity is inherent in the language. This means that evaluations that ignore the context may have impact on the evaluation result. Also, the evaluated word embedding techniques in (Schnabel et al., 2015)— except TSCCA (Dhillon et al., 2015)—generate one vector for each word, and that makes comparisons between two related words from two embedding techniques difficult. For example, the word 'bank' may be embedded by CBOW as a noun in the context of 'he cashed a cheque at the bank' where the related word according to nearest neighbours would be 'financial' or 'finance' whereas the TSCCA might embed the same 'bank' as a noun but in the context of 'they pulled the canoe up on the bank' where related word according to nearest neighbours would be 'slope' or 'incline'. Although all the embedding techniques have been trained with the same corpus, different techniques may encode different explanatory factors of variation present in the data (Gao et al., 2014), and using one embedding vector per word cannot capture the different meanings (Huang et al., 2012), and as a result, not all senses will be conflated into one representation.

If the query word 'bank' is presented to a user with 'financial' and 'incline' as related words, and a user is asked which one is more likely to be a related word, then the user has to choose one word, but she does not know the context. Therefore, if 100 people were asked to evaluate the query word, and 50 persons voted for 'financial' and 50 persons voted for 'incline' to be a related word, then both CBOW and TSCCA have the same score. However, this judgement would be inaccurate as CBOW can embed one vector per word whereas TSCCA can embed multiple vectors for each word. Thus user's choice of a related word does not have sufficient impact on the quality evaluation of the embedding techniques. Note that the word 'bank', as a noun, has 10 senses in WordNet.

Before we introduce our extensions in the next section, we investigate how (Schnabel et al., 2015) accommodates word sense ambiguity. The Turker is presented with a query word and several related words to choose from. If the options presented to the Turker are from different contexts, the Turker has to choose from several correct senses. The Turker could be instructed that multiple senses can be encountered during the experiment, and one of the two alternative solutions could be considered:

1. **Biased** Select the sense that is most likely according to your knowledge of the language
2. **Uniform sampling** Select one sense randomly giving the same preference to all options

The first approach would be more appropriate because senses that are more common would be given higher priority. The second option would be hard to implement in practice because it is not clear if random sampling could be achieved, but this option will be useful to show connections with our method. Certainly, even if the Turker can sample according to a uniform probability, the real samples would depend on which senses contained in the corpus were captured by various word embedding techniques. Overall, using the above options, one could argue that the method accommodates different senses because the evaluation measures how well the word embedding methods recover the sense selection strategy of the user. The biased method would be desirable because it would focus on the most frequent senses, but one should note that this would depend on the subjective judgement of the user and her knowledge.

3 Proposed Extensions

Recent efforts on multiple embeddings for words (Neelakantan et al., 2015; Reisinger and Mooney, 2010) require a more sophisticated evaluation and further motivate our ideas. There are existing works, such as (Song, 2016; Iacobacci et al., 2015), where the sense embedding was proposed as a remedy for the current word embedding limitation on ubiquitous polysemous words, and the method learns a vector for each sense of a word. For words with multiple meanings, it is important to see how many senses a word embedding technique can represent through multiple vectors. To achieve such an evaluation, we have first extended the work of (Schnabel et al., 2015) to include sentential context to avoid word sense ambiguity faced by a human tester. In our method, every query word is accompanied by a context sentence. We then extended the method further so that it is more suitable to evaluate embedding techniques designed for polysemous words with regard to their ability to embed diverse senses.

3.1 First Extension

Our chief idea is to extend the work of (Schnabel et al., 2015) by adding a context sentence for each query term. Using a context sentence for resolving word sense ambiguity is not a new concept, and it has been used by numerous researchers, such as (Melamud et al., 2015; Huang et al., 2012; Stetina et al., 1998; Biemann, 2013). In particular, human judgement based approaches, such as (Huang et al., 2012), have used the sentential context to determine the similarity between two words, and (Biemann, 2013) used sentential context for lexical substitution realising the importance of the word interpretation in the context for crowdsourcing-based evaluations.

Due to limited and potentially insufficient embedded vocabulary used to identify a related sense of the query term, we are also proposing to provide another option of 'None of the above' along with the six words. In fact, (Schnabel et al., 2015) have already considered 'I don't know the meaning of one (or several) of the words'; however, when the context is in place, there may be a situation when none of the embeddings make a good match for the query term, and in that case 'None of the above' is more appropriate. In this way, the user's response will be more justified, and a more reliable evaluation score will be retrieved. Our proposal is based on an observation that human reasoning about a word is based on the context, and in crowdsourcing evaluations, we use a human to interpret the meaning; and based on their judgement, we evaluate embedding techniques. So the human should be presented with the examples in the manner that is consistent with what humans see in real-life.

3.2 Second Extension

In our first extension above, every query word is presented in a context. In order to implement a multi-sense evaluation, every query word is presented in several contexts where contexts represent different senses. The number (p) of the contexts presented, where $p \geq 1$, will depend on the number and frequency of available senses for a particular query word. Note that p contexts for the query word are presented in every round, and the Turker has more senses to choose from when word embeddings encode multiple senses per word.

3.3 Example

The true, related words are those that are retrieved from the embedding techniques using the nearest neighbour algorithm, for example. Below, we show an example word 'bar' together with its context; the context is extracted from WordNet.

Query Word: **Bar**, [Context Sentence: He drowned his sorrows in whiskey at the <u>bar</u>.], {True Related Words: barroom, bar, saloon, ginmill, taproom}

To extend the evaluation for multi-sense embedding capabilities of the embedding techniques, we will extend the example setting above by adding multiple test cases for each query word representing different senses. Note that this is not needed in (Schnabel et al., 2015) where query words are not annotated. In the above example, only one test case per query word was presented. However, for the query word 'Bar' as a noun, there are 15 senses available in WordNet 3.0, and 23 senses available in 2012 version of Wikipedia (Dandala et al., 2013a). For the second extension, the human evaluator will be presented with p context sentences representing p different senses. The criteria for selecting senses, and the corresponding context sentences will be discussed in the next section.

3.4 Context Generation

In every iteration, every word embedding method will return its best match for the query term. Our method will need to determine a context (i.e. an appropriate sentence for the given word). We call this process context generation, and this section introduces two approaches that can be used to implement it.

3.4.1 Informed Matching

In this informed approach, our assumption is that the senses selected for the query word should exist in the training corpus. Below we explain how to implement this feature.

Matching Frequent Senses In this approach, the goal is to use the most frequent senses from WordNet. In this way, we can take into account the frequency of senses embedded in WordNet. For every query word, the most frequent n, where $n \geq 1$, word senses will be selected from WordNet. Note that we have to select only those senses that exist in our training corpus which is Wikipedia in this case. The mapping of the senses between Wikipedia and WordNet will be implemented using a method similar to (Mihalcea, 2007, Section 3.1). In the final step of their method, the labels (Wikipedia senses) are manually (i.e. they are performed by a human) mapped to WordNet senses. An alternative approach would be automated mapping introduced in (Fernando and Stevenson, 2012), which does not require human intervention. One could argue that the manual

mapping would be more accurate because of the incorporation of the human judgement, however, this is expensive and time consuming. As the overlapping, most frequent senses from the Wikipedia and WordNet will be chosen, the correct senses corresponding to the embedded word can be selected by Turkers as long as the word embedding methods are accurate. Since our method presents n senses per run, it is more likely that one or more of the chosen senses were embedded by the embedding techniques. Note that senses in WordNet are generally ordered from the most frequent to the least frequent. WordNet sense frequencies come from the SemCor (Miller et al., 1993) sense-tagged corpus which means that WordNet frequencies are well justified, and they are based on data. The example sentence corresponding to the chosen sense will be taken as a context sentence. As WordNet was annotated by humans, we assume that the context sentences are correct for a particular sense.

Matching Rare Senses In (Vossen et al., 2013), the authors argue that current *sense-tagged* corpora have insufficient support for rare senses and contexts and, as a result, they may not be sufficient for word-sense-disambiguation. For example, WordNet 3.0 has 15 senses for the word 'bar' as a noun, whereas 2012 version of Wikipedia has 23 senses (Dandala et al., 2013a) for this word. As a remedy for this issue, we propose another way to generate contexts where we utilise m, where $m \geq 1$, randomly selected senses from the training corpus (Wikipedia in our case). Note that this section applies to the situation where none of the rare senses exist in WordNet. Since Wikipedia does not contain frequencies for senses, sampling has to be according to a uniform distribution. Overall, Wikipedia can be used as a training corpus for the embedding methods and also for sense annotation.

In (Mihalcea, 2007), the authors showed that links in Wikipedia articles are appropriate for representing a sense. When Wikipedia will be used for selecting rare senses, the context sentence will be retrieved using a similar method to (Mihalcea, 2007, Section 3.1). Specifically, in the final step of the mapping method of (Mihalcea, 2007, Section 3.1), the labels (Wikipedia senses) were mapped to WordNet senses. However, this time we are interested in the word senses that are not available in WordNet; as a result, we will map the selected senses from Wikipedia to the appropri-

ate subsenses in the Oxford Dictionary of English
(ODE) (Soanes and Stevenson, 2003). Note that
ODE provides a hierarchical structure of senses,
and each polysemous sense is divided into a core
sense and a set of subsenses (Navigli, 2006). We
will follow an approach similar to (Navigli, 2006)
where WordNet sense was semantically mapped
to the ODE core senses. They mapped to the core
senses because they were interested in the coarse-
grained sense mapping to resolve granularity inherent in WordNet. In our case, we will do semantic mapping between Wikipedia senses (piped
link or simple link) and ODE subsenses, instead
of mapping the WordNet sense to the ODE core
senses. Then, corresponding context sentences
will be selected from Wikipedia or ODE.

Overall, when the corresponding context sentence for a query term is not available in Word-
Net, the context sentence can be retrieved from
Wikipedia (Mihalcea, 2007; Dandala et al., 2013b)
or ODE using the method described above.

3.4.2 Random Matching

The informed method described above requires either manual matching by humans (which are time
consuming and expensive) or an automated matching which may be inaccurate. An alternative approach is to sample senses randomly from Word-
Net ignoring senses contained in the training corpus. The sampling distribution should be based on
frequencies of senses. In this case, 'None of the
above' option will be used whenever none of the
embedded words are related to the query word according to the presented context. If we consider a
large number of Turkers' evaluations, the evaluation will still give the performance score reflecting
the true performance score of the embedding technique. However, this will be more costly because
more Turkers will be required.

3.5 Merit of our Extensions

At the end of Sec. 2.2, we explained how word
sense ambiguity is accommodated in (Schnabel et
al., 2015). We argued that their evaluation was
in expectation with respect to subjective preferences of the Turkers. Additionally, when the context is not provided, the Turkers may even forget about common senses of the query word. In
our proposal, we argue that query words should
be presented in an appropriate context. Similar to
Sec. 2.2, we can distinguish two ways in which we
can apply our method:

1. **Informed sampling** Sample senses according to their frequency in WordNet
2. **Uniform sampling** Sample senses according
   to a uniform probability distribution if no frequency data is available (e.g. Wikipedia)

We can now draw a parallel with alternative ways
that Turkers may apply to solve the word sense
ambiguity problem. In particular, under certain
conditions (i.e. when word embeddings don't use
sense frequency information), the uniform sampling option in our method would be equivalent
with the uniform sampling method in Sec. 2.2.
This means that asking the Turkers to select senses
randomly according to a uniform probability distribution is the same as sampling contexts according to a uniform distribution. The two approaches differ, however, when non-uniform, informed probability distributions are used. Informed sampling in our approach is based on
WordNet whose sense frequencies are based on
data-driven research. This means that the overall evaluation would be based on real frequencies coming from the data instead of subjective
and idiosyncratic judgements by the Turkers. This
probabilistic argument provides another justifica-
tion for our approach.

4 Conclusion

In this paper, a crowdsourcing-based word embedding evaluation technique of (Schnabel et al.,
2015) was extended to provide data-driven treatment of word sense ambiguity. The method of
(Schnabel et al., 2015) relies on user's subjective
and knowledge dependent ability to select 'preferred' meanings whereas our method would deal
with this problem selecting explicit contexts for
words. The selection is according to the real frequencies of meanings computed from data. With
this data-driven feature, our method could be more
appropriate to evaluate both methods that produce one embedding per *word* as well as methods that produce one embedding per *word sense*.
Our method would provide scores that accommo-
date word sense frequencies in the real use of the
language. Here, we assume that word embeddings should recover the most frequent senses with
higher priority.

Acknowledgement We thank the anonymous
reviewers for stimulating criticism and for point-
ing out important references. We also thank Omer
Levy for being a supportive workshop organiser.

References

Vamshi Ambati, Stephan Vogel, and Jaime Carbonell. 2010. Active learning and crowd-sourcing for machine translation. In *Proceedings of the Seventh International Conference on Language Resources and Evaluation (LREC-2010)*, pages 2169–2174, Valletta, Malta, May. European Languages Resources Association (ELRA). ACL Anthology Identifier: L10-1165.

Vamshi Ambati. 2012. *Active Learning and Crowdsourcing for Machine Translation in Low Resource Scenarios*. Ph.D. thesis, Pittsburgh, PA, USA. AAI3528171.

Chris Biemann. 2013. Creating a system for lexical substitutions from scratch using crowdsourcing. *Language Resources and Evaluation*, 47(1):97–122.

Chris Callison-Burch. 2009. Fast, cheap, and creative: Evaluating translation quality using amazon's mechanical turk. In *Proceedings of the 2009 Conference on Empirical Methods in Natural Language Processing*, pages 286–295, Singapore, August. Association for Computational Linguistics.

Ronan Collobert, Jason Weston, Léon Bottou, Michael Karlen, Koray Kavukcuoglu, and Pavel Kuksa. 2011. Natural language processing (almost) from scratch. *J. Mach. Learn. Res.*, 12:2493–2537, November.

Bharath Dandala, Chris Hokamp, Rada Mihalcea, and Razvan C. Bunescu. 2013a. Sense clustering using wikipedia. In Galia Angelova, Kalina Bontcheva, and Ruslan Mitkov, editors, *Recent Advances in Natural Language Processing, RANLP 2013, 9-11 September, 2013, Hissar, Bulgaria*, pages 164–171. RANLP 2013 Organising Committee / ACL.

Bharath Dandala, Rada Mihalcea, and Razvan Bunescu. 2013b. Word sense disambiguation using wikipedia. In *The People's Web Meets NLP*, pages 241–262. Springer.

Paramveer S. Dhillon, Jordan Rodu, Dean P. Foster, and Lyle H. Ungar. 2012. Two step cca: A new spectral method for estimating vector models of words. In *Proceedings of the 29th International Conference on Machine learning*, ICML'12.

Paramveer S. Dhillon, Dean P. Foster, and Lyle H. Ungar. 2015. Eigenwords: Spectral word embeddings. *Journal of Machine Learning Research*, 16:3035–3078.

Miriam Faust and Christine Chiarello. 1998. Sentence context and lexical ambiguity resolution by the two hemispheres. *Neuropsychologia*, 36(9):827–835.

Samuel Fernando and Mark Stevenson. 2012. Mapping wordnet synsets to wikipedia articles. In *Proceedings of the Eight International Conference on Language Resources and Evaluation (LREC'12)*, Istanbul, Turkey, may. European Language Resources Association (ELRA).

Bin Gao, Jiang Bian, and Tie-Yan Liu. 2014. Wordrep: A benchmark for research on learning word representations. *CoRR*, abs/1407.1640.

Eric H. Huang, Richard Socher, Christopher D. Manning, and Andrew Y. Ng. 2012. Improving word representations via global context and multiple word prototypes. In *Proceedings of the 50th Annual Meeting of the Association for Computational Linguistics: Long Papers - Volume 1*, ACL '12, pages 873–882, Stroudsburg, PA, USA. Association for Computational Linguistics.

Ignacio Iacobacci, Mohammad Taher Pilehvar, and Roberto Navigli. 2015. Sensembed: learning sense embeddings for word and relational similarity. In *Proceedings of ACL*, pages 95–105.

Rémi Lebret and Ronan Lebret. 2013. Word emdeddings through hellinger PCA. *CoRR*, abs/1312.5542.

Ping Li, Trevor J. Hastie, and Kenneth W. Church. 2006. Very sparse random projections. In *Proceedings of the 12th ACM SIGKDD International Conference on Knowledge Discovery and Data Mining*, KDD '06, pages 287–296, New York, NY, USA. ACM.

Oren Melamud, Omer Levy, and Ido Dagan. 2015. A simple word embedding model for lexical substitution. In *Proceedings of the 1st Workshop on Vector Space Modeling for Natural Language Processing*.

Rada Mihalcea. 2007. Using wikipedia for automatic word sense disambiguation. In *HLT-NAACL*, pages 196–203.

Tomas Mikolov, Ilya Sutskever, Kai Chen, Greg S Corrado, and Jeff Dean. 2013. Distributed representations of words and phrases and their compositionality. In C. J. C. Burges, L. Bottou, M. Welling, Z. Ghahramani, and K. Q. Weinberger, editors, *Advances in Neural Information Processing Systems 26*, pages 3111–3119. Curran Associates, Inc.

George A. Miller, Claudia Leacock, Randee Tengi, and Ross T. Bunker. 1993. A semantic concordance. In *Proceedings of the workshop on Human Language Technology*, HLT '93, pages 303–308, Stroudsburg, PA, USA. Association for Computational Linguistics.

George A. Miller. 1995. Wordnet: A lexical database for english. *Commun. ACM*, 38(11):39–41, November.

Roberto Navigli. 2006. Meaningful clustering of senses helps boost word sense disambiguation performance. In *Proceedings of the 21st International Conference on Computational Linguistics and the 44th annual meeting of the Association for Computational Linguistics*, pages 105–112. Association for Computational Linguistics.

Arvind Neelakantan, Jeevan Shankar, Alexandre Passos, and Andrew McCallum. 2015. Efficient non-parametric estimation of multiple embeddings per word in vector space. *arXiv preprint arXiv:1504.06654*.

Siddharth Patwardhan, Satanjeev Banerjee, and Ted Pedersen. 2003. Using measures of semantic relatedness for word sense disambiguation. In *Proceedings of the 4th International Conference on Computational Linguistics and Intelligent Text Processing*, CICLing'03, pages 241–257, Berlin, Heidelberg. Springer-Verlag.

Jeffrey Pennington, Richard Socher, and Christopher Manning. 2014. Glove: Global Vectors for Word Representation. In *Proceedings of the 2014 Conference on Empirical Methods in Natural Language Processing (EMNLP)*, pages 1532–1543, Doha, Qatar, October. Association for Computational Linguistics.

Joseph Reisinger and Raymond J Mooney. 2010. Multi-prototype vector-space models of word meaning. In *Human Language Technologies: The 2010 Annual Conference of the North American Chapter of the Association for Computational Linguistics*, pages 109–117. Association for Computational Linguistics.

Tobias Schnabel, Igor Labutov, David Mimno, and Thorsten Joachims. 2015. Evaluation methods for unsupervised word embeddings. In *Proceedings of the 2015 Conference on Empirical Methods in Natural Language Processing*, pages 298–307, Lisbon, Portugal, September. Association for Computational Linguistics.

Catherine Soanes and Angus Stevenson, editors. 2003. *Oxford Dictionary of English*. Cambridge University Press.

Linfeng Song. 2016. Word embeddings, sense embeddings and their application to word sense induction. The University of Rochester, April.

Jiri Stetina, Sadao Kurohashi, and Makoto Nagao. 1998. General word sense disambiguation method based on a full sentential context. In *In Usage of WordNet in Natural Language Processing, Proceedings of COLING-ACL Workshop*.

Edward Vajda. 2001. Semantics. Webpage for course material of Linguistics 201:INTRODUCTION TO LINGUISTICS.

Piek Vossen, Rubn Izquierdo, and Attila Grg. 2013. Dutchsemcor: in quest of the ideal sense-tagged corpus. In Galia Angelova, Kalina Bontcheva, and Ruslan Mitkov, editors, *RANLP*, pages 710–718. RANLP 2013 Organising Committee / ACL.

Evaluation of acoustic word embeddings

Sahar Ghannay, Yannick Estève, Nathalie Camelin, Paul deléglise
LIUM - University of Le Mans, France
`firstname.lastname@univ-lemans.fr`

Abstract

Recently, researchers in speech recognition have started to reconsider using whole words as the basic modeling unit, instead of phonetic units. These systems rely on a function that embeds an arbitrary or fixed dimensional speech segments to a vector in a fixed-dimensional space, named acoustic word embedding. Thus, speech segments of words that sound similarly will be projected in a close area in a continuous space. This paper focuses on the evaluation of acoustic word embeddings. We propose two approaches to evaluate the intrinsic performances of acoustic word embeddings in comparison to orthographic representations in order to evaluate whether they capture discriminative phonetic information. Since French language is targeted in experiments, a particular focus is made on homophone words.

1 Introduction

Recent studies have started to reconsider the use of whole words as the basic modeling unit in speech recognition and query applications, instead of phonetic units. These systems are based on the use of acoustic word embedding, which are projection of arbitrary or fixed dimensional speech segments into a continuous space, in a manner that preserve acoustic similarity between words. Thus, speech segments of words that sound similarly will have similar embeddings. Acoustic word embedding were successfully used in a query-by-example search system (Kamper et al., 2015; Levin et al., 2013) and in a ASR lattice re-scoring system (Bengio and Heigold, 2014).

The authors in (Bengio and Heigold, 2014) proposed an approach to build acoustic word embeddings from an orthographic representation of the word. This paper focuses on the evaluation of these acoustic word embeddings. We propose two approaches to evaluate the intrinsic performances of acoustic word embeddings in comparison to orthographic representations. In particular we want to evaluate whether they capture discriminative information about their pronunciation, approximated by their phonetic representation. In our experiments, we focus on French language whose particularity is to be rich of homophone words. This aspect is also studied in this work.

2 Acoustic word embeddings

2.1 Building acoustic word embeddings

The approach we used to build acoustic word embeddings is inspired from the one proposed in (Bengio and Heigold, 2014). The deep neural architecture depicted in figure 1 is used to train the acoustic word embeddings. It relies on a convolutional neural network (CNN) classifier over words and on a deep neural network (DNN) trained by using a triplet ranking loss (Bengio and Heigold, 2014; Wang et al., 2014; Weston et al., 2011).

The two architectures are trained using different inputs: speech signal and orthographic representation of the word, which are detailed as follows.

The convolutional neural network classifier is trained independently to predict a word given a speech signal as input. It is composed of convolution and pooling layers, followed by fully connected layers which feed the final softmax layer. The embedding layer is the fully connected layer just below the softmax one, named **s** in the figure 1. This representation contains a compact representation of the acoustic signal. It tends to preserve acoustic similarity between words, such that words are close in this space if they sound alike.

The feedforward neural network (DNN) is used

Proceedings of the 1st Workshop on Evaluating Vector Space Representations for NLP, pages 62–66,
Berlin, Germany, August 12, 2016. ©2016 Association for Computational Linguistics

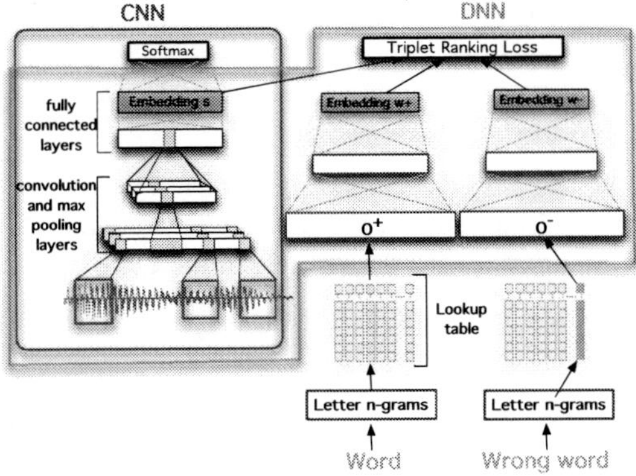

Figure 1: Deep architecture used to train acoustic word embeddings.

with the purpose to build an acoustic word embedding for a word not observed in the audio training corpus, based on its orthographic representation. It is trained using the triplet ranking loss function in order to project orthographic word representations to the same space as the acoustic embeddings $\mathbf{s}$.

The orthographic word representation consists in a bag of n-grams ($n \leq 3$) of letters, with additional special symbols $[$ and $]$ to specify the start and the end of a word. The size of this bag of n-grams vector is reduced using an auto-encoder.

During the training process, this model takes as inputs acoustic embeddings $\mathbf{s}$ selected randomly from the training set and, for each signal acoustic embedding, the orthographic representation of the matching word $\mathbf{o}^+$, and the orthographic representation of a randomly selected word different to the first word $\mathbf{o}^-$. These two orthographic representations supply shared parameters in the DNN.

The resulting DNN model can then be used to build an acoustic word embedding ($\mathbf{w}^+$) from any word, as long as one can extract an orthographic representation from it. This acoustic word embedding can be perceived as a canonical acoustic representation for a word, since different pronunciations imply different signal embeddings $\mathbf{s}$.

2.2 Evaluation

In the literature (Kamper et al., 2015; Levin et al., 2013; Carlin et al., 2011), a word discrimination task was used to evaluate acoustic embeddings $\mathbf{s}$. Given a pair of acoustic segments, this task consists on deciding whether the segments correspond to the same words or not. This evalua-

tion task can be performed on many ways, for example through the use of a dynamic time warping (DTW) to quantify the similarity between two segments when using frame level embeddings (Thiolliere et al., 2015), or by using the euclidean distance or the cosine similarity between embeddings representing the segments.

In (Kamper et al., 2015) the evaluation was conducted on two collections of words (train and test) coming from the Switchboard English corpus. After training the model on the training corpus, the cosine similarity is computed between the embeddings of each pair of words in the test set. These pairs are classified as similar or different by applying a threshold on their distance, and a precision-recall curve is obtained by varying the threshold.

In this study, we propose two approaches to evaluate acoustic word embeddings $\mathbf{w}^+$. We suggest to build different evaluation sets in order to assess the acoustic word embeddings ($\mathbf{w}^+$) performances on *orthographic* and *phonetic similarity* and *homophones detection* tasks. We remind that the acoustic word embedding $\mathbf{w}^+$ is a projection of an orthographic word representation $\mathbf{o}^+$ into the space of acoustic signal embeddings $\mathbf{s}$. In our evaluation, we would like to measure the loss of orthographic information carried by $\mathbf{w}^+$ and the potential gain of acoustic information due to this projection, in comparison to the information carried by $\mathbf{o}^+$.

The evaluation sets are built as follows: given a list L of n frequent words (candidate words) in the vocabulary composed of m words, a list of $n \times m$ word pairs was created. Then, two alignments were performed between each word pair based on their orthographic (letters) and phonetic (phonemes) representations, using the sclite[1] tool.

From these alignment two *edition distances* are computed with respect to the alignment results of orthographic and phonetic representations. The Edition distance is computed as follows:

$$SER = \frac{\#In + \#Sub + \#Del}{\#symbols\ in\ the\ reference\ word} \times 100 \quad (1)$$

where SER stands for Symbol Error rate, *symbols* correspond to the letters for orthographic representations, and to the phonemes for phonetic ones, and In, Sub and Del correspond respectively to insertion, substitution and deletion.

---

[1] http://www.icsi.berkeley.edu/Speech/docs/sctk-1.2/sclite.htm

Next, we compute two *similarity scores* that correspond to the orthographic and phonetic similarity scores *sim_score* attributed for each pair of words, which are defined as:

$$sim\_score = 10 - \min(10, SER/10) \qquad (2)$$

where $\min()$ is a function used to have an edition distance between 0 and 10. Then, for each candidate word in the list L we extract its orthographically and phonetically 10 nearest words. This results in two lists for *orthographic* and *phonetic similarity* tasks. For each candidate word in the list L, the Orthographic list contains its ten closest words in terms of orthographic similarity scores and the Phonetic list contains its ten closest words in terms of phonetic similarity scores. Finally, the Homophones list, used for the *homophone* detection task, contains the homophone words (*i.e.* sharing the same phonetic representation).

Table 1 shows an example of the content of the three lists.

List	Exampls
Orthographic	très près 7.5 très ors 5
Phononetic	très frais 6.67 très traînent 6.67
Homophone	très traie très traient

Table 1: Example of the content of the three lists.

In the case of the orthographic and phonetic similarity tasks, the evaluation of the acoustic embeddings is performed by ranking the pairs according to their cosine similarities and measuring the Spearman's rank correlation coefficient (Spearman's ρ). This approach is used in (Gao et al., 2014; Ji et al., 2015; Levy et al., 2015; Ghannay et al., 2016) to evaluate the linguistic word embeddings on similarity tasks, in which the similarity scores are attributed by human annotators.

For the homophone detection task, the evaluation is performed in terms of precision. For each word w in the Homophones list, let $L_H(w)$ be the list of k homophones of the word w, and $L_{H\_neighbour}(w)$ be the list of k nearest neighbours extracted based on the cosine similarity and $L_{H\_found}(w)$ be the intersection between $L_H(w)$ and $L_{H\_neighbour}(w)$, that corresponds to the list of homophones found of the word w.

The precision P_w of the word w is defined as:

$$P_w = \frac{|L_{H\_found}(w)|}{|L_H(w)|} \qquad (3)$$

where $|.|$ refers to the size of a list. We define the overall homophone detection precision on the Homophones list as the average of the P_w:

$$P = \frac{\sum_{i=1}^{N} P_{w_i}}{N} \qquad (4)$$

where N is the number of candidate words which have a none-empty Homophones list.

3 Experiments on acoustic word embeddings

3.1 Experimental setup

The training set for the CNN consists of 488 hours of French Broadcast News with manual transcriptions. This dataset is composed of data coming from the ESTER1 (Galliano et al., 2005), ESTER2 (Galliano et al., 2009) and EPAC (Estève et al., 2010) corpora.

It contains $52k$ unique words that have been seen at least twice each in the corpus. All of them corresponds to a total of 5.75 millions occurrences. In French language, many words have the same pronunciation without sharing the same spelling, and they can have different meanings; *e.g.* the sound [so] corresponds to four homophones: *sot* (fool), *saut* (jump), *sceau* (seal) and *seau* (bucket), and twice more by taking into account their plural forms that have the same pronunciation: *sots, sauts, sceaux*, and *seaux*. When a CNN is trained to predict a word given an acoustic sequence, these frequent homophones can introduce a bias to evaluate the recognition error. To avoid this, we merged all the homophones existing among the $52k$ unique words of the training corpus. As a result, we obtained a new reduced dictionary containing $45k$ words and classes of homophones.

Acoustic features provided to the CNN are log-filterbanks, computed every 10ms over a 25ms window yielding a 23-dimension vector for each frame. A forced alignment between manual transcriptions and speech signal was performed on the training set in order to detect word boundaries. The statistics computed from this alignment reveal that 99% of words are shorter than 1 second. Hence we decided to represent each word by 100 frames, thus, by a vector of 2300 dimensions.

When words are shorter they are padded with zero equally on both ends, while longer words are cut equally on both ends.

The CNN and DNN deep architectures are trained on 90% of the training set and the remaining 10% are used for validation.

3.2 Acoustic word embeddings evaluation

The embeddings we evaluate are built from two different vocabularies: the one used to train the neural network models (CNN and DNN), composed of $52k$ words present in the manual transcriptions of the 488 hours of audio; and another one composed of $160k$ words. The words present in the $52k$ vocabulary are nearly all present in the $160k$ vocabulary.

The evaluation sets described in section 2.2 are generated from these two vocabularies: in the $52k$ vocabulary, all the acoustic word embeddings w^+ are related to words which have been observed during the training of the CNN. This means that at least two acoustic signal embeddings have been computed from the audio for each one of these words; in the $160k$ vocabulary, about $110k$ acoustic word embeddings were computed for words never observed in the audio data.

3.2.1 Quantitative Evaluation

The quantitative evaluation of the acoustic word embeddings w^+ is performed on orthographic similarity, phonetic similarity, and homophones detection tasks. Results are summarized in table 2.

Task	52K Vocab.		160K Vocab.	
	o^+	w^+	o^+	w^+
Orthographic	**54.28**	49.97	**56.95**	51.06
Phonetic	40.40	**43.55**	41.41	**46.88**
Homophone	64.65	**72.28**	52.87	**59.33**

Table 2: Evaluation results of similarity ($\rho \times 100$) and homophone detection tasks (*precision*).

They show that the acoustic word embeddings w^+ are more relevant for the phonetic similarity task, while o^+ are obviously the best ones on the orthographic similarity task.

These results show that the projection of the orthographic embeddings o^+ into the acoustic embeddings space s changes their properties, since they have captured more information about word pronunciation while they have lost information

about spelling. So, in addition to making possible a measure of similarity distance between the acoustic signal (represented by s) and a word (represented by w^+), acoustic word embeddings are better than orthographic ones to measure the phonetic proximity between two words.

For the homophone detection task, the Homophones list is computed from the $160k$ vocabulary: that results to 53869 homophone pairs in total. The $52k$ vocabulary contains 13561 homophone pairs which are included in the pairs present in the $160k$ vocabulary. As we can see, the w^+ acoustic embeddings outperform the orthographic ones on this task on the two data sets. This confirms that acoustic word embeddings have captured additional information about word pronunciation than the one carried by orthographic word embeddings. For this task we cannot compare the results between the two vocabularies, since the precision measure is dependent to the number of events. For the Spearman's correlation, a comparison is roughly possible and results show that the way to compute w^+ is effective to generalize this computation to word not observed in the audio training data.

3.2.2 Qualitative Evaluation

To give more insight into the difference of the quality of the orthographic word embeddings o^+ and the acoustic ones w^+, we propose an empirical comparison by showing the nearest neighbours of a given set of words. Table 3 shows examples of such neighbour. It can be seen that, as expected, neighbour of any given word share the same spelling with it when they are induced by the orthographic embeddings and arguably sound like it when they are induced by the acoustic word ones.

Candidate word	o^+	w^+
grecs	i-grec, rec, marec	grec, grecque, grecques
ail	aile, trail, fail	aille, ailles, aile
arts	parts, charts, encarts	arte, art, ars
blocs	bloch, blocher, bloche	bloc, bloque, bloquent

Table 3: Candidate words and their nearest neighbours

4 Conclusion

In this paper, we have investigated the intrinsic evaluation of acoustic word embeddings. These latter offer the opportunity of an *a priori* acoustic representation of words that can be compared, in terms of similarity, to an embedded representation of the audio signal. We have proposed two approaches to evaluate the performances of these acoustic word embeddings and compare them to their orthographic embeddings: orthographic and phonetic performance by ranking pairs and measuring the Spearman's rank correlation coefficient (Spearman's ρ), and by measuring the precision in a homophone detection task.

Experiments show that the acoustic word embeddings are better than orthographic ones to measure the phonetic proximity between two words. More, they are better too on homophone detection task. This confirms that acoustic word embeddings have captured additional information about word pronunciation.

Acknowledgments

This work was partially funded by the European Commission through the EUMSSI project, under the contract number 611057, in the framework of the FP7-ICT-2013-10 call, by the French National Research Agency (ANR) through the VERA project, under the contract number ANR-12-BS02-006-01, and by the Région Pays de la Loire.

References

Samy Bengio and Georg Heigold. 2014. Word embeddings for speech recognition. In *INTERSPEECH*, pages 1053–1057.

Michael A Carlin, Samuel Thomas, Aren Jansen, and Hynek Hermansky. 2011. Rapid Evaluation of Speech Representations for Spoken Term Discovery. In *INTERSPEECH*, pages 821–824.

Yannick Estève, Thierry Bazillon, Jean-Yves Antoine, Frédéric Béchet, and Jérôme Farinas. 2010. The EPAC Corpus: Manual and Automatic Annotations of Conversational Speech in French Broadcast News. In *LREC, Malta, 17-23 may 2010*.

Sylvain Galliano, Edouard Geoffrois, Djamel Mostefa, Khalid Choukri, Jean-François Bonastre, and Guillaume Gravier. 2005. The ESTER phase II evaluation campaign for the rich transcription of French Broadcast News. In *Interspeech*, pages 1149–1152.

Sylvain Galliano, Guillaume Gravier, and Laura Chaubard. 2009. The ESTER 2 evaluation campaign for the rich transcription of French radio broadcasts. In *Interspeech*, volume 9, pages 2583–2586.

Bin Gao, Jiang Bian, and Tie-Yan Liu. 2014. Wordrep: A benchmark for research on learning word representations. *CoRR*, abs/1407.1640.

Sahar Ghannay, Benoit Favre, Yannick Estève, and Nathalie Camelin. 2016. Word embedding evaluation and combination. In *10th edition of the Language Resources and Evaluation Conference (LREC 2016)*, Portorož (Slovenia), 23-28 May.

Shihao Ji, Hyokun Yun, Pinar Yanardag, Shin Matsushima, and S. V. N. Vishwanathan. 2015. Wordrank: Learning word embeddings via robust ranking. *CoRR*, abs/1506.02761.

Herman Kamper, Weiran Wang, and Karen Livescu. 2015. Deep convolutional acoustic word embeddings using word-pair side information. In *arXiv preprint arXiv:1510.01032*.

Keith Levin, Katharine Henry, Anton Jansen, and Karen Livescu. 2013. Fixed-dimensional acoustic embeddings of variable-length segments in low-resource settings. In *Automatic Speech Recognition and Understanding (ASRU), 2013 IEEE Workshop on*, pages 410–415. IEEE.

Omer Levy, Yoav Goldberg, and Ido Dagan. 2015. Improving distributional similarity with lessons learned from word embeddings. *Transactions of the Association for Computational Linguistics*, 3:211–225.

Roland Thiolliere, Ewan Dunbar, Gabriel Synnaeve, Maarten Versteegh, and Emmanuel Dupoux. 2015. A hybrid dynamic time warping-deep neural network architecture for unsupervised acoustic modeling. In *Proc. Interspeech*.

Jiang Wang, Yang Song, Thomas Leung, Chuck Rosenberg, Jingbin Wang, James Philbin, Bo Chen, and Ying Wu. 2014. Learning fine-grained image similarity with deep ranking. In *Proceedings of the IEEE Conference on Computer Vision and Pattern Recognition*, pages 1386–1393.

Jason Weston, Samy Bengio, and Nicolas Usunier. 2011. Wsabie: Scaling up to large vocabulary image annotation. In *IJCAI*, volume 11, pages 2764–2770.

Evaluating Embeddings using Syntax-based Classification Tasks as a Proxy for Parser Performance

Arne Köhn
Deparment of Informatics
Universität Hamburg
`koehn@informatik.uni-hamburg.de`

Abstract

Most evaluations for vector space models are semantically motivated, e.g. by measuring how well they capture word similarity. If one is interested in syntax-related downstream applications such as dependency parsing, a syntactically motivated evaluation seems preferable. As we show, the choice of embeddings has a noticeable impact on parser performance. Since evaluating embeddings directly in a parser is costly, we analyze the correlation between the full parsing task and a simple linear classification task as a potential proxy.

1 Introduction

Many complex tasks in NLP are solved using embeddings as additional features. In some pipelines, pre-trained embeddings are used as-is, in others they are learned as an integral part of training the pipeline (examples for this would be e. g. RNNLMs(Mikolov et al., 2010) or parsers that learn their own embeddings (e. g. Chen and Manning (2014))). We focus on the first type. If we want to run a system that can be enhanced using pre-trained embeddings, the question arises which embedding actually works best.

Since it is computationally infeasible to evaluate all embeddings on all pipelines, usually simple tasks are used to demonstrate the strengths of embeddings and an embedding for use in a pipeline is picked based on these proxy tasks. Most of these tasks are semantically motivated and English dominates as language of choice for the tasks. Last year, we proposed a more syntactically motivated evaluation task *syneval*, which uses morpho-syntactic information across a variety of languages (see Section 2).

Morphological information helps syntactic parsers, but usually there is no gold-standard information available during parsing (with the exception of parser evaluation). Using embeddings that are good predictors of the missing morphological information should alleviate the problem of missing morphology.

It is reasonable to assume that the classification problems in syneval are a good proxy for syntax-related tasks because they describe how well an embedding is able to capture morphological information which is helpful to the parser. To test this assumption, we evaluate the performance of RBGParser (Lei et al., 2014; Zhang et al., 2014) using different embeddings as additional features. The parser performance using a specific embedding should then reflect the embedding's performance on the classification tasks. We know that embeddings yield only marginal improvements if the parser also has access to gold standard morphological information but benefits significantly if no morphological information is present (Lei et al., 2014; Köhn et al., 2014). Therefore, we experiment with stripping the information that is used as classification target in syneval.

2 Syneval

In previous work, we proposed to make use of treebanks to extract simple syntactic evaluation tasks (Köhn, 2015) but somehow didn't assign a catchy name. We now make up for this and call this approach *syneval* throughout this paper. For a given syntactic feature type F (e.g. tense or case), a classification task is created as follows: Let W be the set of words forms and $V \subseteq \mathbb{R}^n$ the vector space of a given embedding $W \to V$. Using a treebank where some words[1] are annotated with

---

[1] Some words are not annotated with features of certain types, e. g. nouns are usually annotated without tense markers.

Proceedings of the 1st Workshop on Evaluating Vector Space Representations for NLP, pages 67–71,
Berlin, Germany, August 12, 2016. ©2016 Association for Computational Linguistics

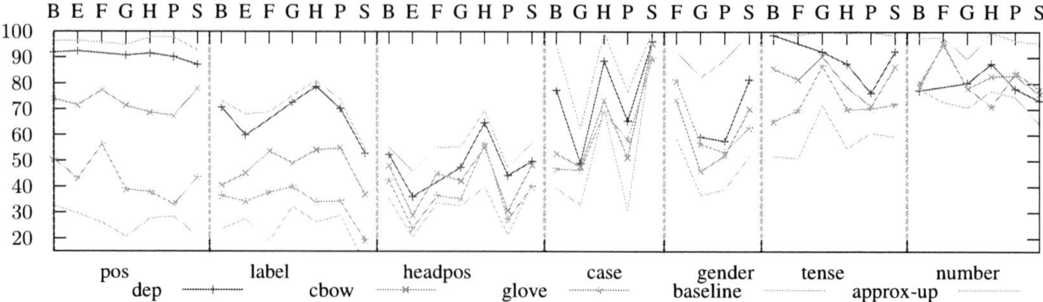

Figure 1: Accuracies for the proxy task *syneval* evaluated on **B**asque, **E**nglish, **F**rench, **G**erman, **H**ungarian, **P**olish, and **S**wedish. Note that dep was not evaluated on French. All results are from Köhn (2015). Results for embeddings not discussed in this paper have been omitted.

a syntactic feature of the given type $f \in F$, we combine the syntactic information with the word vector $v \in V$ of the word, obtaining a pair (v, f) for each word. In other words, we perform an inner join of the embedding and the syntactic annotation on the word and project on V and F.

Note that there is no functional dependence $W \rightarrow F$ because the same word form can have different syntactic features depending on the context. Therefore, there is also no functional dependence between the word vectors and the syntactic features.

A linear classifier is trained on (v, f) pairs to predict the syntactic feature given the word embedding. If the classifier yields a high accuracy, the embeddings encode structure with respect to the syntactic feature type. The vector space is partitioned by the classifier into convex polytopes which each represent one syntactic feature (such as NN for the PoS classification task) and if the classifier has a high accuracy, these polytopes accurately describe the features. Since the classifier does not use any context features and a word vector can be paired with different syntactic features, the upper bound for classification accuracy can be approximated by classification based on the word form. The lower bound is the majority baseline, i.e. using no features at all.

The syntactic features used in syneval are: *pos* (the PoS of the word), *label* (the dependency label), *headpos* (the PoS of the word's head) as well as the morphological features *case*, *gender*, *tense*, and *number*. Syneval results for a selected set of embeddings are depicted in Figure 1.

Syneval has several advantages over other em-

bedding evaluation methods: First of all, it uses several languages instead of being centered on English. It does not need manually generated data such as similarity judgments as the treebanks used for evaluation have already been built for other purposes. Syneval covers much more lexical items than other evaluations: SimLex-999 (Hill et al., 2015, one of the larger word similarity corpora) contains 1030 word forms whereas syneval performs an evaluation on nearly 30.000 word forms for English.

3 Data and Embeddings

To limit the amount of computation, we select four languages out of the seven evaluated by Köhn (2015), namely Basque, German, Hungarian, and Swedish, and three embeddings out of six. Even with these reductions, the experiments for this paper needed about 500 CPU-days. All experiments are performed on data from the SPMRL 2014 (Seddah et al., 2014), using the full training set for each language and the dev set for evaluation.

The embeddings are taken from Köhn (2015). We use the ten-dimensional embeddings, as the differences between the approaches are more pronounced there, and we can be sure that the parser does not drain in high dimensional features (Lei et al. (2014) used 25 and 50 dimensional vectors). Again, we limit the number of embeddings to three: skip-gram using dependency contexts (*dep*, (Levy and Goldberg, 2014)), *GloVe* (Pennington et al., 2014), and word2vec using *cbow* (Mikolov et al., 2013). In the syneval evaluation, dep performed best, GloVe worst, and cbow in between (see Fig-

		dep	cbow	GloVe	none			dep	cbow	GloVe	none
Basque	+all	89.77	89.13	89.79	**90.07**	Hungarian	+all	**88.66**	88.54	88.24	88.39
	-case	89.43	88.12	88.30	88.41		-case	87.52	87.37	87.46	87.10
	-tense	89.81	88.80	89.71	**89.97**		-tense	**87.50**	87.41	87.59	87.26
	-number	89.88	88.86	89.26	89.86		-number	87.59	87.34	87.60	87.07
	-PoS	**88.22**	86.39	87.94	87.99		-PoS	**85.97**	85.72	85.80	85.42
	-all	**85.51**	80.99	81.68	79.24		-all	**81.18**	78.69	78.24	76.08
German	+all	94.87	94.67	94.89	94.82	Swedish	+all	85.17	85.06	84.83	85.17
	-case	94.38	94.20	94.40	94.42		-case	85.20	84.94	84.97	85.15
	-tense	94.87	94.66	94.81	94.76		-tense	84.94	84.94	**85.27**	85.15
	-number	94.84	94.60	94.77	94.83		-number	85.07	84.81	85.06	**85.19**
	-PoS	91.24	90.15	91.15	91.22		-PoS	**79.53**	78.21	78.65	78.68
	-all	**88.26**	86.68	87.72	87.35		-all	**76.55**	73.79	73.41	71.11

Table 1: Unlabeled parsing accuracies using different embeddings as well as no embeddings with varying amounts of gold-standard morphological information available. Results better than the second best by a margin of at least .1 are highlighted.

ure 1). For some tasks, GloVe barely outperforms the majority baseline, i.e. it does not contain much information that can be extracted with a linear classifier.

4 Using Embeddings in a Parser

To evaluate the benefit of using the embeddings mentioned in the previous section in a parser, the parser needs to fulfill several requirements: The parser needs to work both with and without embeddings, it needs to use pre-trained embeddings, and it should make use of morphological features. If all these requirements are fulfilled, it is possible to measure the benefit of different embeddings as well as using embeddings at all, and whether morphological information supersedes such benefits.

Based on the requirements, we chose RBGParser for the evaluation. RBGParser uses embeddings for scoring edges using low-rank tensors. To score edges, the function uses the embedding, form, lemma, pos, and morphological information of the words as well as arc length and direction. In addition to the low-rank tensor, it uses the same features as TurboParser (Martins et al., 2013) as well as some features encoding global properties. Both components are weighted using a hyperparameter which we keep fixed at the default value. Since the embeddings are only used in the tensor component, the quality of the embeddings only affect this component.

Nevertheless, we chose to use the whole parser including all features instead of just measuring the

impact on the low-rank tensor component because it is possible that improvements in this component don't translate to an improvement of the whole parser.

5 Experiments

The basic idea is as follows: If an embedding encodes a morphological feature well, it should be a good drop-in replacement of that feature. Therefore, if we strip a morphological feature from the data, using a well-performing embedding should yield higher parsing accuracies than using a worse performing one.

We use the following setups with each embedding (as well as without embeddings):

- no case information (-case)
- no tense information (-tense)
- no number information (-number)
- no PoS information (-PoS)
- morphology (including PoS) completely stripped (-all)
- all gold standard information as-is (+all)

We train RBGParser on the gold standard for each language using the settings mentioned above, i.e. stripping the morphological information corresponding to the setting from both training and test data. For each setting and language, we trained the parser in for modes: Without Embeddings, with dep, with GloVe, and with cbow. The resulting accuracies are listed in Table 1. No embedding is able to provide a benefit to the parser with complete gold-standard annotations (the +all rows), which is consistent with previous findings.

Even when stripping morphological information, the embeddings only yield relevant improvements with respect to not using embeddings in -PoS and -all settings. In both these cases, dep clearly outperforms the other embeddings, which is consistent with the syneval results (Figure 1). In contrast, cbow, which performs better than GloVe in syneval, yields worse results than GloVe on average. Both differences are significant (two-sided sign test; dep $\neq$ glove: $p < 0.05$; GloVe $\neq$ cbow: $p < 0.01$). The absolute difference between dep and GloVe is much larger than the absolute difference between GloVe and cbow. The difference between GloVe and cbow is especially striking in the -PoS case where cbow outperforms GloVe by a large margin in syneval but is consistently beaten in the parsing task for every language, even those where cbow outperforms GloVe in the +all case.

Stripping a single morphological feature (other than PoS) has little impact on parsing accuracy. On the other hand, stripping all morphological information leads to much worse accuracies than just parsing without PoS. This hints at some redundancy provided by the morphological annotations.

6 Conclusions

Syneval and the downstream parser evaluation both reveal large differences between the different embeddings. dep outperforms all other embeddings in syneval for all tasks except number-Polish and number-Spain and also is most helpful to the parser with considerable margin. The embeddings are only consistently helpful to the parser if no PoS-tags are provided.

Despite the consistency of the dep result between syneval and the parsing task, our findings are inconclusive overall. On the one hand, the by far best performing approach on the proxy task also performed best for parsing, on the other hand cbow performed worse than GloVe in the parsing task despite performing better in the proxy task. This indicates that there is helpful information encoded that is not captured by the proxy task, but which interestingly can not be realized when parsing with full gold-standard morphological annotation.

Code and data for this work is available under http://arne.chark.eu/repeval2016.

References

Danqi Chen and Christopher Manning. 2014. A fast and accurate dependency parser using neural networks. In *Proceedings of the 2014 Conference on Empirical Methods in Natural Language Processing (EMNLP)*, pages 740–750, Doha, Qatar, October. Association for Computational Linguistics.

Felix Hill, Roi Reichart, and Anna Korhonen. 2015. Simlex-999: Evaluating semantic models with (genuine) similarity estimation. *Computational Linguistics*, 41(4):665–695, Sep.

Arne Köhn, U Chun Lao, AmirAli B Zadeh, and Kenji Sagae. 2014. Parsing morphologically rich languages with (mostly) off-the-shelf software and word vectors. In *Proceedings of the 2014 Shared Task of the COLING Workshop on Statistical Parsing of Morphologically Rich Languages*.

Arne Köhn. 2015. What's in an embedding? analyzing word embeddings through multilingual evaluation. In *Proceedings of the 2015 Conference on Empirical Methods in Natural Language Processing*, pages 2067–2073, Lisbon, Portugal, September. Association for Computational Linguistics.

Tao Lei, Yu Xin, Yuan Zhang, Regina Barzilay, and Tommi Jaakkola. 2014. Low-rank tensors for scoring dependency structures. In *Proceedings of the 52nd Annual Meeting of the Association for Computational Linguistics (Volume 1: Long Papers)*, pages 1381–1391, Baltimore, Maryland, June. Association for Computational Linguistics.

Omer Levy and Yoav Goldberg. 2014. Dependency-based word embeddings. In *Proceedings of the 52nd Annual Meeting of the Association for Computational Linguistics (Volume 2: Short Papers)*, pages 302–308, Baltimore, Maryland, June. Association for Computational Linguistics.

André Martins, Miguel Almeida, and Noah A. Smith. 2013. Turning on the turbo: Fast third-order non-projective turbo parsers. In *Proceedings of the 51st Annual Meeting of the Association for Computational Linguistics (Volume 2: Short Papers)*, pages 617–622, Sofia, Bulgaria, August.

Tomáš Mikolov, Martin Karafiát, Lukáš Burget, Jan Černocký, and Sanjeev Khudanpur. 2010. Recurrent neural network based language model. In *Proceedings of INTERSPEECH-2010*, pages 1045–1048.

Tomáš Mikolov, Kai Chen, Greg Corrado, and Jeffrey Dean. 2013. Efficient estimation of word representations in vector space. *arXiv preprint arXiv:1301.3781*.

Jeffrey Pennington, Richard Socher, and Christopher Manning. 2014. GloVe: Global vectors for word representation. In *Proceedings of the*

2014 Conference on Empirical Methods in Natural Language Processing (EMNLP), pages 1532–1543, Doha, Qatar, October. Association for Computational Linguistics.

Djamé Seddah, Reut Tsarfaty, Sandra Kübler, Marie Candito, Jinho Choi, Matthieu Constant, Richárd Farkas, Iakes Goenaga, Koldo Gojenola, Yoav Goldberg, Spence Green, Nizar Habash, Marco Kuhlmann, Wolfgang Maier, Joakim Nivre, Adam Przepiorkowski, Ryan Roth, Wolfgang Seeker, Yannick Versley, Veronika Vincze, Marcin Woliński, Alina Wróblewska, and Eric Villemonte de la Clérgerie. 2014. Overview of the SPMRL 2014 shared task on parsing morphologically rich languages. In *Notes of the SPMRL 2014 Shared Task on Parsing Morphologically-Rich Languages*, Dublin, Ireland.

Yuan Zhang, Tao Lei, Regina Barzilay, Tommi Jaakkola, and Amir Globerson. 2014. Steps to excellence: Simple inference with refined scoring of dependency trees. In *Proceedings of the 52nd Annual Meeting of the Association for Computational Linguistics (Volume 1: Long Papers)*, pages 197–207, Baltimore, Maryland, June. Association for Computational Linguistics.

Evaluating vector space models using human semantic priming results

Allyson Ettinger
Department of Linguistics
University of Maryland
aetting@umd.edu

Tal Linzen
LSCP & IJN, École Normale Supérieure
PSL Research University
tal.linzen@ens.fr

Abstract

Vector space models of word representation are often evaluated using human similarity ratings. Those ratings are elicited in explicit tasks and have well-known subjective biases. As an alternative, we propose evaluating vector spaces using implicit cognitive measures. We focus in particular on semantic priming, exploring the strengths and limitations of existing datasets, and propose ways in which those datasets can be improved.

1 Introduction

Vector space models of meaning (VSMs) represent the words of a vocabulary as points in a multidimensional space. These models are often evaluated by assessing the extent to which relations between pairs of word vectors mirror relations between the words that correspond to those vectors. This evaluation method requires us to select a word relation metric that can serve as ground truth, and it requires us to identify the particular types of relations that we would like our models to represent accurately.

Typical approaches to VSM evaluation use human annotations as ground truth: in particular, similarity ratings for pairs of words. Some evaluation datasets focus on similarity *per se*: *hot-scalding* would rate highly, while antonyms like *hot-cold* and associates like *hot-stove* would not (Hill et al., 2015). Others do not distinguish similarity from other types of relations: synonyms, antonyms and associates can all receive high ratings (Bruni et al., 2014).

While the distinction between similarity and relatedness is important, it represents only a preliminary step toward a more precise understanding of what we mean—and what we should mean—when we talk about relations between words. The notions of "similarity" and "relatedness" are fairly vaguely defined, and as a result human raters asked to quantify these relations must carry out some interpretations of their own with respect to the task, in order to settle upon a judgment schema and apply that schema to rate word pairs. The fact that the definition of the relation structure is left to the annotator's judgment introduces inter-annotator variability as well as potentially undesirable properties of human similarity judgments: for example, the fact that they are not symmetric (Tversky, 1977).

The subjectivity of this task, and the involvement of the conscious reasoning process needed to arrive at a rating (Batchkarov et al., 2016), raise the question: to what extent does the relation structure that emerges from such rating tasks reliably reflect the relation structure that underlies human language understanding? After all, humans process language effortlessly, and natural language comprehension does not require reasoning about how similar or related words are.

This does not mean that the brain does not perform computations reflecting relations between words—evidence suggests that such computations occur constantly in language processing, but that these computations occur on a subconscious level (Kutas and Federmeier, 2011). Fortunately, there are psycholinguistic paradigms that allow us to tap into this level of processing. If we can make use of these subconscious cognitive measures of relatedness, we may be able to continue taking advantage of humans as the source of ground truth on word relations—while avoiding the subjectivity and bias introduced by conscious rating tasks.

We propose to evaluate VSMs using semantic priming, a cognitive phenomenon understood to reflect word-level relation structure in the human brain. We show some preliminary results

Proceedings of the 1st Workshop on Evaluating Vector Space Representations for NLP, pages 72–77,
Berlin, Germany, August 12, 2016. ©2016 Association for Computational Linguistics

exploring the ability of various VSMs to predict this measure, and discuss the potential for finer-grained differentiation between specific types of word relations. Finally, we argue that existing datasets (both explicit similarity judgments and semantic priming) are too small to meaningfully compare VSMs, and propose creating a larger semantic priming resource tailored to the needs of VSM evaluation.

2   Semantic priming

Semantic priming refers to the phenomenon in which, when performing a language task such as deciding whether a string is a word or a nonword (lexical decision), or pronouncing a word aloud (naming), humans show speeded performance if the word to which they are responding is preceded by a semantically related word (Meyer and Schvaneveldt, 1971; McNamara, 2005). For instance, response times are quicker to a word like *dog* (referred to as the "target" word) when it is preceded by a word like *cat* (referred to as the "prime"), than when it is preceded by a prime like *table*. This facilitation of the response to *dog* is taken to be an indication of the relation between *dog* and *cat*, and the magnitude of the speed-up can be interpreted as reflecting the strength of the relation.

Since priming results provide us with a human-generated quantification of relations between word pairs, without requiring participants to make conscious decisions about relatedness—the task that participants are performing is unrelated to the question of relatedness—this measure is a strong candidate for tapping into subconscious properties of word relations in the human brain.

Several studies have already shown correspondence between priming magnitude and VSM measures of relation such as cosine similarity or neighbor rank (Mandera et al., 2016; Lapesa and Evert, 2013; Jones et al., 2006; Padó and Lapata, 2007; Herdağdelen et al., 2009; McDonald and Brew, 2004). These positive results suggest that some of the implicit relation structure in the human brain is already reflected in current vector space models, and that it is in fact feasible to evaluate relation structure of VSMs by testing their ability to predict this implicit human measure.

However, to our knowledge, there has not yet been an effort to identify or tailor a priming dataset such that it is ideally suited to evaluation of VSMs.

Semantic priming experiments make use of many different methodologies, and test many different types of relations between words. In selecting or constructing a priming dataset, we want to be informed about the methodologies that are best-suited to generating data for purposes of VSM evaluation, and we want in addition to have control over—or at least annotation of—the types of relations between the word pairs being tested.

3   Experimental setup

3.1   Cognitive measurements

Most previous work has modeled small priming datasets. By contrast, we follow Mandera et al. (2016) in taking advantage of the online database of the Semantic Priming Project (SPP), which compiles priming data from 768 subjects for over 6000 word pairs (Hutchison et al., 2013). This dataset's size alone is advantageous, as it potentially allows us to draw more confident conclusions about differences between models (as discussed below), and it ensures broader coverage in the vocabulary.

The SPP has two additional advantages that are relevant for our purposes. First, it contains data for four methodological variations on the semantic priming paradigm: all combinations of two tasks, lexical decision and naming, and two stimulus onset asynchronies (SOA), 200 ms and 1200 ms, which represent the amount of time between the start of the prime word and the start of the target word. We assess the usefulness of each of the methods for evaluating VSMs, in order to identify the methodological choices that generate optimal data for evaluation. A second advantage of the SPP is that it contains annotations of the relation types of the word pairs; this property can allow for finer-grained analyses that focus on relations of particular interest, as we will discuss in greater detail below.

3.2   Vector-space models

We trained four word-level VSMs for testing: skip-gram (Mikolov et al., 2013) with window sizes of 5 and 15 words (referred to as SG5 and SG15 below) and GloVe (Pennington et al., 2014) with window sizes of 5 and 15 words (Gl5 and Gl15). All models were trained on a concatenation of English Wikipedia and English GigaWord using their default parameters and dimensionality of 100. A fifth model (referred to as SG5n) was generated by adding uniform random noise $\mathcal{U}(-2,2)$ to the vectors of the SG5 model, as an example of a model that we would expect to perform poorly.

3.3 Evaluation

We evaluated the VSMs by fitting linear regression models to the human response times, with cosine similarity between prime and target as the predictor of interest.[1] As a simple baseline model, we entered only word frequency as a predictor. Word frequency is widely recognized as a strong predictor of reaction time in language tasks (Rubenstein et al., 1970). While it is only one among the factors known to affect the speed of word recognition (Balota et al., 2004), it is by far the most important, and unlike factors such as word length, it is represented in many vector space models (Schnabel et al., 2015), making it all the more important to control for here.

4 Results

4.1 Cognitive measures

We first compare the four methodological variations on the semantic priming paradigm. Figure 1 shows the r^2 values, which quantify the proportion of the variance explained by the regression model. Recall that the baseline regression model ("base") contains only frequency as a predictor of response time, while the other regression models contain as predictors both frequency and cosine similarity between prime and target, as determined by each of the respective VSMs.

The greatest amount of variance is accounted for in the lexical decision task, with somewhat more variance accounted for with the 200 ms SOA. There is a more substantial margin of improvement over the frequency baseline in the 200 ms SOA, suggesting that the results of the LDT-200 ms paradigm constitute the most promising metric for assessing the extent to which VSMs reflect cognitive relation structure.

The four normally-trained VSMs (SG5, SG15, Gl5, Gl15) perform quite similarly to one another on this metric. Within those conditions in which we do see improvement over the frequency baseline—that is, primarily the lexical decision task conditions—the introduction of noise (SG5n)

Relation	Example pair
Synonym	*presume, assume*
Antonym	*asleep, awake*
Forward phrasal associate	*human, being*
Script	*ambulance, emergency*
Category	*celery, carrot*
Supraordinate	*disaster, earthquake*
Instrument	*rake, leaves*
Functional property	*airplane, fly*
Backward phrasal associate	*lobe, ear*
Perceptual property	*fire, hot*
Action	*quench, thirst*

Table 1: Annotated relations in SPP

nullifies that improvement. This suggests that the additional variance accounted for by the four normal VSMs is indeed a reflection of their quality.

4.2 Relation types

Each word pair in the Semantic Priming Project is additionally annotated for the category of the relation between the words in the pair (see Table 1 for examples). Having access to information about the particular relations embodied by a given word pair can be quite important for maximizing the utility of our evaluation metrics, as we are likely to care about different relations depending upon the downstream task to which we intend to apply our vector representations. For instance, we may care more about faithfulness to script relations when performing document-level tasks, but care more about performance on synonym and antonym relations for word- and sentence-level tasks such as sentiment analysis and entailment.

With this in mind, we run preliminary experiments testing our VSMs as predictors of response time within the specific relation categories. In Figure 2, we show a sample of results on the per-relation level. These suggest that the spaces may vary in interesting ways, both within and between relation types. However, the small sample sizes lead to large confidence intervals; in particular, the drop in performance resulting from the addition of noise is dwarfed by the size of the error bars. As such, we cannot at this point draw firm conclusions from the results. To make conclusive use of the advantages potentially afforded by the relation annotation in the SPP, it would be necessary to collect additional relation-annotated priming data.

---

[1]Lapesa and Evert's (2013) result suggests that rank of the target among the vector space neighbors of the prime may model priming results more closely; we intend to experiment with this measure in future work.

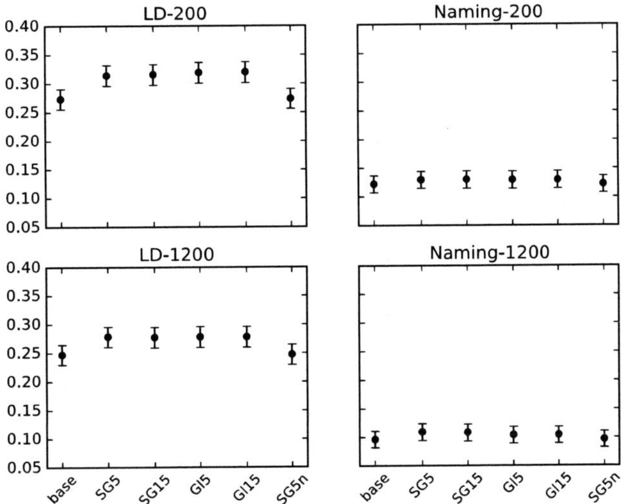

Figure 1: r^2 values for linear models fit to priming results in full SPP dataset, under different priming conditions. Baseline model ("base") contains only frequency as a predictor, while other models contain cosine values from the indicated VSMs. Error bars represent bootstrapped 95% confidence intervals.

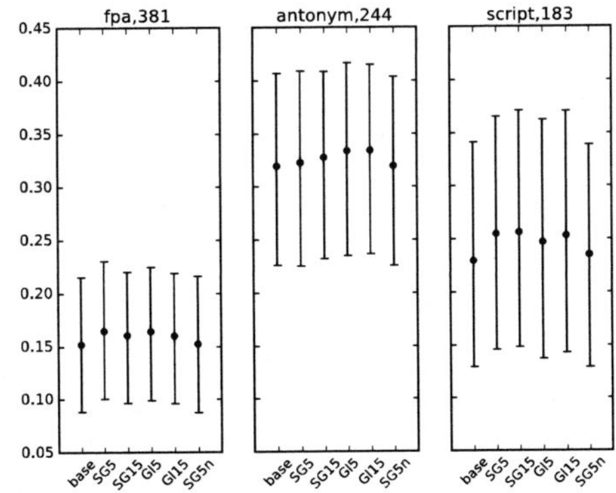

Figure 2: r^2 values for linear models fit to priming results in specific relation categories. Number of items in category is indicated in subplot title.

4.3 Similarity datasets

Finally, for the sake of comparison with conventional metrics, we include Figure 3, which shows the same baseline and vector space regression models, assessed as predictors of the ratings in the MEN (Bruni et al., 2014) and Sim-Lex (Hill et al., 2015) datasets. Frequency appears to be a poorer predictor of explicit similarity ratings than of the implicit cognitive measures. Although there is some variation in performance be-

tween the four normally-trained VSMs, it is less straightforward to distinguish between them once we take confidence intervals into account; this issue of overlapping confidence intervals is much more pronounced with smaller datasets such as RG-65 (Rubenstein and Goodenough, 1965) and MC-30 (Miller and Charles, 1991).

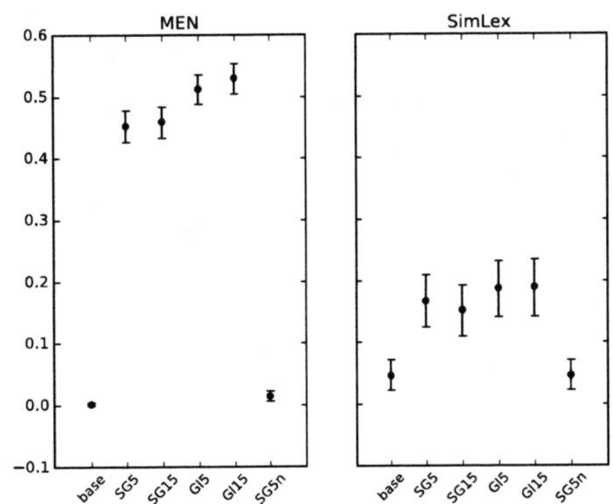

Figure 3: r^2 values, with 95% confidence intervals, for linear models fit to MEN/SimLex explicit similarity ratings.

5 Discussion

We have presented here a proposal to leverage implicit measures of relation structure in the human brain to evaluate VSMs. Such measures can sidestep the subjectivity introduced by standard similarity rating tasks, and tap more directly into the relation structure fundamental to language processing by humans.

In our exploratory results above we find, consistent with previous studies, that VSMs can predict priming beyond the variance explained by frequency alone, at least in certain cognitive measurements (in particular, lexical decision with a short SOA), suggesting that priming magnitude could be used as a VSM evaluation metric. We have also reported preliminary results taking advantage of the relation-specific annotation in the SPP. Relation-specific evaluation sets could prove valuable for finer-grained understanding of the relations captured in a given VSM. We see, however, that if we are to make statistically valid conclusions about differences between models, we must extend our dataset substantially. This could be accomplished by the same basic procedures used to build the SPP, extended to a massive scale using an online platform such as Mechanical Turk.

Finally, it may be useful to experiment with other implicit cognitive measures known to reflect relation structure. A prominent example is the N400, a neural response elicited by every word during sentence comprehension (Kutas and Federmeier, 2011). The amplitude of the N400 response is modulated by the relation of the word to its context: the worse the fit to context, the larger the N400 amplitude. As a result, the N400 is often used to study the effects of context on word processing. There is existing evidence that vector space model representations of preceding context and target words can predict N400 amplitude (Parviz et al., 2011; Ettinger et al., 2016). In future work, the N400 may therefore prove useful for assessing VSM relation structure above the word level.

Acknowledgments

This work was supported in part by an NSF Graduate Research Fellowship to Allyson Ettinger under Grant No. DGE 1322106. Any opinions, findings, and conclusions or recommendations expressed are those of the authors and do not necessarily reflect the views of the NSF. Tal Linzen's research was supported by the European Research Council (grant ERC-2011-AdG 295810 BOOTPHON) and the Agence Nationale pour la Recherche (grants ANR-10-IDEX-0001-02 PSL and ANR-10-LABX-0087 IEC). This work benefited from the helpful comments of two anonymous reviewers, and from discussions with Philip Resnik, Colin Phillips, and other members of the University of Maryland language science community.

References

David A. Balota, Miachael J. Cortese, Susan D. Sergent-Marshall, Daniel H. Spieler, and Melvin J. Yap. 2004. Visual word recognition of single-syllable words. *Journal of Experimental Psychology: General*, 133(2):283.

Miroslav Batchkarov, Thomas Kober, Jeremy Reffin, Julie Weeds, and David Weir. 2016. A critique of word similarity as a method for evaluating distributional semantic models. In *Proceedings of the First Workshop on Evaluating Vector Space Representations for NLP*.

Elia Bruni, Nam-Khanh Tran, and Marco Baroni. 2014. Multimodal distributional semantics. *Journal of Artificial Intelligence Research*, 49:1–47.

Allyson Ettinger, Naomi H. Feldman, Philip Resnik, and Colin Phillips. 2016. Modeling N400 amplitude using vector space models of word representation. In *Proceedings of the Annual Meeting of the Cognitive Science Society*.

Amaç Herdağdelen, Katrin Erk, and Marco Baroni. 2009. Measuring semantic relatedness with vector space models and random walks. In *Proceedings of the 2009 Workshop on Graph-based Methods for Natural Language Processing*, pages 50–53.

Felix Hill, Roi Reichart, and Anna Korhonen. 2015. Simlex-999: Evaluating semantic models with (genuine) similarity estimation. *Computational Linguistics*.

Keith A Hutchison, David A Balota, James H Neely, Michael J Cortese, Emily R Cohen-Shikora, Chi-Shing Tse, Melvin J Yap, Jesse J Bengson, Dale Niemeyer, and Erin Buchanan. 2013. The semantic priming project. *Behavior research methods*, 45(4):1099–1114.

Michael N Jones, Walter Kintsch, and Douglas JK Mewhort. 2006. High-dimensional semantic space accounts of priming. *Journal of Memory and Language*, 55(4):534–552.

Marta Kutas and Kara D Federmeier. 2011. Thirty years and counting: finding meaning in the N400 component of the event-related brain potential (ERP). *Annual review of psychology*, 62:621–647.

Gabriella Lapesa and Stefan Evert. 2013. Evaluating neighbor rank and distance measures as predictors of semantic priming. In *Proceedings of the ACL Workshop on Cognitive Modeling and Computational Linguistics (CMCL 2013)*, pages 66–74.

Paweł Mandera, Emmanuel Keuleers, and Marc Brysbaert. 2016. Explaining human performance in psycholinguistic tasks with models of semantic similarity based on prediction and counting: A review and empirical validation. *Journal of Memory and Language*.

Scott McDonald and Chris Brew. 2004. A distributional model of semantic context effects in lexical processing. In *Proceedings of the Annual Meeting of the Association for Computational Linguistics*, page 17.

Timothy P McNamara. 2005. *Semantic priming: Perspectives from memory and word recognition*. Psychology Press.

D.E. Meyer and R.W. Schvaneveldt. 1971. Facilitation in recognizing pairs of words: evidence of a dependence between retrieval operations. *Journal of experimental psychology*, 90(2):227.

Tomas Mikolov, Kai Chen, Greg Corrado, and Jeffrey Dean. 2013. Efficient estimation of word representations in vector space. *arXiv preprint arXiv:1301.3781*.

George A Miller and Walter G Charles. 1991. Contextual correlates of semantic similarity. *Language and Cognitive Processes*, 6(1):1–28.

Sebastian Padó and Mirella Lapata. 2007. Dependency-based construction of semantic space models. *Computational Linguistics*, 33(2):161–199.

Mehdi Parviz, Mark Johnson, Blake Johnson, and Jon Brock. 2011. Using language models and latent semantic analysis to characterise the n400m neural response. In *Proceedings of the Australasian Language Technology Association Workshop 2011*, pages 38–46.

Jeffrey Pennington, Richard Socher, and Christopher D. Manning. 2014. Glove: Global vectors for word representation. In *Empirical Methods in Natural Language Processing (EMNLP)*, pages 1532–1543.

Herbert Rubenstein and John B Goodenough. 1965. Contextual correlates of synonymy. *Communications of the ACM*, 8(10):627–633.

Herbert Rubenstein, Lonnie Garfield, and Jane A Millikan. 1970. Homographic entries in the internal lexicon. *Journal of verbal learning and verbal behavior*, 9(5):487–494.

Tobias Schnabel, Igor Labutov, David Mimno, and Thorsten Joachims. 2015. Evaluation methods for unsupervised word embeddings. In *Proceedings of the Conference on Empirical Methods in Natural Language Processing*.

Amos Tversky. 1977. Features of similarity. *Psychological Review*, 84(4):327.

Evaluating embeddings on dictionary-based similarity

Judit Ács
Department of Automation
Budapest University of Technology
Magyar Tudósok krt 2
1111 Budapest, Hungary
judit@aut.bme.hu

András Kornai
Institute for Computer Science
Hungarian Academy of Sciences
Kende u. 13-17
1111 Budapest, Hungary
andras@kornai.com

Abstract

We propose a method for evaluating embeddings against dictionaries with tens or hundreds of thousands of entries, covering the entire gamut of the vocabulary.

1 Introduction

Continuous vector representations (embeddings) are, to a remarkable extent, supplementing and potentially taking over the role of detail dictionaries in a broad variety of tasks ranging from POS tagging (Collobert et al., 2011) and parsing (Socher et al., 2013) to MT (Zou et al., 2013), and beyond (Karpathy, Joulin, and Li, 2014). Yet an evaluation method that directly compares embeddings on their ability to handle word similarity at the entire breadth of a dictionary has been lacking, which is all the more regrettable in light of the fact that embeddings are normally generated from gigaword or larger corpora, while the state of the art test sets surveyed in Chiu, Korhonen, and Pyysalo (2016) range between a low of 30 (MC-30) and a high of 3,000 word pairs (MEN).

We propose to develop a dictionary-based standard in two steps. First, given a dictionary such as the freely available Collins-COBUILD (Sinclair, 1987), which has over 77,400 headwords, or Wiktionary (162,400 headwords), we compute a frequency list F that lists the probabilities of the headwords (this is standard, and discussed only briefly), and a dense similarity matrix M or an embedding ψ, this is discussed in Section 2. Next, in Section 3 we consider an arbitrary embedding ϕ, and we systematically compare both its frequency and its similarity predictions to the gold standard embodied in F and ψ, building on the insights of Arora et al. (2015). Pilot studies conducted along these lines are discussed in Section 4.

Before turning to the details, in the rest of this Introduction we attempt to evaluate the proposed evaluation itself, primarily in terms of the criteria listed in the call. As we shall see, our method is *highly replicable for other researchers* for English, and to the extent monolingual dictionaries are available, for other other languages as well. Low resource languages will typically lack a monolingual dictionary, but this is less of a perceptible problem in that they also lack larger corpora so building robust embeddings is already out of the question for these. *The costs are minimal*, since we are just running software on preexisting dictionaries. Initially, dictionaries are hard to assemble, require a great deal of manual labor, and are often copyrighted, but here our point is to leverage the manual (often crowdsourced) work that they already embody.

The proposed algorithm, as we present it here, is aimed primarily at *word-level* evaluation, but there are standard methods for extending these from word to sentence similarity (Han et al., 2013). Perhaps the most attractive *downstream application* we see is MT, in particular word sense disambiguation during translation. As for *linguistic/semantic/psychological properties*, dictionaries, both mono- and bilingual, are crucial resources not only for humans (language learners, translators, etc.) but also for a variety of NLP applications, including MT, cross-lingual information retrieval, cross-lingual QA, computer-assisted language learning, and many more. The mandate of lexicographers is to capture a huge number of linguistic phenomena ranging from gross synonymy to subtle meaning distinctions, and at the semantic level the *inter-annotator agreement is very high*, a point we discuss in greater detail below. Gladkova and Drozd (2016) quote Schütze (2016) that "human linguistic judgments (...) are subject to over 50 potential linguistic, psychologi-

Proceedings of the 1st Workshop on Evaluating Vector Space Representations for NLP, pages 78–82,
Berlin, Germany, August 12, 2016. ©2016 Association for Computational Linguistics

cal, and social confounds", and many of these taint the crowd-sourced dictionaries, but lexicographers are annotators of a highly trained sort, and their work gives us valuable data, as near to laboratory purity as it gets.

2   Constructing the standard

Our main inputs are a frequency list F, ideally generated from a corpus we consider representative of the text of interest (the expected input to the downstream task), and a preexisting dictionary D which is not assumed to be task-specific. For English, we use both the Collins-COBUILD dictionary (CED) and Wiktionary, as these are freely available, but other general-purpose dictionaries would be just as good, and for specific tasks (e.g. medical or legal texts) it may make sense to add in a task-specific dictionary if available. Neither D nor F need contain the other, but we assume that they are stemmed using the same stemmer.

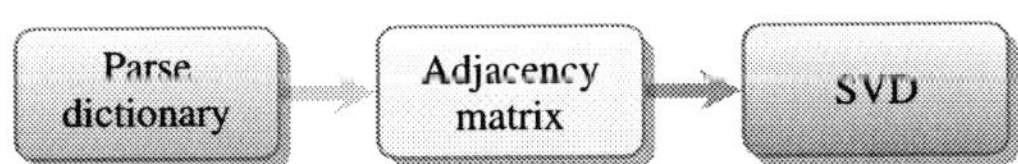

Figure 1: Building the standard

The first step is to parse D into ⟨word, definition⟩ stanzas. (This step is specific to the dictionary at hand, see e.g. Mark Lieberman's *readme.* for CED). Next, we turn the definitions into dependency graphs. We use the Stanford dependency parser (Chen and Manning, 2014) at this stage, and have not experimented with alternatives. This way, we can assign to each word a graph with dependency labels, see Fig 2 for an example, and Recski (2016) for details. The dependency graphs are not part of the current incarnation of the evaluation method proposed here, but are essential for our future plans of extending the evaluation pipeline (see Section 4).

In the second step we construct two global graphs: the *definitional dependency* graph DD which has a node for each word in the dictionary, and directed edges running from w_i to w_j if w_j appears in the definition of w_i; and the *headword graph* HG which only retains the edge running from the definiendum to the head of the definiens. We take the head to be the 'root' node returned by the Stanford parser, but in many dictionaries the syntactic head of the definition is typographically set aside and can be obtained directly from the raw D.

At first blush it may appear that the results of this process are highly dependent on the choice of D, and perhaps on the choice of the parser as well. Consider the definition of *client* taken from four separate sources: 'someone who gets services or advice from a professional person, company, or organization' (Longman); 'a person who pays a professional person or organization for services' (Webster); 'a person who uses the services or advice of a professional person or organization' (Oxford); 'a person or group that uses the professional advice or services of a lawyer, accountant, advertising agency, architect, etc.' (dictionary.com).

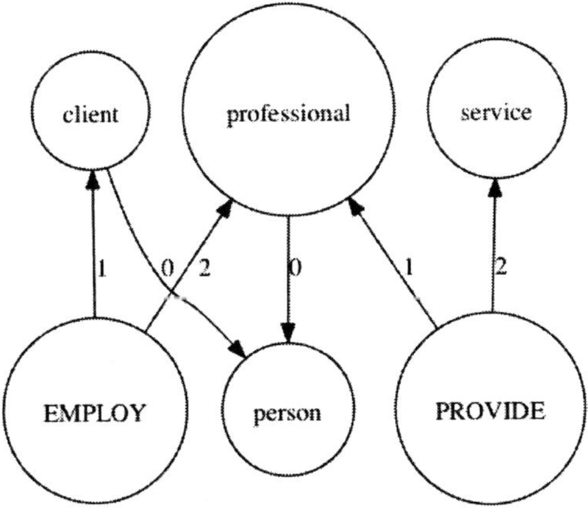

Figure 2: Graph assigned to *client*. Edge labels are 0=isa; 1=nsubj; 2=dobj

The definitions do not literally preserve the headword (hypernym, genus, IS_A): in three cases we have 'person', in one 'somebody'. But semantically, these two headwords are very close synonyms, distinguished more by POS than by content. Similarly, the various definitions do not present the exact same verbal pivot, 'engage/hire/pay for/use the services of', but their semantic relatedness is evident. Finally, there are differences in attachment, e.g. is the service rendered professional, or is the person/organization rendering the service professional? In Section 3 we will present evidence that the proposed method is not overly sensitive to these differences, because the subsequent steps wipe out such subtle distinctions.

In the third step, by performing SVD on the Laplacian of the graphs DD and HG we obtain two embeddings we call the *definitional* and the *head* embedding. For any embedding ψ, a (symmetric, dense) similarity matrix $M_{i,j}$ is given by the cosine similarity of $\psi(w_i)$ and $\psi(w_j)$. Other methods for computing the similarity matrix M are also possible, and the embedding could also be obtained by direct computation, setting the context window of each word to its definition – we defer the discussion of these and similar alternatives to the concluding Section 4.

Now we define the *direct* similarity of two embeddings ϕ and ψ as the average of the (cosine) similarities of the words that occur in both:

$$S(\phi, \psi) = (\sum_w \frac{\phi(w)\psi(w)}{\|\phi(w)\|\|\psi(w)\|})/|D| \qquad (1)$$

It may also make sense to use a frequency-weighted average, since we already have a frequency table F – we return to this matter in Section 3. In and of itself, S is not a very useful measure, in that even random seeding effects are sufficient to destroy similarity between near-identical embeddings, such as could be obtained from two halves of the same corpus. For example, the value of S between 300-dimensional GloVe (Pennington, Socher, and Manning, 2014) embeddings generated from the first and the second halves of the UMBC Webbase (Han et al., 2013) is only 0.0003. But for any two embeddings, it is an easy matter to compute the rotation (orthonormal transform) R and the general linear transform G that would maximize $S(\phi, R(\psi))$ and $S(\phi, G(\psi))$ respectively, and it is these *rotational* resp. *general* similarities S_R and S_G that we will use. For the same embeddings, we obtain $S_R = 0.709, S_G = 0.734$. Note that only S_R is symmetrical between embeddings of the same dimension, for S_G the order of arguments matters.

With this, the essence of our proposal should be clear: we generate ψ from a dictionary, and measure the goodness of an arbitrary embedding ϕ by means of computing S_R or S_G between ϕ and ψ. What remains to be seen is that different dictionary-based embeddings are close to one another, and measure the same thing.

3   Using the standard

In the random walk on context space model of Arora et al. (2015), we expect the log frequency of words to have a simple linear relation to the length of the word vectors:

$$\log(p(w)) = \frac{1}{2d}\|\vec{w}\|^2 - \log Z \pm o(1) \qquad (2)$$

Kornai and Kracht (2015) compared GloVe to the Google 1T frequency count (Brants and Franz, 2006) and found a correlation of 0.395, with the frequency model failing primarily in distinguishing mid- from low-frequency words. The key insight we take from Arora et al. (2015) is that an embedding is both a model of frequency, whose merit can be tested by direct comparison to F, and a model of cooccurrence, given by $\log p(w, w') = \frac{1}{2d}\|\vec{w} + \vec{w'}\|^2 - 2\log Z \pm o(1)$.

Needless to say, the ⟨word, definition⟩ stanzas of a dictionary do not constitute a random walk: to the contrary, they amount to statements of semantic, rather than cooccurrence-based, similarity between definiendum and definiens, and this is precisely what makes dictionaries the appropriate yardstick for evaluating embeddings.

State of the art on Simlex-999 was $\rho = 0.64$ (Banjade et al., 2015), obtained by combining many methods and data sources. More recently, Wieting et al. (2015) added paraphrase data to achieve 0.69, and Recski et al. (2016) added dictionary data to get to 0.76. Standard, widely used embeddings used in isolation do not come near this, the best we tested was `GoogleNews-vectors-negative300`, which gets only $\rho = 0.44$; `senna` gets 0.27; and `hpca.2B.200d` gets 0.16, very much in line with the design goals of Simlex-999. The purely dictionary-based embeddings are even worse, the best obtains only $\rho = 0.082$ at 300 dimensions, $\rho = 0.079$ at 30 dimensions.

A heuristic indication of the observation that choice of dictionary will be a secondary factor comes from the fact that dictionary-based embeddings are close to one another. Table 1 shows S_R for three dictionaries, CED, Wikt, and My (not in the public domain). The numbers above the diagonal at 300 dim, below at 30 dim.

	CED	Wikt	My
CED	1.0	.127	.124
Wikt	.169	1.0	.131
My	.202	.168	1.0

Table 1 S_R for dictionary-based embeddings

A more solid indication comes from evaluating embeddings under Simlex-999, under the dictionary-based similarities, and under some other test sets.

emb.tr.dim	SL999	CED	Wikt	MEN	RW	size ∩
GN-vec-neg.300	.442	.078	.044	.770	.508	1825
glove.840B.300	.408	.058	.047	.807	.449	1998
glove.42B.300	.374	.009	.045	.742	.371	2013
glove.6B.300	.360	.065	.127	.734	.389	1782
glove.6B.200	.340	.060	.118	.725	.383	1782
glove.6B.100	.298	.059	.112	.697	.362	1782
senna.300	.270	.052	.098	.568	.385	1138
glove.6B.50	.265	.040	.087	.667	.338	1782
hpca.2B.200	.164	.040	.140	.313	.176	1315

Table 2: Comparing embeddings by Simlex-999, dictionary S_R, MEN, and RareWord

As can be seen, the ρ and S_R numbers largely, though not entirely, move together. This is akin to the astronomers' method of building the 'distance ladder' starting from well-understood measurements (in our case, Simlex-999), and correlating these to the new technique proposed here. While Chiu, Korhonen, and Pyysalo (2016) make a rather compelling case that testsets such as MEN, Mtruk-28, RareWord, and WS353 are not reliable for predicting downstream results, we present here ρ values for the two largest tasks, MEN, with 3,000 word pairs, and RareWord, ideally 2,034, but in practice considerably less, depending on the intersection of the embedding vocabulary with the Rare Word vocabulary (given in the last column of Table 2). We attribute the failure of the lesser test sets, amply demonstrated by Chiu, Korhonen, and Pyysalo (2016), simply to undersampling: a good embedding will have 10^5 or more words, and the idea of assessing the quality on less than 1% simply makes no sense, given the variability of the data. A dictionary-wide evaluation improves this by an order of magnitude or more.

4 Conclusions, further directions

An important aspect of the proposal is the possibility of making better use of F. By optimizing the frequency-weighted rotation we put the emphasis on the function words, which may be very appropriate for some tasks. In other tasks, we may want to simply omit the high frequency words, or give them very low weights. In medical texts we may want to emphasize the words that stand out from the background English frequency counts. To continue with astronomy, the method proposed in this paper is akin to a telescope, which can be pointed at various phenomena.

It is clear from the foregoing that we are offering not a single measurement yardstick but rather a family of these. Lexicographers actually include information that we are only beginning to explore, such as the NSUBJ and DOBJ relations that are also returned in the dependency parse. These can also be built into, or even selectively emphasized, in the similarity matrix M, which would offer a more direct measurement of the potential of individual embeddings in e.g. semantic role labeling tasks. We can also create large-scale systematic evaluations of paraphrase quality, using definitions of the same word coming from different dictionaries – Wieting et al. (2015) already demonstrated the value of paraphrase information on Simlex-999.

We have experimented with headword graphs that retain only the head of a definition, typically the genus. Since the results were very bad, we do not burden the paper with them, but note the following. HGs are very sparse, and SVD doesn't preserve a lot of information from them (the ultimate test of an embedding would be the ability to reconstruct the dictionary relations from the vectors). Even in the best of cases, such as hypernyms derived from WordNet, the relative weight of this information is low (Banjade et al., 2015; Recski et al., 2016). That said, the impact of hypernym/genus on the problem of hubness (Dinu, Lazaridou, and Baroni, 2015) is worth investigating further.

One avenue of research opened up by dictionary-based embeddings is to use not just the definitional dependency graph, but an enriched graph that contains the unification of all definition graphs parsed from the definitions. This will, among other issues, enable the study of *selectional restrictions* (Chomsky, 1965), e.g. that the subject of *elapse* must be a time interval, the object of *drink* must be a liquid, and so on. Such information is routinely encoded in dictionaries. Consider the definition of *wilt* '(of a plant) to become weak and begin to bend towards the ground, or (of a person) to become weaker, tired, or less confident'. To the extent the network derived from the dictionary already contains selectional restriction information, a better fit with the dictionary-based embedding is good news for any downstream task.

References

Arora, Sanjeev et al. (2015). "Random Walks on Context Spaces: Towards an Explanation of the Mysteries of Semantic Word Embeddings". In: *arXiv:1502.03520v1*.

Banjade, Rajendra et al. (2015). "Lemon and Tea Are Not Similar: Measuring Word-to-Word Similarity by Combining Different Methods". In: *Proc. CICLING15*. Ed. by Alexander Gelbukh. Springer, pp. 335–346.

Brants, Thorsten and Alex Franz (2006). *Web 1T 5-gram Version 1*. Philadelphia: Linguistic Data Consortium.

Chen, Danqi and Christopher D Manning (2014). "A Fast and Accurate Dependency Parser using Neural Networks." In: *EMNLP*, pp. 740–750.

Chiu, Billy, Anna Korhonen, and Sampo Pyysalo (2016). "Intrinsic Evaluation of Word Vectors Fails to Predict Extrinsic Performance". In: *Proc. RepEval (this volume)*. Ed. by Omer Levy. ACL.

Chomsky, Noam (1965). *Aspects of the Theory of Syntax*. MIT Press.

Collobert, R. et al. (2011). "Natural Language Processing (Almost) from Scratch". In: *Journal of Machine Learning Research (JMLR)*.

Dinu, Georgiana, Angeliki Lazaridou, and Marco Baroni (2015). "Improving Zero-shot Learning by Mitigating the Hubness Problem". In: *ICLR 2015, Workshop Track*.

Gladkova, Anna and Aleksandr Drozd (2016). "Intrinsic Evaluations of Word Embeddings: What Can We Do Better?" In: *Proc. RepEval (this volume)*. Ed. by Omer Levy. ACL.

Han, Lushan et al. (2013). "UMBC_EBIQUITY-CORE: Semantic textual similarity systems". In: *Proceedings of the 2nd Joint Conference on Lexical and Computational Semantics*, pp. 44–52.

Karpathy, Andrej, Armand Joulin, and Fei Fei F Li (2014). "Deep Fragment Embeddings for Bidirectional Image Sentence Mapping". In: *Advances in Neural Information Processing Systems 27*. Ed. by Z. Ghahramani et al. Curran Associates, Inc., pp. 1889–1897.

Kornai, András and Marcus Kracht (2015). "Lexical Semantics and Model Theory: Together at Last?" In: *Proceedings of the 14th Meeting on the Mathematics of Language (MoL 14)*. Chicago, IL: Association for Computational Linguistics, pp. 51–61.

Pennington, Jeffrey, Richard Socher, and Christopher Manning (2014). "Glove: Global Vectors for Word Representation". In: *Conference on Empirical Methods in Natural Language Processing (EMNLP 2014)*.

Recski, Gábor (2016). "Computational methods in semantics". PhD thesis. Eötvös Loránd University, Budapest.

Recski, Gábor et al. (2016). "Measuring semantic similarity of words using concept networks". to appear in RepL4NLP. URL: `http://hlt.bme.hu/en/publ/Recski%5C_2016c`.

Schütze, Carson T. (2016). *The empirical base of linguistics*. 2nd ed. Vol. 2. Classics in Linguistics. Berlin: Language Science Press.

Sinclair, John M. (1987). *Looking up: an account of the COBUILD project in lexical computing*. Collins ELT.

Socher, R. et al. (2013). "Zero-shot learning through cross-modal transfer". In: *International Conference on Learning Representations (ICLR)*.

Wieting, John et al. (2015). "From Paraphrase Database to Compositional Paraphrase Model and Back". In: *TACL* 3, pp. 345–358.

Zou, Will Y et al. (2013). "Bilingual Word Embeddings for Phrase-Based Machine Translation." In: *EMNLP*, pp. 1393–1398.

Evaluating multi-sense embeddings for semantic resolution monolingually and in word translation

Gábor Borbély
Department of Algebra
Budapest University of Technology
Egry József u. 1
1111 Budapest, Hungary
borbely@math.bme.hu

Márton Makrai
Institute for Linguistics
Hungarian Academy of Sciences
Benczúr u. 33
1068 Budapest, Hungary
makrai.marton@nytud.mta.hu

Dávid Nemeskey
Institute for Computer Science
Hungarian Academy of Sciences
Kende u. 13-17
1111 Budapest, Hungary
nemeskeyd@sztaki.mta.hu

András Kornai
Institute for Computer Science
Hungarian Academy of Sciences
Kende u. 13-17
1111 Budapest, Hungary
andras@kornai.com

Abstract

Multi-sense word embeddings (MSEs) model different meanings of word forms with different vectors. We propose two new methods for evaluating MSEs, one based on monolingual dictionaries, and the other exploiting the principle that words may be ambiguous as far as the postulated senses translate to different words in some other language.

1 Introduction

Gladkova and Drozd (2016) calls polysemy "the elephant in the room" as far as evaluating embeddings are concerned. Here we attack this problem head on, by proposing two methods for evaluating multi-sense word embeddings (MSEs) where polysemous words have multiple vectors, ideally one per sense. Section 2 discusses the first method, based on sense distinctions made in traditional monolingual dictionaries. We investigate the correlation between the number of senses of each word-form in the embedding and in the manually created inventory as a proxy measure of how well embedding vectors correspond to concepts in speakers' (or at least, the lexicographers') mind.

The other evaluation method, discussed in Section 3, is bilingual, based on the method of Mikolov et al. (2013b), who formulate word translation as a linear mapping from the source language embedding to the target one, trained on a seed of a few thousand word pairs. Our proposal is to perform such translations from MSEs, with the idea that what are different senses in the source language will very often translate to different words in the target language. This way, we can use single-sense embeddings on the target side and thereby reduce the noise of MSEs.

Altogether we present a preliminary evaluation of four MSE implementations by these two methods on two languages, English and Hungarian: the released result of the spherical context clustering method huang (Huang et al., 2012); the learning process of Neelakantan et al. (2014) with adaptive sense numbers (we report results using their release MSEs and their tool itself, calling both neela); the parametrized Bayesian learner of Bartunov et al. (2015) where the number of senses is controlled by a parameter α for semantic resolution, here referred to as AdaGram; and jiweil (Li and Jurafsky, 2015). MSEs with multiple instances are suffixed with their most important parameters, i.e. the learning rate for AdaGram ($a = 0.5$); the number of multi-prototype words and whether the model is adaptive (NP) for release neela; and the number of induced word senses ($s = 4$) for our non-adaptive neela runs.

Some very preliminary conclusions are offered in Section 4, more in regards to the feasibility of the two evaluation methods we propose than about the merits of the systems we evaluated.

2 Comparing lexical headwords to multiple sense vectors

Work on the evaluation of MSEs (for lexical relatedness) goes back to the seminal Reisinger and Mooney (2010), who note that usage splits words

Proceedings of the 1st Workshop on Evaluating Vector Space Representations for NLP, pages 83–89,
Berlin, Germany, August 12, 2016. ©2016 Association for Computational Linguistics

more finely (with synonyms and near-synonyms ending up in distant clusters) than semantics. The differentiation of word senses is fraught with difficulties, especially when we wish to distinguish homophony, using the same written or spoken form to express different concepts, such as Russian *mir* 'world' and *mir* 'peace' from polysemy, where speakers feel that the two senses are very strongly connected, such as in Hungarian *nap* 'day' and *nap* 'sun'. To quote Zgusta (1971) "Of course it is a pity that we have to rely on the subjective interpretations of the speakers, but we have hardly anything else on hand". Etymology makes clear that different languages make different lump/split decisions in the conceptual space, so much so that translational relatedness can, to a remarkable extent, be used to recover the universal clustering (Youna et al., 2016).

Another confounding factor is part of speech (POS). Very often, the entire distinction is lodged in the POS, as in *divorce* (Noun) and *divorce* (Verb), while at other times this is less clear, compare the verbal *to bank* 'rely on a financial institution' and *to bank* 'tilt'. Clearly the former is strongly related to the nominal *bank* 'financial institution' while the semantic relation 'sloping sideways' that connects the tilting of the airplane to the side of the river is some-

what less direct, and not always perceived by the speakers. This problem affects our sources as well: the Collins-COBUILD (CED, Sinclair (1987)) dictionary starts with the semantic distinctions and subordinates POS distinctions to these, while the Longman dictionary (LDOCE, Boguraev and Briscoe (1989)) starts with a POS-level split and puts the semantic split below. Of the Hungarian lexicographic sources, the Comprehensive Dictionary of Hungarian (NSZ, Ittzés (2011)) is closer to CED, while the Explanatory Dictionary of Hungarian (EKSZ, Pusztai (2003)), is closer to LDOCE in this regard. The corpora we rely on are UMBC Webbase (Han et al., 2013) for English and Webkorpusz (Halácsy et al., 2004) for Hungarian. For the Hungarian dictionaries, we relied on the versions created in Miháltz (2010); Recski et al. (2016). We simulate the case of languages without a machine-readable monolingual dictionary with OSub, a dictionary extracted from the OpenSubtitles parallel corpus (Tiedemann, 2012) automatically: the number of the senses of a word in a source language is the number of words it translates to, averaged among many languages. More precisely, we use the unigram perplexity of the translations instead of their count to reduce the considerable noise present in automatically created dictionaries.

Resource	1	2	3	4	5	6+	Size	Mean	Std
CED	80,003	1,695	242	69	13	2	82,024	1.030	0.206
LDOCE	26,585	3,289	323	56	11	1	30,265	1.137	0.394
OSub	58,043	14,849	2,259	431	111	25	75,718	1.354	0.492
AdaGram	122,594	330,218	11,341	5,048	7,626	0	476,827	1.836	0.663
huang	94,070	0	0	0	0	6,162	100,232	1.553	2.161
neela.30k	69,156	0	30,000	0	0	0	99,156	1.605	0.919
neela.NP.6k	94,165	2,967	1,012	383	202	427	99,156	1.101	0.601
neela.NP.30k	71,833	20,175	4,844	1,031	439	834	99,156	1.411	0.924
neela.s4	574,405	0	0	4,000	0	0	578,405	1.021	0.249
EKSZ	66,849	628	57	11	1	0	121,578	1.012	0.119
NSZ (b)	5,225	122	13	3	0	0	5,594	1.029	0.191
OSub	159,843	9,169	229	3	0	0	169,244	1.144	0.199
AdaGram	135,052	76,096	15,353	5,448	6,513	0	238,462	1.626	0.910
jiweil	57,109	92,263	75,710	39,624	15,153	5,997	285,856	2.483	1.181
neela.s2	767,870	4,000	0	0	0	0	99,156	1.005	0.072
neela.s4	767,870	0	0	4,000	0	0	99,156	1.016	0.215

Table 1: Sense distribution, size (in words), mean, and standard deviation of the English and Hungarian lexicographic and automatically generated resources

Table 1 summarizes the distribution of word senses (how many words with 1,...,6+ senses) and the major statistics (size, mean, and variance) both for our lexicographic sources and for the automatically generated MSEs.

While the lexicographic sources all show roughly exponential decay of the number of senses, only some of the automatically generated MSEs replicate this pattern, and only at well-chosen hyperparameter settings. `huang` has a hard switch between single-sense (94% of the words) and 10 senses (for the remaining 6%), and the same behavior is shown by the released Neela.300D.30k (70% one sense, 30% three senses). The English AdaGram and the Hungarian `jiweil` have the mode shifted to two senses, which makes no sense in light of the dictionary data. Altogether, we are left with only two English candidates, the adaptive (NP) `neelas`; and one Hungarian, AdaGram, that replicate the basic exponential decay.

The figure of merit we propose is the correlation between the number of senses obtained by the automatic method and by the manual (lexicographic) method. We experimented both with Spearman ρ

Resources compared	n	ρ
LDOCE vs CED	23702	0.266
EKSZ vs NSZ (b)	3484	0.648
neela.30k vs CED	23508	0.089
neela.NP.6k vs CED	23508	0.084
neela.NP.30k vs CED	23508	0.112
neela.30k vs LDOCE	21715	0.226
neela.NP.6k vs LDOCE	21715	**0.292**
neela.NP.30k vs LDOCE	21715	0.278
huang vs CED	23706	0.078
huang vs LDOCE	21763	**0.280**
neela.s4 vs EKSZ	45401	0.067
jiweil vs EKSZ	32007	0.023
AdaGram vs EKSZ	26739	0.086
AdaGram.a05 vs EKSZ	26739	0.088
neela.30k vs huang	99156	0.349
neela.NP.6k vs huang	99156	**0.901**
neela.NP.30k vs huang	99156	0.413
neela.s4 vs jiweil	283083	0.123
AdaGram vs neela.s4	199370	**0.389**
AdaGram vs jiweil	201291	0.140

Table 2: Word sense distribution similarity between various resources

and Pearson r values, the entropy-based measures Jensen-Shannon and KL divergence, and cosine similarity and Cohen's κ. The entropy-based measures failed to meaningfully distinguish between the various resource pairs. The cosine similarities and κ values would also have to be taken with a grain of salt: the former does not take the exact number of senses into account, while the latter penalizes all disagreements the same, regardless of how far the guesses are. On the other hand, the Spearman and Pearson values are so highly correlated that Table 2 shows only ρ of sense numbers attributed to each word by different resources, comparing lexicographic resources to one another (top panel); automated to lexicographic (mid panel); and different forms of automated English (bottom panel). The top two values in each column are highlighted in the last two panels, n is the number of headwords shared between the two resources.

The dictionaries themselves are quite well correlated with each other. The Hungarian values are considerably larger both because we only used a subsample of NSZ (the letter b) so there are only 5,363 words to compare, and because NSZ and EKSZ come from the same Hungarian lexicographic tradition, while CED and LDOCE never shared personnel or editorial outlook. Two English systems, `neela` and `huang`, show perceptible correlation with a lexical resource, LDOCE, and only two systems, AdaGram and `neela`, correlate well with each other (ignoring different parametrizations of the same system, which of course are often well correlated to one another).

2.1 Parts of speech and word frequency

Since no gold dataset exists, against which the results could be evaluated and the errors analyzed, we had to consider if there exist factors that might have affected the results. In particular, the better correlation of the adaptive methods with LDOCE than with CED raises suspicions. The former groups entries by part of speech, the latter by meaning, implying that the methods in question might be counting POS tags instead of meanings.

Another possible bias that might have influenced the results is word frequency (Manin, 2008). This is quite apparent in the release version of the non-adaptive methods `huang` and `neela`: the former expressly states in the README that the 6,162 words with multiple meanings "roughly cor-

Resources compared	n	ρ
CED vs POS	42532	0.052
LDOCE vs POS	28549	**0.206**
OSub vs POS	48587	**0.141**
EKSZ vs POS	52158	0.080
NSZ vs POS	3532	0.046
huang vs POS	98405	0.026
AdaGram vs freq	399985	0.343
huang vs freq	94770	0.376
CED vs freq	36709	0.124
LDOCE vs freq	27859	0.317
neela.s4 vs freq	94044	**0.649**
neela.NP.30k vs freq	94044	0.368
neela.NP.6k vs freq	94044	**0.635**
UMBC POS vs freq	136040	-0.054

Table 3: Word sense distribution similarity with POS tag perplexity (top panel) and word frequency (bottom panel)

respond to the most frequent words".

To examine the effect of these factors, we measured their correlation with the number of meanings reported by the methods above. For each word, the frequency and the POS perplexity was taken from the same corpora we ran the MSEs on: UMBC for English and Webkorpusz for Hungarian. Table 3 shows the results for both English and Hungarian. The correlation of automatically generated resources with POS tags is negligible: all other embeddings correlate even weaker than huang, the only one shown. From the English dictionaries, LDOCE produces the highest correlation, followed by OSub; the correlation with CED, as expected, is very low. The Hungarian dictionaries are around the level of CED.

In comparison, the correlation between sense numbers and word frequency is much more evident. Almost all English resources correlate with the word frequency by at least 0.3 (the notable exception being CED which is the closest to a gold standard we have); furthermore, the highest correlation we measured are between two versions of neela and the word frequency. Adding to this the low correlation of the gold CED against the other resources (see Table 2), it appears the multi-prototype embeddings included in the study were trained to assign more vectors to frequent words instead of trying this for truly polysemous ones.

To disentangle these factors further, we performed partial correlation analysis with the effect of frequency (or its log) or POS perplexity removed. Recall that LDOCE and CED originally correlated only to $\rho = 0.266$. After removing POS, we obtain 0.545, removing frequency yields 0.546, and removing log frequency brings this up to 0.599. Full discussion would stretch the bounds of this paper, but on select embeddings such as neela.NP.6k correlations with CED improve from a negligible 0.093 to a respectable 0.397 if POS, and an impressive 0.696 if log frequency is factored out.

3 Cross-linguistic treatment of concepts

Since monolingual dictionaries are an expensive resource, we also propose an automatic evaluation of MSEs based on the discovery of Mikolov et al. (2013b) that embeddings of different languages are so similar that a linear transformation can map vectors of the source language words to the vectors of their translations.

The method uses a seed dictionary of a few thousand words to learn translation as a linear mapping $W : \mathbb{R}^{d_1} \to \mathbb{R}^{d_2}$ from the source (monolingual) embedding to the target: the translation $z_i \in \mathbb{R}^{d_2}$ of a source word $x_i \in \mathbb{R}^{d_1}$ is approximately its image Wx_i by the mapping. The translation model is trained with linear regression on the seed dictionary

$$\min_W \sum_i ||Wx_i - z_i||^2$$

and can be used to collect translations for the whole vocabulary by choosing z_i to be the nearest neighbor of Wx_i.

We follow Mikolov et al. (2013b) in using different metrics, Euclidean distance in training and cosine similarity in collection of translations. Though this choice is theoretically unmotivated, it

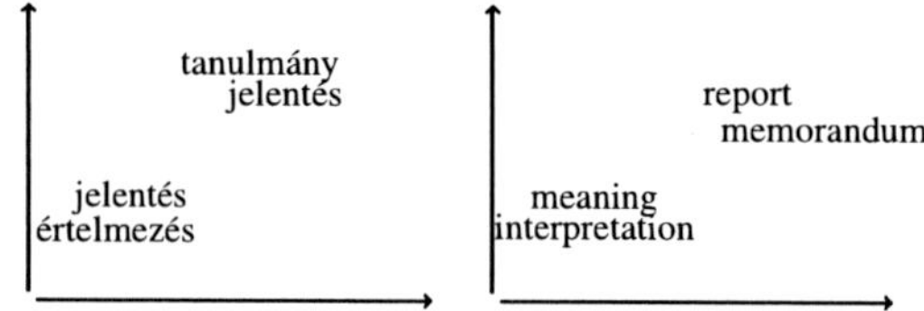

Figure 1: Linear translation of word senses. The Hungarian word *jelentés* is ambiguous between 'meaning' and 'report'. The two senses are identified by the "neighboring" words *értelmezés* 'interpretation' and *tanulmány* 'memorandum'.

seems to work better than more consistent use of metrics; but see (Xing et al., 2015) for opposing results.

In a multi-sense embedding scenario, we take a multi-sense embedding as source model, and a single-sense embedding as target model. We evaluate a specific source MSE model in two ways referred as *single*, and *multiple*.

The tools that generate MSEs all provide fallbacks to singe-sense embeddings in the form of so called global vectors. The method *single* can be considered as a baseline; a traditional, single-sense translation between the global vectors and the target vectors. Note that the seed dictionary may contain overlapping translation pairs: one word can have multiple translations in the gold data, and more than one word can have the same translation. In the *multiple* method we used the same translation matrix, trained on the global vectors, and inspected the translations of the different senses of the same source word. Exploiting the multiple sense vectors one word can have more than one translation.

Two evaluation metrics were considered, *lax* and *strict*. In lax evaluation a translation is taken to be correct if any of the source word's senses are translated into any of its gold translations. In strict evaluation the translations of the source word are expected to cover all of its gold translations. For example if *jelentés* has two gold translations, *report* and *meaning*, and its actual translations are 'report' and some word other than 'meaning', then it has a lax score of 2, but a strict score of 1.

The quality of the translation was measured by training on the most frequent 5k word pairs and evaluating on another 1k seed pairs. We used `OSub` as our seed dictionary. Table 4 shows the percentage of correctly translated words for single-sense and multi-sense translation.

embedding		lax	strict
AdaGram 800 a.05 m100	s	26.0%	21.7%
	m	30.5%	25.1%
AdaGram 800 a.01 m100	s	12.8%	10.8%
	m	24.4%	21.0%
jiweil	s	39.1%	32.2%
	m	9.7%	8.3%

Table 4: Hungarian to English translation. Target embedding from Mikolov et al. (2013a)

4 Conclusions

To summarize, we have proposed evaluating word embeddings in terms of their semantic resolution (ability to distinguish multiple senses) both monolingually and bilingually. Our monolingual task, match with the sense-distribution of a dictionary, yields an intrinsic measure in the sense of Chiu et al. (2016), while the bilingual evaluation is extrinsic, as it measures an aspect of performance on a downstream task, MT. For now, the two are not particularly well correlated, though the low/negative result of `jiweil` in Table 1 could be taken as advance warning for the low performance in Table 4. The reason, we feel, is that both kinds of performance are very far from expected levels, so little correlation can be expected between them: only if the MSE distribution of senses replicates the exponential decay seen in dictionaries (both professional lexicographic and crowdsourced products) is there any hope for further progress.

The central linguistic/semantic/psychological property we wish to capture is that of a *concept*, the underlying word sense unit. To the extent standard lexicographic practice offers a reasonably robust notion (this is of course debatable, but we consider a straight correlation of 0.27 and and a frequency-effect-removed correlation of 0.60 over a large vocabulary a strong indication of consistency), this is something that MSEs should aim at capturing. We leave the matter of aligning word senses in different dictionaries for future work, but we expect that by (manual or automated) alignment the inter-dictionary (inter-annotator) agreement can be improved considerably, to provide a more robust gold standard.

At this point everything we do is done in software, so other researchers can accurately reproduce these kinds of evaluations. Some glue code for this project can be found at `https://github.com/hlt-bme-hu/multiwsi`. Whether a 'gold' sense-disambiguated dictionary should be produced beyond the publicly available CED is not entirely clear, and we hope workshop participants will weigh in on this matter.

Acknowledgments

Research partially supported by National Research, Development, and Innovation Office NKFIH grant #115288.

References

Sergey Bartunov, Dmitry Kondrashkin, Anton Osokin, and Dmitry Vetrov. 2015. Breaking sticks and ambiguities with adaptive skip-gram. *ArXiv preprint* .

Branimir K. Boguraev and Edward J. Briscoe. 1989. *Computational Lexicography for Natural Language Processing*. Longman.

Billy Chiu, Anna Korhonen, and Sampo Pyysalo. 2016. Intrinsic evaluation of word vectors fails to predict extrinsic performance. In Omer Levy, editor, *Proc. RepEval (this volume)*. ACL.

Anna Gladkova and Aleksandr Drozd. 2016. Intrinsic evaluations of word embeddings: What can we do better? In Omer Levy, editor, *Proc. RepEval (this volume)*. ACL.

Péter Halácsy, András Kornai, László Németh, András Rung, István Szakadát, and Viktor Trón. 2004. Creating open language resources for Hungarian. In *Proc. LREC2004*. pages 203–210.

Lushan Han, Abhay Kashyap, Tim Finin, James Mayfield, and Jonathan Weese. 2013. UMBC_EBIQUITY-CORE: Semantic textual similarity systems. In *Proceedings of the 2nd Joint Conference on Lexical and Computational Semantics*. pages 44–52.

Eric H. Huang, Richard Socher, Christopher D. Manning, and Andrew Y. Ng. 2012. Improving word representations via global context and multiple word prototypes. In *Proceedings of the 50th Annual Meeting of the Association for Computational Linguistics: Long Papers - Volume 1*. Association for Computational Linguistics, Stroudsburg, PA, USA, ACL '12, pages 873–882.

Nóra Ittzés, editor. 2011. *A magyar nyelv nagyszótára III-IV*. Akadémiai Kiadó.

Jiwei Li and Dan Jurafsky. 2015. Do multi-sense embeddings improve natural language understanding? In *EMNLP*.

Dmitrii Y. Manin. 2008. Zipf's law and avoidance of excessive synonymy. *Cognitive Science* .

Márton Miháltz. 2010. *Semantic resources and their applications in Hungarian natural language processing*. Ph.D. thesis, Pázmány Péter Catholic University.

Tomas Mikolov, Kai Chen, Greg Corrado, and Jeffrey Dean. 2013a. Efficient estimation of word representations in vector space. In Y. Bengio and Y. LeCun, editors, *Proceedings of the ICLR 2013*.

Tomas Mikolov, Quoc V Le, and Ilya Sutskever. 2013b. Exploiting similarities among languages for machine translation. Xiv preprint arXiv:1309.4168.

Arvind Neelakantan, Jeevan Shankar, Alexandre Passos, and Andrew McCallum. 2014. Efficient non-parametric estimation of multiple embeddings per word in vector space. In *EMNLP*.

Ferenc Pusztai, editor. 2003. *Magyar értelmező kéziszótár*. Akadémiai Kiadó.

Gábor Recski, Gábor Borbély, and Attila Bolevácz. 2016. Building definition graphs using monolingual dictionaries of Hungarian. In Attila Tanács, Viktor Varga, and Veronika Vincze, editors, *XI. Magyar Számitógépes Nyelvészeti Konferencia [11th Hungarian Conference on Computational Linguistics]*.

Joseph Reisinger and Raymond J Mooney. 2010. Multi-prototype vector-space models of word meaning. In *The 2010 Annual Conference of the North American Chapter of the Association for Computational Linguistics*. Association for Computational Linguistics, pages 109–117.

John M. Sinclair. 1987. *Looking up: an account of the COBUILD project in lexical computing*. Collins ELT.

Jörg Tiedemann. 2012. Parallel data, tools and interfaces in OPUS. In Nicoletta Calzolari (Conference Chair), Khalid Choukri, Thierry Declerck, Mehmet Ugur Dogan, Bente Maegaard, Joseph Mariani, Jan Odijk, and Stelios Piperidis, editors, *Proceedings of the Eight International Conference on Language Resources and Evaluation (LREC'12)*. European Language Resources Association (ELRA), Istanbul, Turkey.

Chao Xing, Chao Liu, RIIT CSLT, Dong Wang, China TNList, and Yiye Lin. 2015. Normalized word embedding and orthogonal transform for bilingual word translation. In *NAACL*.

Hyejin Youna, Logan Sutton, Eric Smith, Cristopher Moore, Jon F. Wilkins, Ian Maddieson, William Croft, and Tanmoy Bhattacharya.

2016. On the universal structure of human lexical semantics. *PNAS* 113(7):1766–1771.

Ladislav Zgusta. 1971. *Manual of lexicography.* Academia, Prague.

Subsumption Preservation as a Comparative Measure for Evaluating Sense-Directed Embeddings

A. Patrice Seyed
3M HIS
Silver Spring, MD
apseyed@gmail.com

Abstract

While there has been a growing body of work on word embeddings, and recent directions better reflect sense-level representations, evaluation remains a challenge. We propose a method of query inventory generation for embedding evaluation that recasts the principle of subsumption preservation, a desirable property of semantic graph-based similarity measures, as a comparative similarity measure as applied to existing lexical resources. We aim that this method is immediately applied to populate query inventories and perform evaluation with the ordered triple-based approach set forth, and inspires future refinements to existing notions of evaluating sense-directed embeddings.

1 Introduction

Work in the area of word embeddings has exploded in the last several years. Approaches based on word prediction (Mikolov et al., 2013) show improvement over traditional and recent work on count based vectors (Baroni et al., 2014). There has been gradual movement toward sense-directed or sense-level embeddings (Huang et al., 2012; Faruqui et al., 2015; Trask et al., 2015) while existing evaluation strategies based on applications, human rankings, and solving word choice problems have limitations (Schnabel et al., 2015). A limitation of relying on downstream applications for evaluation is that results vary depending on the application (Schnabel et al., 2015). In recent work, Tsvetkov (2015) leverages alignment with existing manually crafted lexical resources as a standard for evaluation, which shows a strong correlation with downstream applications.

Along this vein, there is an increasing need for methodologies for word-sense level evaluation measures. The utility of word embeddings is to reflect notions of similarity and relatedness, and word embeddings intended to represent senses should in turn reflect structured relations like hypernymy and meronymy. Most existing resources on lexical similarity and relatedness rely on subjective scores assigned between word pairs. This style of evaluation suffers from limited size of the evaluation sets and subjectivity of annotators. To address the first issue, we propose a method for exploiting existing knowledge formalized in lexical resources and ontologies as a means to automating the process of populating a query inventory. To address the second issue, we propose an evaluation approach that, instead of human scoring of word pairs, relies on comparative similarity given a semantic ordering represented as 3-tuples (henceforth triples). The method applies the principle of subsumption preservation as a standard by which to generate a query inventory and evaluate word embedding by geometric similarity. For example, subsumption is preserved when the similarity score of embeddings representing *ferry* and *boat* is greater than that of *ferry* and *vessel*. In the following section we illuminate the method, evaluation approach, an exploratory experiment, its results, related work, and next steps.

2 Method

The foundation of the method is the principle of *subsumption preservation* (Lehmann and Turhan, 2012).[1] We define this principle with axiom schemata as follows:

---

[1] We reference the two principles of subsumption and reverse subsumption atomically via the disjunction. *Transitive* serves as syntactic shorthand for the corresponding axiom. We assume the relationship between A and C is not asserted but inferred by transitivity.

Proceedings of the 1st Workshop on Evaluating Vector Space Representations for NLP, pages 90–93,
Berlin, Germany, August 12, 2016. ©2016 Association for Computational Linguistics

$$SP_{sim_{rel}}(A,B,C) =_{def}$$
$$rel(A,B) \wedge rel(B,C) \wedge Transitive(rel) \rightarrow$$
$$sim(A,B) \vee sim(B,C) \geq sim(A,C)$$

$SP_{sim_{rel}}(A,B,C)$ means that similarity measure *sim* conforms to the subsumption preservation principle with respect to relation *rel* for all triples $\langle A,B,C \rangle$, just in case for any tuple $\langle A,B,C \rangle$ of *rel* related via transitivity, the similarity score of $\langle A,B \rangle$ and that of $\langle B,C \rangle$ is greater than or equal to that of $\langle A,C \rangle$. The property of subsumption preservation provides a link between subsumption and similarity in that it expresses the constraint that A and B (B and C) are more similar than A and C since the former pair(s) are 'closer' in the corresponding graph. Note that *rel* serves as relational schema that is satisfied by transitive, generalization relations. This includes taxonomic or partonomic inclusion that are the foundation of lexical resources and ontologies (e.g., WordNet, Gene Ontology).

The original intent of the subsumption preservation principle is that any quantitative semantic similarity measure *sim* is constrained by this desirable formal property. For instance, *Path* (Rada et al., 1989) abides by the subsumption preservation principle, and is defined as Path(A,B) $=_{def}$ 1/p, where p is the length of the path separating two concepts, *A* and *B*. A weakness of this and similar measures is that the length of path between two concepts is often a reflection of variability in the knowledge modeling technique or scope and not necessary a reflection of relatedness. To account for this shortcoming, Resnik (1995) applies the notion of information content: IC_{corpus} = -log(freq(A)), the inverse log of a concept *A*'s frequency in a given corpus, of a concept pair's least common subsumer as the similarity measure. There are other, varied approaches to semantic similarity that are based on a combination of corpus statistics and lexical taxonomy (Jiang and Conrath, 1997). Ultimately these approaches produce a score that is to some extent dependent on graph-based distances.

In the present work we take a different approach by proposing comparative similarity that hinges on semantic graph order preservation as the unit of evaluation. The intent is to apply only a basic geometric similarity measure (e.g., cosine) as *sim* within our definition of subsumption preservation, in order to provide a measure of how well embeddings abstract to the knowledge structure expected of a sense-directed embedding.

Thus given word embeddings, a knowledge resource and a similarity measure over the embedding space, an embedding does not conform to the subsumption preserving principle, if for example, the similarity score between terms *sparrow* and *bird* or *bird* and *vertebrate* is less than that of *sparrow* and *vertebrate*. A set of sense embeddings do not conform to the subsumption preserving principle to the proportion of cases that are violated. By adhering to the subsumption preserving principle a set of sense embeddings reflects notions of foundational semantic relationships and comparative similarity explicitly formalized in lexical and ontological resources. Thus, evaluation based on this method can serve as an indicator of how well approaches for learning embeddings can reflect relationships that are not present in knowledge resources.

3 Evaluation Approach

Traditionally word pairs of a query inventory are scored by similarity with a value between 0-1. We propose a different approach based on the unit of ordered triple instead of pairs, and that is relative rather than absolute and quantitative. Given a set of tuples of a relation *rel* that *sim* is potentially constrained by under subsumption preservation, we consider the candidate triples as instances of a query inventory for evaluation.

A similar approach has been applied in the evaluation of machine translation. Kahn (2009) describes a family of dependency pair match measures that are composed of precision and recall over various decompositions of a syntactic dependency tree. A dependency parser determines the relevant word triples where the relation is the second element. Reference and hypothesis sentences are converted to a labeled syntactic dependence tree, and the relations from each tree are extracted and compared. We draw inspiration from this approach, where the unit of evaluation is the ordered triple. Given the nature of our task we apply the measure of accuracy on the triples.

4 Exploratory Experiment Setup

For evaluation the BLESS dataset is selected as the basis for selecting a triple-based query inventory, (Baroni and Lenci, 2011), focusing on hypernymy and leaving meronymy as a future consideration. For pairs that are related by hypernymy we identify intermediate words within the hypernym graph to generate candidate triples, including only nouns. For embeddings we used word2vec-based embeddings generated from google corpora.[2] For the similarity measure we selected cosine similarity, although the evaluation approach assumes embeddings and a similarity measure are two variables. So for example the score of sim(broccoli, vegetable) is greater than sim(broccoli,produce), therefore one part of the subsumption preservation principle is conformed to for the triple ⟨broccoli, vegetable, produce⟩. Also, sim(vegetable, produce) is greater than sim(broccoli, produce), therefore the triple is also in conformance with the other part of the subsumption preserved principle, namely reverse subsumption preservation.

We consider two approaches for calculating cosine similarity between words within the word2vec generated embeddings. The first is the simple approach and is performed by calculating the cosine between two word embeddings. The second is the aggregate approach, and requires, for each of the two words, exhaustively collecting all sister lemmas for the senses each word is a lemma of, calculating the centroid for all corresponding embeddings, and calculating cosine similarity between the resultant pair of centroid embeddings. The aggregate approach is in effort to simulate sense level embeddings for this exploration. We also consider the role of word generality in the evaluation.

5 Results

The results of the exploratory evaluation are shown in Table 5. SS, RSS, AS, and RAS represent subsumption and reserve subsumption preservation by the simple and aggregate approaches. The triple inventory *w/o abstract* represents where triples including highly abstract terms *object* and *artifact* were removed, and the inventory *IC threshold* represents where triples only included terms with Information Content above 3.0. Therefore the number of triples in the three inventories are approximately 1900, 900, and 300, respectively. In all three cases 5k was used as the unigram frequency cutoff for all terms in the triples, and it was observed that increasing above this value did not improvement accuracy. The results of the latter two runs illustrate where the most

<hr>

[2]https://code.google.com/archive/p/word2vec/

triple inventory	SS	RSS	AS	RAS
baseline	.67	.68	.73	.68
w/o abstract	.78	.72	.78	.69
IC threshold	.88	.73	.78	.65

Table 1: Accuracy figures for the triple-based query inventory generated from the BLESS dataset and WordNet.

general term in the triples is more likely a domain concept, which coincides which better overall accuracy.

6 Related Work

Newman (2010) applies semantic similarity measures leveraging WordNet, among other resources, for measuring coherence of topic models. Word pairs of a topic's top N terms are scored by similarity measures, where all synset pairs for a word pair are exhaustively applied prior to calculating their mean. The goal is to determine, based on topics previously selected by Mechanical Turkers as coherent, how well similarity measures reflect the coherence. It was found that WordNet-based similarity measures varied greatly, while non-graph similarity measures using Wikipedia and more generally applying pointwise mutual information performed the best.

Schnabel (2015) performs a comparative intrinsic evaluation based on selected word embeddings and nearest neighbor terms by cosine similarity for different word embedding learning approaches. Mechanical Turk participants were asked to select the most similar term from nearest neighbors for a given target term. Embedding learning approaches are compared by average win ratio.

7 Discussion and Future Work

In this paper we put forth a method for generating a triple-based query inventory and evaluation to assist in determining how well word embedding abstract to the sense, conceptual level. This approach provides an evaluation of relative rather than absolute similarity, the latter of which can lead to drastic differences in similarity scoring. The results improved by applying filters to the BLESS-derived query inventory aimed at where the most general term in the triples are more "meaningful", or put simply, where we increased the proportion of domain knowledge being tested. Since this occurred at the cost of the size of the triple set, it is worth considering other heuristics for augmenting the generated candidate triples to improve their utility. We hope that this approach be ultimately treated as a sort of unit test for embeddings aimed at the open or a particular domain.

In future work we will perform the evaluation on sense embeddings (Trask et al., 2015), and on embeddings that integrate with lexical resources (Faruqui et al., 2015; Rothe and Schütze, 2015). We will also investigate the use of other broader relations, such as meronymy, as well as consider other lexical and ontological resources that are more comprehensive for the domains we aim to evaluate. Another consideration is evaluating embeddings with other similarity measures that account for asymmetry. Further, we aim to test if the accuracy conforming to subsumption preservation correlates with an evaluation of a downstream task, to confirm whether it can serve as a valid proxy.

8   Acknowledgements

Many thanks to Amitai Axelrod, Omer Levy, and the reviewers for fruitful feedback.

References

Marco Baroni and Alessandro Lenci. 2011. How we blessed distributional semantic evaluation. In *Processings of the GEMS 2011 Workshop on Geometrical Models of Natural Language Semantics*, page 110. Association for Computational Linguistics.

Marco Baroni, Georgiana Dinu, and Germán Kruszewski. 2014. Don't count, predict! A systematic comparison of context-counting vs. context-predicting semantic vectors. In *Proceedings of the 52nd Annual Meeting of the Association for Computational Linguistics, ACL 2014, June 22-27, 2014, Baltimore, MD, USA, Volume 1: Long Papers*, pages 238–247.

Manaal Faruqui, Jesse Dodge, Sujay Kumar Jauhar, Chris Dyer, Eduard H. Hovy, and Noah A. Smith. 2015. Retrofitting word vectors to semantic lexicons. In *NAACL HLT 2015, The 2015 Conference of the North American Chapter of the Association for Computational Linguistics: Human Language Technologies, Denver, Colorado, USA, May 31 - June 5, 2015*, pages 1606–1615.

Eric H. Huang, Richard Socher, Christopher D. Manning, and Andrew Y. Ng. 2012. Improving word representations via global context and multiple word prototypes. In *The 50th Annual Meeting of the Association for Computational Linguistics, Proceedings of the Conference, July 8-14, 2012, Jeju Island, Korea - Volume 1: Long Papers*, pages 873–882.

Jay J Jiang and David W Conrath. 1997. Semantic similarity based on corpus statistics and lexical taxonomy. *arXiv preprint cmp-lg/9709008*.

Jeremy G. Kahn, Matthew G. Snover, and Mari Ostendorf. 2009. Expected dependency pair match: predicting translation quality with expected syntactic structure. *Machine Translation*, 23(2-3):169–179.

Karsten Lehmann and Anni-Yasmin Turhan. 2012. A framework for semantic-based similarity measures for {ELH} concepts. In *Logics in Artificial Intelligence*, pages 307–319. Springer.

Tomas Mikolov, Kai Chen, Greg Corrado, and Jeffrey Dean. 2013. Efficient estimation of word representations in vector space. *CoRR*, abs/1301.3781.

David Newman, Jey Han Lau, Karl Grieser, and Timothy Baldwin. 2010. Automatic evaluation of topic coherence. In *Human Language Technologies: The 2010 Annual Conference of the North American Chapter of the Association for Computational Linguistics*, pages 100–108. Association for Computational Linguistics.

Roy Rada, Hafedh Mili, Ellen Bicknell, and Maria Blettner. 1989. Development and application of a metric on semantic nets. *Systems, Man and Cybernetics, IEEE Transactions on*, 19(1):17–30.

Philip Resnik. 1995. Using information content to evaluate semantic similarity in a taxonomy. *arXiv preprint cmp-lg/9511007*.

Sascha Rothe and Hinrich Schütze. 2015. Autoextend: Extending word embeddings to embeddings for synsets and lexemes. *arXiv preprint arXiv:1507.01127*.

Tobias Schnabel, Igor Labutov, David M. Mimno, and Thorsten Joachims. 2015. Evaluation methods for unsupervised word embeddings. In *Proceedings of the 2015 Conference on Empirical Methods in Natural Language Processing, EMNLP 2015, Lisbon, Portugal, September 17-21, 2015*, pages 298–307.

Andrew Trask, Phil Michalak, and John Lui. 2015. "sense2vec-a fast and accurate method for word sense disambiguation. *Neural Word Embeddings*.

Yulia Tsvetkov, Manaal Faruqui, Wang Ling, Guillaume Lample, and Chris Dyer. 2015. Evaluation of word vector representations by subspace alignment. In *Proceedings of the 2015 Conference on Empirical Methods in Natural Language Processing, EMNLP 2015, Lisbon, Portugal, September 17-21, 2015*, pages 2049–2054.

Evaluating Informal-Domain Word Representations With UrbanDictionary

Naomi Saphra
University of Edinburgh
n.saphra@ed.ac.uk

Adam Lopez
University of Edinburgh
alopez@inf.ed.ac.uk

Abstract

Existing corpora for intrinsic evaluation are not targeted towards tasks in informal domains such as Twitter or news comment forums. We want to test whether a representation of informal words fulfills the promise of eliding explicit text normalization as a preprocessing step. One possible evaluation metric for such domains is the proximity of spelling variants. We propose how such a metric might be computed and how a spelling variant dataset can be collected using UrbanDictionary.

1 Introduction

Recent years have seen a surge of interest in training effective models for informal domains such as Twitter or discussion forums. Several new works have thus targeted social media platforms by learning word representations specific to such domains (Tang et al., 2014); (Benton et al., 2016).

Traditional NLP techniques have often relied on text normalization methods when applied to informal domains. For example, "u want 2 chill wit us 2nite" may be transcribed as "you want to chill with us tonight", and the normalized transcription would be used as input for a text processing system. This method makes it easier to apply models that are successful on formal language to more informal language. However, there are several drawbacks to this method.

Building an accurate text normalization component for a text processing pipeline can require substantial engineering effort and collection of manually annotated training data. Even evaluating text normalization models is a difficult problem and often subjective (Eisenstein, 2013b).

Even when the model accurately transcribes informal spelling dialects to a standard dialect, text normalization methods may not be appropriate.

Converting text to a style more consistent with The Wall Street Journal than Twitter may make parsing easier, but it loses much of the nuance in a persona deliberately adopted by the writer. Twitter users often express their spoken dialect through spelling, so regional and demographic information may also be lost in the process of text normalization (Eisenstein, 2013a).

Distributional word representations hold promise to replace this flawed preprocessing step. By making the shared semantic content of spelling variants implicit in the representation of words, text processing models can be more flexible. They can extract persona or dialect information while handling the semantic or syntactic features of words (Benton et al., 2016).

In this proposal, we will present a method of evaluating whether a particular set of word representations can make text normalization unnecessary. Because the intrinsic evaluation we present is inexpensive and simple, it can be easily used to validate representations during training. An evaluation dataset can be collected easily from UrbanDictionary by methods we will outline.

2 Evaluating By Spelling Variants

Several existing metrics for evaluating word representations assume that similar words will have similar representations in an ideal embedding space. A natural question is therefore whether a representation of words in social media text would place spelling variants of the same word close to each other. For example, while the representation of "ur" may appear close to "babylon" and "mesopotamia" in a formal domain like Wikipedia, on Twitter it should be closer to "your".

We can evaluate these representations based on the proximity of spelling variants. Given a corpus of common spelling variant pairs (one informal variant and one formal), we will accept

Proceedings of the 1st Workshop on Evaluating Vector Space Representations for NLP, pages 94–98,
Berlin, Germany, August 12, 2016. ©2016 Association for Computational Linguistics

or reject each word pair's relative placement in our dictionary. For example, we may consider (ur, your) to be such a pair. To evaluate this pair, we rank the words in our vocabulary by cosine-similarity to ur.

We could then count the pair correct if your appears in the top k most similar tokens. A similar method is common in assessing performance on analogical reasoning tasks (Mikolov et al., 2013). Having thus accepted or rejected the relationship for each pair, we can summarize our overall performance as accuracy statistic.

The disadvantage of this method is that performance will not be robust to vocabulary size. Adding more informal spelling variants of the same word may push the formal variant down the ranked list (for example, yr may be closer to ur than your is). However, if these new variants are not in the formal vocabulary, they should not affect the ability to elide text normalization into the representation.

To make the metric robust to vocabulary size, instead of ranking all tokens by similarity to the first word in the variant pair, we rank only tokens that we consider to be formal. We consider a token to be formal if it appears on a list of formal vocabulary. Such a list can be collected, for example, by including all vocabulary appearing in Wikipedia or the Wall Street Journal.

3   Gathering Spelling Variants

If we have an informal text corpus, we can use it to generate a set of likely spelling variants to validate by hand. An existing unsupervised method to do so is outlined as part of the text normalization pipeline described by (Gouws et al., 2011).

This technique requires a formal vocabulary corpus such as Wikipedia as well as a social media corpus such as Twitter. They start by exhaustively ranking all word pairs by their distributional similarity in both Wikipedia and Twitter. The word pairs that are distributionally similar in Twitter but not in Wikipedia are considered to be candidate spelling variants. These candidates are then re-ranked by lexical similarity, providing a list of likely spelling variants.

This method is inappropriate when collecting datasets for the purpose of evaluation. When we rely on co-occurrence information in a social media corpus to identify potential spelling variants, we provide an advantage to representations learned using co-occurrence information. When we rely on lexical similarity to find variants, we also offer an unfair advantage to representations that include character-level similarity as part of the model, such as (Dhingra et al., 2016).

We therefore collected a dataset from an independent source of spelling variants, UrbanDictionary.

UrbanDictionary

UrbanDictionary is a crowd-compiled dictionary of informal words and slang with over 7 million entries. We can use UrbanDictionary as a resource for identifying likely spelling variants. One advantage of this system is that UrbanDictionary will typically be independent of the corpus used for training, and therefore we will not use the same training features for evaluation.

To identify spelling variants on UrbanDictionary, we scrape all words and definitions from the site. In the definitions, we search for a number of common strings that signal spelling variants. To cast a very wide net, we could search for all instances of "spelling" and then validate a large number of results by hand. More reliably, we can search for strings like:

- misspelling of [your][1]

- misspelling of "your"

- way of spelling [your]

- spelling for [your]

A cursory filter will yield thousands of definitions that follow similar templates. The word pairs extracted from these definitions can then be validated by Mechanical Turk or study participants.

Scripts for scraping and filtering UrbanDictionary are released with this proposal, along with a small sample of hand-validated word pairs selected in this way[2].

4   Experiments

Restricting ourselves to entries for ASCII-only words, we identified 5289 definitions on Urban-Dictionary that contained the string "spelling". Many entries explicitly describe a word as a spelling variant of a different "correctly" spelled word, as in the following definition of "neice":

---

[1]Brackets indicate a link to another page of definitions, in this case for "your".

[2]https://github.com/nsaphra/urbandic-scraper

```
spelling[^\.,]* (’|\"|\[)(?P<variant>\w+)(\1)
```

Figure 1: Regular expression to identify spelling variants.

Neice is a common misspelling of the word niece, meaning the daughter of one's brother or sister. The correct spelling is niece.

Even this relatively wide net misses many definitions that identify a spelling variant, including this one for "definately":

The wrong way to spell definitely.

We extracted respelling candidates using the regular expression in Figure 1, where the group `variant` contains the candidate variant. We thus required the variant word to be either quoted or a link to a different word's page, in order to simplify the process of automatically extracting the informal-formal word pairs, as in the following definition of "suxx":

[Demoscene] spelling of "Sucks".

We excluded all definitions containing the word "name" and definitions of words that appeared less than 100 times in a 4-year sample of English tweets. This template yielded 923 candidate pairs. 7 of these pairs were people's names, and thus excluded. 760 (83%) of the remaining candidate pairs were confirmed to be informal-to-formal spelling variant pairs.

Some definitions that yielded false spelling variants using this template, with the candidate highlighted, were:

1. recieve: The spelling bee champion of his 1st grade class above me neglected to correctly spell "*acquired*", so it seems all of you who are reading this get a double-dose of spelling corrections.

2. Aryan: The ancient spelling of the word "*Iranian*".

3. moran: The correct spelling of moran when posting to [*fark*]

4. mosha: …However, the younger generation (that were born after 1983) think it is a great word for someone who likes "Nu Metal" And go around calling people fake moshas (or as the spelling was originally "*Moshers*".

Most of the false spelling variants were linked to commentary about usage, such as descriptions of the typical speaker (e.g., "ironic") or domains (e.g., "YouTube" or "Fark").

When using the word pairs to evaluate trained embeddings, we excluded examples where the second word in the pair was not on a formal vocabulary list (e.g., "Eonnie", a word borrowed from Korean meaning "big sister", was mapped to an alternative transcription, "unni").

4.1 Filtering by a Formal Vocabulary List

Some tokens which UrbanDictionary considers worth mapping to may not appear in the formal corpus. For example, UrbanDictionary considers the top definition of "braj" to be:

Pronounced how it is spelled. Means bro, or dude. Developed over numerous times of misspelling [brah] over texts and online chats.

Both "braj" and "brah" are spelling variants of "bro", itself an abbreviation of "brother". If we extract (`braj, brah`) as a potential spelling pair based on this definition, we cannot evaluate it if `brah` does not appear in the formal corpus. Representations of these words should probably reflect their similarity, but using the method described in Section 2, we cannot evaluate spelling pairs of two informal words.

Using a vocabulary list compiled from English Wikipedia, we removed 140 (18%) of the remaining pairs. Our final set of word pairs contained 620 examples.

4.2 Results on GloVe

As a test, we performed an evaluation on embeddings trained with GloVe (Pennington et al., 2014) on a 121GB English Twitter corpus. We used a formal vocabulary list based on English Wikipedia. We found that 146 (24%) of the informal word representations from the word pairs in our dataset had the target formal word in the top 20 most similar formal words from the vocabulary. Only 70 (11%) of the informal word representations had the target formal word as the most similar formal word.

The word pairs with representations that appeared far apart often featured an informal word that appeared closer to words that were related by topic, but not similar in meaning. The representation of "orgasim" was closer to a number of medical terms, including "abscess", "hysterectomy", "hematoma", and "cochlear", than it was to "orgasm".

Other word pairs were penalized when the "formal" vocabulary list failed to filter out informal words that appeared in the same online dialect. The five closest "formal" words to "qurl" ("girl"), which were "coot", "dht", "aaw", "luff", and "o.k".

Still other word pairs were counted as wrong, but were in fact polysemous. The representation of "tarp" did not appear close to "trap", which was its formal spelling according to UrbanDictionary. Instead, the closest formal word was "tarpaulin", which is commonly abbreviated as "tarp".

These results suggest that current systems based exclusively on distributional similarity may be insufficient for the task of representing informal-domain words.

5   Biases and Drawbacks

Evaluating performance on spelling variant pairs could predict performance on a number of tasks that are typically solved with a text normalization step in the system pipeline. In a task like sentiment analysis, however, the denotation of the word is not the only source of information. For example, a writer may use more casual spelling to convey sarcasm:

> I see women who support Trump or Brock Turner and I'm like "wow u r such a good example for ur daughter lol not poor bitch" (Twitter, 18 Jun 2016)

or whimsy:

> *taking a personalitey test*
> ugh i knew i shoud have studied harder for this (Twitter, 6 Jun 2016)

An intrinsic measure of spelling variant similarity will not address these aspects.

Some of the disadvantages of metrics based on cosine similarity, as discussed in Faruqui et al. (2016), apply here as well. In particular, we do not know if performance would correlate well with extrinsic metrics; we do not account for the role of word frequency in cosine similarity; and we cannot handle polysemy. Novel issues of polysemy also emerge in cases such as "tarp"; "wit", which represents either cleverness or a spelling variant of "with"; and "ur", which maps to both "your" and "you are".

However, compared to similarity scores in general (Gladkova and Drozd, 2016), spelling variant pairs are less subjective.

6   Conclusions

The heuristics used to collect the small dataset released with this paper were restrictive. It is possible to collect more spelling variant pairs by choosing more common patterns (such as the over 5000 entries containing the string "spelling") to pick candidate definitions. We could then use more complex rules, a learned model, or human participants to extract the spelling variants from the definitions. However, the simplicity of our system, which requires minimal human labor, makes it a practical option for evaluating specialized word embeddings for social media text.

Our experiments with GloVe indicate that models based only on the distributional similarity of words may be limited in their ability to represent the semantics of online speech. Some recent work has learned representations of embeddings for Twitter using character sequences as well as distributional information (Dhingra et al., 2016); (Vosoughi et al., 2016). These models should have a significant advantage in any metric relying on spelling variants, which are likely to exhibit character-level similarity.

References

Adrian Benton, Raman Arora, and Mark Dredze. 2016. Learning multiview embeddings of twitter users. ACL.

Bhuwan Dhingra, Zhong Zhou, Dylan Fitzpatrick, Michael Muehl, and William W Cohen. 2016. Tweet2vec: Character-based distributed representations for social media. In *Proceedings of ACL*.

Jacob Eisenstein. 2013a. Phonological factors in social media writing. In *Proc. of the Workshop on Language Analysis in Social Media*, pages 11–19.

Jacob Eisenstein. 2013b. What to do about bad language on the internet. In *HLT-NAACL*, pages 359–369.

Manaal Faruqui, Yulia Tsvetkov, Pushpendre Rastogi, and Chris Dyer. 2016. Problems with evaluation of word embeddings using word similarity tasks. In *RepEval*.

Anna Gladkova and Aleksandr Drozd. 2016. Intrinsic evaluations of word embeddings: What can we do better? In *RepEval*.

Stephan Gouws, Dirk Hovy, and Donald Metzler. 2011. Unsupervised mining of lexical variants from noisy text. In *Proceedings of the First Workshop on Unsupervised Learning in NLP*, EMNLP '11, pages 82–90, Stroudsburg, PA, USA. Association for Computational Linguistics.

Tomas Mikolov, Ilya Sutskever, Kai Chen, Greg S Corrado, and Jeff Dean. 2013. Distributed representations of words and phrases and their compositionality. In *Advances in neural information processing systems*, pages 3111–3119.

Jeffrey Pennington, Richard Socher, and Christopher D Manning. 2014. Glove: Global vectors for word representation. In *EMNLP*, volume 14, pages 1532–43.

Duyu Tang, Furu Wei, Nan Yang, Ming Zhou, Ting Liu, and Bing Qin. 2014. Learning sentiment-specific word embedding for twitter sentiment classification. In *ACL (1)*, pages 1555–1565.

Soroush Vosoughi, Prashanth Vijayaraghavan, and Deb Roy. 2016. Tweet2vec: Learning tweet embeddings using character-level cnn-lstm encoder-decoder. In *SIGIR*.

Thematic fit evaluation: an aspect of selectional preferences

Asad Sayeed, Clayton Greenberg, and Vera Demberg
Computer Science / Computational Linguistics and Phonetics
Saarland University
66117 Saarbrücken, Germany
`{asayeed,claytong,vera}@coli.uni-saarland.de`

Abstract

In this paper, we discuss the *human thematic fit judgement correlation* task in the context of real-valued vector space word representations. Thematic fit is the extent to which an argument fulfils the selectional preference of a verb given a role: for example, how well "cake" fulfils the patient role of "cut". In recent work, systems have been evaluated on this task by finding the correlations of their output judgements with human-collected judgement data. This task is a representation-independent way of evaluating models that can be applied whenever a system score can be generated, and it is applicable wherever predicate-argument relations are significant to performance in end-user tasks. Significant progress has been made on this cognitive modeling task, leaving considerable space for future, more comprehensive types of evaluation.

1 Introduction

In this paper, we discuss a way of evaluating real-valued semantic representations: *human thematic fit judgement correlations*. This evaluation method permits us to model the relationship between the construction of these semantic representation spaces and the cognitive decision-making process that goes into predicate-argument compositionality in human language users. We focus here on verb-noun compositionality as a special case of thematic fit judgement evaluation.

A verb typically evokes expectations regarding the participants in the event that the verb describes. By generalizing over different verbs, we can create a scheme of *thematic roles*, which characterize different ways to be a participant. Schemes vary,

but most contain *agent, patient, instrument,* and *location* (Aarts, 1997). The verb "cut" creates an expectation, among others, for a *patient* role that is to be fulfilled by something that is cuttable. This role-specific expectation is called the *patient selectional preference* of "cut". The noun "cake" fulfils the patient selectional preference of "cut", "form" less so. As such, we can see that selectional preferences are likely to be graded.

We define *thematic fit* to be the extent to which a noun fulfils the selectional preference of a verb given a role. This can be quantified in *thematic fit ratings*, human judgements that apply to combinations of verb, role, and noun[1]. One of the goals of this type of evaluation is both for cognitive modeling and for future application. From a cognitive modeling perspective, thematic fit judgements offer a window into the decision-making process of language users in assigning semantic representations to complex expressions. Psycholinguistic work has shown that these introspective judgements map well to underlying processing notions (Padó et al., 2009; Vandekerckhove et al., 2009).

One of our goals in developing this type of evaluation is to provide another method of testing systems designed for applications in which predicate-argument relations may have a significant effect on performance, especially in user interaction. This particularly applies in tasks where non-local dependencies have semantic relevance, for example, such as in judging the plausibility of a candidate coreferent from elsewhere in the discourse. Such applications include statistical sentence generation in spoken dialog contexts, where systems must make plausible lexical choices in context. This is particularly important as dialog systems grow steadily less task-specific. Indeed, applications that depends on predicting or generating match-

---

[1] Sometimes roles can be fulfilled by clausal arguments, which we leave for the future.

Proceedings of the 1st Workshop on Evaluating Vector Space Representations for NLP, pages 99–105,
Berlin, Germany, August 12, 2016. ©2016 Association for Computational Linguistics

ing predicate-argument pairs in a human-plausible
way, such as question-answering, summarization,
or machine translation, may benefit from this form
of thematic fit evaluation.

Both from the cognitive modeling perspective
and from the applications perspective, there is still
significant work to be done in constructing models, including distributional representations. We
thus need to determine whether and how we can
find judgements that are a suitable gold standard
for evaluating automatic systems. We seek in this
paper to shed some light on the aspects of this
problem relevant to vector-space word representation and to highlight the evaluation data currently
available for this task.

This task differs from other ways of evaluating word representations because it focuses partly
on the psychological plausibility of models of
predicate-argument function application. Analogy task evaluations, for example, involve comparisons of word representations that are similar
in their parts of speech (Mikolov et al., 2013b).
Here we are evaluating relations between words
that are "counterparts" of one another and that exist overall in complementary distribution to one
another. There are other forms of evaluation that
attempt to replicate role assignments or predict
more plausible role-fillers given observed text data
(Van de Cruys, 2014), but this does not directly
capture human biases as to plausibility: infrequent
predicate-argument combinations can nevertheless
have high human ratings. Consequently, we view
this task as a useful contribution to the family
of evaluations that would test different aspects of
general-purpose word representations.

2   Existing datasets

The first datasets of human judgements were obtained in the context of a larger scientific discussion on human sentence processing. In particular,
McRae et al. (1998) proposed incremental evaluation of thematic fit for the arguments in potential
parses as a method of parse comparison. Human
judgements of thematic fit were needed for incorporation into this model.

McRae et al. (1997) solicited thematic fit ratings on a scale from 1 (least common) to 7 (most
common) using "How common is it for a {*snake,
nurse, monster, baby, cat*} to *frighten* some-
one/something?" (for agents) and "How common
is it for a {*snake, nurse, monster, baby, cat*} to *be*

verb	role-filler	agent	patient
accept	friend	6.1	5.8
accept	student	5.9	5.3
accept	teenager	5.5	4.1
accept	neighbor	5.4	4.4
accept	award	1.1	6.6
admire	groupie	6.9	1.9
admire	fan	6.8	1.7
admire	disciple	5.6	4.1
admire	athlete	4.8	6.4
admire	actress	4.6	6.4

Table 1: Sample of McRae et al. (1997) ratings.

frightened by someone/something?" (for patients).
A small sample of scores from this dataset is given
in Table 1. Each (*role-filler, verb, role*) triple received ratings from 37 different participants. The
37 ratings for each triple were averaged to generate a final thematic fit score. The verbs were all
transitive, thus allowing an agent rating and patient rating for each verb-noun pair. As shown,
many nouns were chosen such that they fit at least
one role very well. This meant that some verb-
roles in this dataset have no poorly-fitting role-
fillers, e.g., patients of "accept" and "agents of
"admire". This had strong ramifications for the
"difficulty" of this dataset for correlation with automatic systems because extreme differences in
human judgements are much easier to model than
fine-grained ones.

MST98, a 200 item subset of the McRae et al.
(1997) dataset created for McRae et al. (1998), has
two animate role-fillers for each verb. The first
was a good agent and a poor patient, and the other
a poor agent and a good patient. The ratings were
still well-distributed, but these conditions made
correlation with automatic systems easier.

Ferretti et al. (2001) created a dataset of 248 instrument ratings (**F-Inst**) and a dataset of 274 location ratings (**F-Loc**) using questions of the form
"How common is it for someone to use each of the
following to perform the action of *stirring*?" (instruments) and "How common is it for someone to
skate in each of the following locations?". 40 participants supplied ratings on a seven point scale.

Ken McRae, Michael Spivey-Knowlton,
Maryellen MacDonald, Mike Tanenhaus, Neal
Pearlmutter and Ulrike Padó compiled a master
list of thematic fit judgements from Pearlmutter
and MacDonald (1992), Trueswell et al. (1994),

McRae et al. (1997), a replication of Binder et al. (2001) [Experiment B], and follow-up studies of Binder et al. (2001) [Experiment C]. These studies had slightly different requirements for the kinds of verbs and nouns used and significant overlap in stimuli due to collaboration. This represents the largest to-date dataset of agent-patient thematic fit ratings (1,444 single-word verb/noun judgements), referenced herein as **MSTNN**.

Padó (2007) created a new dataset of 414 agent and patient ratings (**P07**) to be included in a sentence processing model. The verbs were chosen based on their frequencies in the Penn Treebank and FrameNet. Role-fillers were selected to give a wide distribution of scores within each verb. The final dataset contains fine-grained distinctions from FrameNet, which many systems map to familiar agent and patient roles. Judgements were obtained on a seven point scale using questions of the form "How common is it for an *analyst* to *tell* [something]?" (subject) and "How common is it for an *analyst* to be *told*?" (object).

Finally, Greenberg et al. (2015a) created a dataset of 720 patient ratings (**GDS-all**) that were designed to be different from the others in two ways. First, they changed the format of the judgement elicitation question, since they believed that asking how common/typical something is would lead the participants to consider frequency of occurrence rather than semantic plausibility. Instead, they asked participants how much they agreed on a 1-7 scale with statements such as "*cream* is something that is *whipped*". This dataset was constructed to vary word frequency and verb polysemy systematically; the experimental subset of the dataset contained frequency-matched monosemous verbs (**GDS-mono**) and polysemous verbs (**GDS-poly**). Synonymous pairs of nouns (one frequent and one infrequent) were chosen to fit a frequent sense, an infrequent sense (for polysemous verbs only), or no senses per verb.

3 Evaluation approaches

The dominant approach in recent work in thematic fit evaluation has been, given a verb/role/noun combination, to use the vector space to construct a prototype filler of the given role for the given verb, and then to compare the given noun to that prototype (Baroni and Lenci, 2010). The prototype fillers are constructed by averaging some number of "typical" (e.g., most common by frequency or by some information statistic) role-fillers for that verb—the verb's vector is not itself directly used in the comparison. Most recent work instead varies in the construction of the vector space and the use of the space to build the prototype.

The importance of the vector space A semantic model should recognize that cutting a cake with an improbable item like a sword is still highly plausible, even if cakes and swords rarely appear in the same genres or discourses; that is, it should recognize that swords and knives (more typically used to cut cakes) are both cutting-instruments, even if their typical genre contexts are different.

Because of their indirect relationship to probability, real-valued vector spaces have produced the most successful recent high-coverage models for the thematic fit judgement correlation task. Even if cakes and swords may rarely appear in the same discourses, swords and knives sometimes may. A robust vector space allows the representation of unseen indirect associations between these items. In order to understand the progress made on the thematic fit question, we therefore look at a sample of recent attempts at exploring the feature space and the handling of the vector space as a whole.

Comparing recent results In table 2, we sample results from recent vector-space modeling efforts in the literature in order to understand the progress made. The table contains:

BL2010 Results from the TypeDM system of Baroni and Lenci (2010). This space is constructed from counts of rule-selected dependency tree snippets taken from a large web crawl corpus, adjusted via local mutual information (LMI) but is otherwise unsupervised. The approach they take generates a vector space above a 100 million dimensions. The top 20 typical role-fillers by LMI are chosen for prototype construction. Some of the datasets presented were only created and tested later by Sayeed et al. (2015) (*) and Greenberg et al. (2015a) (**).

BDK2014 Tests of word embedding spaces from Baroni et al. (2014), constructed via word2vec (Mikolov et al., 2013a). These are the best systems reported in their paper. The selection of typical role-fillers for constructing the prototype role-filler comes from TypeDM, which is not consulted for the vectors themselves.

Dataset	BL2010	BDK2014	GSD2015	GDS2015	SDS2015-avg	SDS2015-swap
P07	28	41	50	-	59	48
MST98	51	27	-	-	-	-
MSTNN	33*	-	36	-	34	25
F-Loc	23*	-	29	-	21	19
F-Inst	36*	-	42	-	39	45
GDS-all	53**	-	-	55	51	50
GDS-mono	41**	-	-	43	-	-
GDS-poly	66**	-	-	67	-	-

Table 2: Spearman's ρ values ($\times 100$) for different datasets with results collected from different evaluation attempts. All models evaluated have coverage higher than 95% over all datasets.

GSD2015 The overall best-performing system from Greenberg et al. (2015b), which is TypeDM from BL2010 with a hierarchical clustering algorithm that automatically clusters the typical role-fillers into verb senses relative to the role. For example, "cut" has multiple senses relative to its patient role, in one of which "budget" may be typical, while in another sense "cake" may be typical.

GSD2015 The overall best-performing system from Greenberg et al. (2015a). This is the same TypeDM system with hierarchical clustering as in GSD2015, but applied to a new set of ratings intended to detect the role of verb polysemy in human decision-making about role-fillers.

SDS2015-avg Sayeed et al. (2015) explore the contribution of semantics-specific features by using a semantic role labeling (SRL) tool to label a corpus similar to that of BL2010 and constructing a similar high-dimensional vector space. In this case, they average the results of their system, SDDM, with TypeDM and find that SRL-derived features make an additional contribution to the correlation with human ratings. Prototypes are constructed using typical role-fillers from the new corpus, weighted, like TypeDM, by LMI.

SDS2015-swap This is similar to SDS2015-avg, but instead, the typical role-fillers of SDDM are used to retrieve the vectors of TypeDM for prototype construction.

It should be emphasized that each of these papers tested a number of parameters, and some of them (Baroni and Lenci, 2010; Baroni et al., 2014) used vector-space representations over a number of tasks. Baroni et al. (2014) found that trained, general-purpose word embeddings—BDK2014—

systematically outperform count-based representations on most of these tasks. However, they also found that the thematic fit correlation task was one of the few for which the same word embedding spaces underperform. We confirm this by observing that every system in Table 2 dramatically outperforms BDK2014.

One hint from this overview as to why trained word embedding spaces underperform on this task is that the best performing systems involve very large numbers of linguistically-interpretable dimensions (features)[2]. SDS2015-avg involves the combination of two different systems with high-dimensional spaces, and it demonstrates top performance on the high-frequency agent-patient dataset of Padó (2007) and competitive performance on the remainder of evaluated datasets. SDS2015-swap, on the other hand, involves the use of one high-dimensional space with the typical role-filler selection of another one, and performs comparatively poorly on all datasets except for instrument roles. Note that the typical role-fillers are themselves chosen by the magnitudes of their (LMI-adjusted) frequency dimensions in the vector space itself, relative to their dependency relationships with the given verb, as per the evaluation procedure of Baroni and Lenci (2010). In other words, not only do many meaningful dimensions seem to matter in comparing the vectors, the selection of vectors is itself tightly dependent on the model's own magnitudes.

What these early results in thematic fit evaluation suggest is that, more so than many other kinds

---

[2]Baroni and Lenci provide a reduction to 5000-dimensions via random indexing (Kanerva et al., 2000) on their web site derived from TypeDM that performs competitively. Most high-performing general-purpose trained word embeddings, including those in (Baroni et al., 2014), have a much smaller dimensionality, and they tend not to be trained from linguistically-rich feature sets.

of lexical-semantic tasks, thematic fit modeling is particularly sensitive to linguistic detail and interpretability of the vector space.

4 Future directions

In the process of proposing this evaluation task, we have presented in this paper an overview of the issues involved in vector-space approaches to human thematic fit judgement correlation. Thematic fit modeling via real-valued vector-space word representations has made recent and significant progress. But in the interest of building evaluations that truly elucidate the cognitive underpinnings of human semantic "decision-making" in a potentially application-relevant way, there are a number of areas in which such evaluations could be strengthened. We present some suggestions here:

Balanced datasets In order to investigate the apparent relationship between the linguistic interpretability of the vector space dimensions and the correlations with human judgements, we need more evaluation data sets balanced for fine-grained linguistic features. The data collected in Greenberg et al. (2015a) is a step in this direction, as it was used to investigate the relationship between polysemy, frequency, and thematic fit, and so it was balanced between polysemy and frequency. However, a thematic role like location—on which all systems reported here perform poorly—could be similarly investigated by collecting data balanced by, for example, the preposition that typically indicates the location relation ("in the kitchen" vs. "on the bus").

Compositionality Both the currently available thematic fit judgements and the vector spaces used to evaluate them are not designed around compositionality, as they have very limited flexibility in combining the subspaces defined by typical role-filler prototypes (Lenci, 2011). Language users may have the intuition that cutting a budget and cutting a cake are both highly plausible scenarios. However, if we were to introduce an agent role-filler such as "child", the human ratings may be quite different, as children are not typical budget-cutters. The thematic fit evaluation tasks of the future will have to consider compositionality more systematically, possibly by taking domain and genre into account.

Perceptuomotor knowledge A crucial question in the use of distributional representations for thematic fit evaluation is the extent to which the distributional hypothesis really applies to predicting predicate-argument relations. Humans presumably have access to world-knowledge that is beyond the mere texts that they have consumed in their lifetimes. While there is evidence from psycholinguistic experimentation that both forms of knowledge are involved in the neural processing of linguistic input (Amsel et al., 2015), the boundary between world-knowledge and distributional knowledge is not at all clear. However, thematic fit judgement data represents the output of the complete system. An area for future work would be to see whether the distinction between these two types of knowledge (such as image data or explicitly-specified logical features) can be incorporated into the evaluation itself. However, the single rating approach has its own advantages, in that we expect an optimal vector-space (or other) representation will also include the means by which to combine these forms of linguistic knowledge.

Rating consistency 240 items, containing the most frequent verbs from the **MSTNN** dataset, were deliberately included in the **GDS-all** dataset, in order to evaluate consistency of judgements between annotators, especially when the elicitation method varied. There was a significant positive correlation between the two sets of ratings, Pearson's $r(238)$ 95% CI [0.68, 0.80], $p < 2.2 \times 10^{-16}$. The residuals appeared normal with homogeneous variances, and the Spearman's ρ was 0.75. This high correlation provides a possible upper-bound on computational estimators of thematic fit. The fact that it is well above the state of the art for any dataset and estimator configuration suggests that there is still substantial room for development for this task.

Acknowledgments

This research was funded by the German Research Foundation (DFG) as part of SFB 1102: "Information Density and Linguistic Encoding" as well as the Cluster of Excellence "Multimodal Computing and Interaction" (MMCI). Also, the authors wish to thank the two anonymous reviewers whose valuable ideas contributed to this paper.

References

Bas Aarts. 1997. *English syntax and argumentation*. St. Martin's Press, New York.

Ben D Amsel, Katherine A DeLong, and Marta Kutas. 2015. Close, but no garlic: Perceptuomotor and event knowledge activation during language comprehension. *Journal of memory and language* 82:118–132.

Marco Baroni, Georgiana Dinu, and Germán Kruszewski. 2014. Don't count, predict! a systematic comparison of context-counting vs. context-predicting semantic vectors. In *Proceedings of the 52nd Annual Meeting of the Association for Computational Linguistics (Volume 1: Long Papers)*. Association for Computational Linguistics, Baltimore, Maryland, pages 238–247.

Marco Baroni and Alessandro Lenci. 2010. Distributional memory: A general framework for corpus-based semantics. *Computational Linguistics* 36(4):673–721.

Katherine S. Binder, Susan A. Duffy, and Keith Rayner. 2001. The effects of thematic fit and discourse context on syntactic ambiguity resolution. *Journal of Memory and Language* 44(2):297–324.

Todd R. Ferretti, Ken McRae, and Andrea Hatherell. 2001. Integrating verbs, situation schemas, and thematic role concepts. *Journal of Memory and Language* 44(4):516–547.

Clayton Greenberg, Vera Demberg, and Asad Sayeed. 2015a. Verb polysemy and frequency effects in thematic fit modeling. In *Proceedings of the 6th Workshop on Cognitive Modeling and Computational Linguistics*. Association for Computational Linguistics, Denver, Colorado, pages 48–57.

Clayton Greenberg, Asad Sayeed, and Vera Demberg. 2015b. Improving unsupervised vector-space thematic fit evaluation via role-filler prototype clustering. In *Proceedings of the 2015 Conference of the North American Chapter of the Association for Computational Linguistics: Human Language Technologies*. Association for Computational Linguistics, Denver, Colorado, pages 21–31.

Pentti Kanerva, Jan Kristofersson, and Anders Holst. 2000. Random indexing of text samples for latent semantic analysis. In *Proceedings of the 22nd annual conference of the cognitive science society*. Citeseer, volume 1036.

Alessandro Lenci. 2011. Composing and updating verb argument expectations: A distributional semantic model. In *Proceedings of the 2nd Workshop on Cognitive Modeling and Computational Linguistics*. Association for Computational Linguistics, Portland, Oregon, USA, pages 58–66.

Ken McRae, Todd R. Ferretti, and Liane Amyote. 1997. Thematic roles as verb-specific concepts. *Language and cognitive processes* 12(2-3):137–176.

Ken McRae, Michael J. Spivey-Knowlton, and Michael K. Tanenhaus. 1998. Modeling the influence of thematic fit (and other constraints) in on-line sentence comprehension. *Journal of Memory and Language* 38(3):283–312.

Tomas Mikolov, Ilya Sutskever, Kai Chen, Greg S Corrado, and Jeff Dean. 2013a. Distributed representations of words and phrases and their compositionality. In *Advances in Neural Information Processing Systems*. pages 3111–3119.

Tomas Mikolov, Wen tau Yih, and Geoffrey Zweig. 2013b. Linguistic regularities in continuous space word representations. In *Proceedings of the 2013 conference of the North American Chapter of the Association for Computational Linguistics: Human Language Technologies (NAACL-HLT 2013)*. Association for Computational Linguistics.

Ulrike Padó. 2007. *The integration of syntax and semantic plausibility in a wide-coverage model of human sentence processing*. Ph.D. thesis, Saarland University.

Ulrike Padó, Matthew W. Crocker, and Frank Keller. 2009. A probabilistic model of semantic plausibility in sentence processing. *Cognitive Science* 33(5):794–838.

Neal J. Pearlmutter and Maryellen C. MacDonald. 1992. Plausibility and syntactic ambiguity resolution. In *Proceedings of the 14th Annual Conference of the Cognitive Science Society*. Lawrence Erlbaum Associates, Inc., Hillsdale, New Jersey, pages 498–503.

Asad Sayeed, Vera Demberg, and Pavel Shkadzko. 2015. An exploration of semantic features in an unsupervised thematic fit evaluation framework. *Italian Journal of Computational Linguistics* 1(1).

John C. Trueswell, Michael K. Tanenhaus, and Susan M. Garnsey. 1994. Semantic influences on parsing: Use of thematic role information in syntactic ambiguity resolution. *Journal of memory and language* 33(3):285–318.

Tim Van de Cruys. 2014. A neural network approach to selectional preference acquisition. In *Proceedings of the 2014 Conference on Empirical Methods in Natural Language Processing (EMNLP)*. pages 26–35.

Bram Vandekerckhove, Dominiek Sandra, and Walter Daelemans. 2009. A robust and extensible exemplar-based model of thematic fit. In *Proceedings of the 12th Conference of the European Chapter of the ACL (EACL 2009)*. Association for Computational Linguistics, Athens, Greece, pages 826–834.

Improving Reliability of Word Similarity Evaluation
by Redesigning Annotation Task and Performance Measure

Oded Avraham and **Yoav Goldberg**
Computer Science Department
Bar-Ilan University
Ramat-Gan, Israel
{oavraham1,yoav.goldberg}@gmail.com

Abstract

We suggest a new method for creating and using gold-standard datasets for word similarity evaluation. Our goal is to improve the reliability of the evaluation, and we do this by redesigning the annotation task to achieve higher inter-rater agreement, and by defining a performance measure which takes the reliability of each annotation decision in the dataset into account.

1 Introduction

Computing similarity between words is a fundamental challenge in natural language processing. Given a pair of words, a similarity model $sim(w_1, w_2)$ should assign a score that reflects the level of similarity between them, e.g.: $sim(singer, musician) = 0.83$. While many methods for computing sim exist (e.g., taking the cosine between vector embeddings derived by word2vec (Mikolov et al., 2013)), there are currently no reliable measures of quality for such models. In the past few years, word similarity models show a consistent improvement in performance when evaluated using the conventional evaluation methods and datasets. But are these evaluation measures really reliable indicators of the model quality? Lately, Hill et al (2015) claimed that the answer is no. They identified several problems with the existing datasets, and created a new dataset – SimLex-999 – which does not suffer from them. However, we argue that there are inherent problems with conventional datasets and the method of using them that were not addressed in SimLex-999. We list these problems, and suggest a new and more reliable way of evaluating similarity models. We then report initial experiments on a dataset of Hebrew nouns similarity that we created according to our proposed method.

2 Existing Methods and Datasets for Word Similarity Evaluation

Over the years, several datasets have been used for evaluating word similarity models. Popular ones include RG (Rubenstein and Goodenough, 1965), WordSim-353 (Finkelstein et al., 2001), WS-Sim (Agirre et al., 2009) and MEN (Bruni et al., 2012). Each of these datasets is a collection of word pairs together with their similarity scores as assigned by human annotators. A model is evaluated by assigning a similarity score to each pair, sorting the pairs according to their similarity, and calculating the correlation (Spearman's ρ) with the human ranking. Hill et al (2015) had made a comprehensive review of these datasets, and pointed out some common shortcomings they have. The main shortcoming discussed by Hill et al is the handling of *associated but dissimilar* words, e.g. (*singer, microphone*): in datasets which contain such pairs (WordSim and MEN) they are usually ranked high, sometimes even above pairs of similar words. This causes an undesirable penalization of models that apply the correct behavior (i.e., always prefer similar pairs over associated dissimilar ones). Other datasets (WS-Sim and RG) do not contain pairs of associated words pairs at all. Their absence makes these datasets unable to evaluate the models' ability to distinct between associated and similar words. Another shortcoming mentioned by Hill et al (2015) is *low inter-rater agreement* over the human assigned similarity scores, which might have been caused by unclear instructions for the annotation task. As a result, state-of-the-art models reach the agreement ceiling for most of the datasets, while a simple manual evaluation will suggest that these models are still inferior to humans. In order to solve these shortcomings, Hill et al (2015) developed a new dataset – Simlex-999 – in which the instructions

Proceedings of the 1st Workshop on Evaluating Vector Space Representations for NLP, pages 106–110,
Berlin, Germany, August 12, 2016. ©2016 Association for Computational Linguistics

presented to the annotators emphasized the difference between the terms associated and similar, and managed to solve the discussed problems.

While SimLex-999 was definitely a step in the right direction, we argue that there are more fundamental problems which all conventional methods, including SimLex-999, suffer from. In what follows, we describe each one of these problems.

3 Problems with the Existing Datasets

Before diving in, we define some terms we are about to use. Hill et al (2015) used the terms *similar* and *associated but dissimilar*, which they didn't formally connected to fine-grained semantic relations. However, by inspecting the average score per relation, they found a clear preference for hyponym-hypernym pairs (e.g. the scores of the pairs (*cat, pet*) and (*winter, season*) are much higher than those of the cohyponyms pair (*cat, dog*) and the antonyms pair (*winter, summer*)). Referring hyponym-hypernym pairs as *similar* may imply that a good similarity model should prefer hyponym-hypernym pairs over pairs of other relations, which is not always true since the desirable behavior is task-dependent. Therefore, we will use a different terminology: we use the term *preferred-relation* to denote the relation which the model should prefer, and *unpreferred-relation* to denote any other relation.

The first problem is *the use of rating scales*. Since the level of similarity is a relative measure, we would expect the annotation task to ask the annotator for a ranking. But in most of the existing datasets, the annotators were asked to assign a numeric score to each pair (e.g. 0-7 in SimLex-999), and a ranking was derived based on these scores. This choice is probably due to the fact that a ranking of hundreds of pairs is an exhausting task for humans. However, using rating scales makes the annotations vulnerable to a variety of biases (Friedman and Amoo, 1999). Bruni et al (2012) addressed this problem by asking the annotators to rank each pair in comparison to 50 randomly selected pairs. This is a reasonable compromise, but it still results in a daunting annotation task, and makes the quality of the dataset depend on a random selection of comparisons.

The second problem is *rating different relations on the same scale*. In Simlex-999, the annotators were instructed to assign low scores to unpreferred-relation pairs, but the decision of *how low* was still up to the annotator. While some of these pairs were assigned very low scores (e.g. sim(*smart, dumb*) = 0.55), others got significantly higher ones (e.g. sim(*winter, summer*) = 2.38). A difference of 1.8 similarity scores should not be underestimated – in other cases it testifies to a true superiority of one pair over another, e.g.: sim(*cab, taxi*) = 9.2, sim(*cab, car*) = 7.42. The situation where an arbitrary decision of the annotators affects the model score, impairs the reliability of the evaluation: a model shouldn't be punished for preferring (*smart, dumb*) over (*winter, summer*) or vice versa, since this comparison is just ill-defined.

The third problem is *rating different target-words on the same scale*. Even within preferred-relation pairs, there are ill-defined comparisons, e.g.: (*cat, pet*) vs. (*winter, season*). It's quite unnatural to compare between pairs that have different target-words, in contrast to pairs which share the target word, like (*cat, pet*) vs. *cat, animal*). Penalizing a model for preferring (*cat, pet*) over (*winter, season*) or vice versa impairs the evaluation reliability.

The fourth problem is that *the evaluation measure does not consider annotation decisions reliability*. The conventional method measures the model score by calculating Spearman correlation between the model ranking and the annotators average ranking. This method ignores an important information source: the reliability of each annotation decision, which can be determined by the agreement of the annotators on this decision. For example, consider a dataset containing the pairs (*singer, person*), (*singer, performer*) and (*singer, musician*). Now let's assume that in the average annotator ranking, (*singer, performer*) is ranked above (*singer, person*) after 90% of the annotators assigned it with a higher score, and (*singer, musician*) is ranked above (*singer, performer*) after 51% percent of the annotators assigned it with a higher score. Considering this, we would like the evaluation measure to severely punish a model which prefers (*singer, person*) over (*singer, performer*), but be almost indifferent to the model's decision over (*singer, performer*) vs. (*singer, musician*) because it seems that even humans cannot reliably tell which one is more similar. In the conventional datasets, no information on reliability of ratings is supplied except for the overall agreement, and each average rank has the same weight in the evaluation measure. The problem of reliability is addressed by Luong et al (2013) which included many rare words in their dataset, and thus allowed an annotator to indicate "Don't know" for a pair if they does not know one of the words. The problem with applying this approach as a more general reliability indicator is that the annotator confidence level is subjective and not absolute.

4 Proposed Improvements

We suggest the following four improvements for handling these problems.

(1) The annotation task will be an explicit ranking task. Similarly to Bruni et al (2012), each pair will be directly compared with a subset of the other pairs. Unlike Bruni et al, each pair will be compared with only a few carefully selected pairs, following the principles in (2) and (3).

(2) A dataset will be focused on a single preferred-relation type (we can create other datasets for tasks in which the preferred-relation is different), and only preferred-relation pairs will be presented to the annotators. We suggest to spare the annotators the effort of considering the *type* of the similarity between words, in order to let them concentrate on the *strength* of the similarity. Word pairs following unpreferred-relations will not be included in the annotation task but will still be a part of the dataset – we always add them to the bottom of the ranking. For example, an annotator will be asked to rate (*cab, car*) and (*cab, taxi*), but not (*cab, driver*) – which will be ranked last since it's an unpreferred-relation pair.

(3) Any pair will be compared only with pairs sharing the same target word. We suggest to make the pairs ranking more reliable by splitting it into multiple target-based rankings, e.g.: (*cat, pet*) will be compared with (*cat, animal*), but not with (*winter, season*) which belongs to another ranking.

(4) The dataset will include a reliability indicator for each annotators decision, based on the agreement between annotators. The reliability indicator will be used in the evaluation measure: a model will be penalized more for making wrong predictions on reliable rankings than on unreliable ones.

4.1 A Concrete Dataset

In this section we describe the structure of a dataset which applies the above improvements. First, we need to define the preferred-relation (to apply improvement (2)). In what follows we use the hyponym-hypernym relation. The dataset is

	w_t	w_1	w_2	$R_>(w_1, w_2; w_t)$
P	singer	person	musician	0.1
P	singer	artist	person	0.8
P	singer	musician	performer	0.6
D	singer	musician	song	1.0
R	singer	musician	laptop	1.0

Table 1: Binary Comparisons for the target word *singer*. P: positive pair; D: distractor pair; R: random pair.

based on *target words*. For each target word we create a group of *complement words*, which we refer to as the *target-group*. Each complement word belongs to one of three categories: *positives* (related to the target, and the type of the relation is the preferred one), *distractors* (related to the target, but the type of the relation is not the preferred one), and *randoms* (not related to the target at all). For example, for the target word *singer*, the target group may include *musician, performer, person* and *artist* as positives, *dancer* and *song* as distractors, and *laptop* as random. For each target word, the human annotators will be asked to rank the positive complements by their similarity to the target word (improvements (1) & (3)). For example, a possible ranking may be: *musician > performer > artist > person*. The annotators responses allow us to create the actual dataset, which consists of a collection of *binary comparisons*. A binary comparison is a value $R_>(w_1, w_2; w_t)$ indicating how likely it is to rank the pair (w_t, w_1) higher than (w_t, w_2), where w_t is a target word and w_1, w_2 are two complement words. By definition, $R_>(w_1, w_2; w_t) = 1 - R_>(w_2, w_1; w_t)$. For each target-group, the dataset will contain a binary comparison for any possible combination of two positive complements w_{p1} and w_{p2}, as well as for positive complements w_p and negative ones (either distractor or random) w_n. When comparing positive complements, $R_>(w_1, w_2; w_t)$ is the portion of annotators who ranked (w_t, w_1) over (w_t, w_2). When comparing to negative complements, the value of $R_>(w_p, w_n; w_t)$ is 1. This reflects the intuition that a good model should always rank preferred-relation pairs above other pairs. Notice that $R_>(w_1, w_2; w_t)$ is the reliability indicator for each of the dataset key answers, which will be used to apply improvement (4). For some example comparisons, see Table 1.

4.2 Scoring Function

Given a similarity function between words $sim(x, y)$ and a triplet (w_t, w_1, w_2) let $\delta = 1$ if

$sim(w_t, w_1) > sim(w_t, w_2)$ and $\delta = -1$ otherwise. The score $s(w_t, w_1, w_2)$ of the triplet is then: $s(w_t, w_1, w_2) = \delta(2R_>(w_1, w_2; w_t) - 1)$. This score ranges between -1 and 1, is positive if the model ranking agrees with more than 50% of the annotators, and is 1 if it agrees with all of them. The score of the entire dataset C is then:

$$\frac{\sum_{w_t, w_1, w_2 \in C} \max(s(w_t, w_1, w_2), 0)}{\sum_{w_t, w_1, w_2 \in C} |s(w_t, w_1, w_2)|}$$

The model score will be 0 if it makes the wrong decision (i.e. assign a higher score to w_1 while the majority of the annotators ranked w_2 higher, or vice versa) in every comparison. If it always makes the right decision, its score will be 1. Notice that the *size* of the majority also plays a role. When the model takes the wrong decision in a comparison, nothing is being added to the numerator. When it takes the right decision, the numerator increase will be larger as reliable as the key answer is, and so is the general score (the denominator does not depend on the model decisions).

It worth mentioning that a score can also be computed over a subset of C, as comparisons of specific type (positive-positive, positive-distractor, positive-random). This allows the user of the dataset to make a finer-grained analysis of the evaluation results: it can get the quality of the model in specific tasks (preferring similar words over less similar, over words from unpreferred-relation, and over random words) rather than just the general quality.

5 Experiments

We created two datasets following the proposal discussed above: one preferring the hyponym-hypernym relation, and the other the cohyponym relation. The datasets contain Hebrew nouns, but such datasets can be created for different languages and parts of speech – providing that the language has basic lexical resources. For our dataset, we used a dictionary, an encyclopedia and a thesaurus to create the hyponym-hypernym pairs, and databases of word association norms (Rubinsten et al., 2005) and categories norms (Henik and Kaplan, 1988) to create the distractors pairs and the cohyponyms pairs, respectively. The hyponym-hypernym dataset is based on 75 target-groups, each contains 3-6 positive pairs, 2 distractor pairs and one random pair, which sums up to 476 pairs. The cohyponym dataset is based on 30

target-groups, each contains 4 positive pairs, 1-2 distractor pairs and one random pair, which sums up to 207 pairs. We used the target groups to create 4 questionnaires: 3 for the hyponym-hypernym relation (each contains 25 target-groups), and one for the cohyponyms relation. We asked human annotators to order the positive pairs of each target-group by the similarity between their words. In order to prevent the annotators from confusing between the different aspects of similarity, each annotator was requested to answer only one of the questionnaires, and the instructions for each questionnaire included an example question which demonstrates what the term "similarity" means in that questionnaire (as shown in Figure 1).

Each target-group was ranked by 18-20 annotators. We measured the average pairwise inter-rater agreement, and as done in (Hill et al., 2015) – we excluded any annotator which its agreement with the other was more than one standard deviation below that average (17.8 percent of the annotators were excluded). The agreement was quite high (0.646 and 0.659 for hyponym-hypernym and co-hyponyms target-groups, respectively), especially considering that in contrast to other datasets – our annotation task did not include pairs that are "trivial" to rank (e.g. random pairs). Finally, we used the remaining annotators responses to create the binary comparisons collection. The hyponym-hypernym dataset includes 1063 comparisons, while the cohyponym dataset includes 538 comparisons. To measure the gap between a human and a model performance on the dataset, we trained a word2vec (Mikolov et al., 2013) model [1] on the Hebrew Wikipedia. We used two methods of measuring: the first is the conventional way (Spearman correlation), and the second is the scoring method we described in the previous section, which we used to measure general and per-comparison-type scores. The results are presented in Table 2.

6 Conclusions

We presented a new method for creating and using datasets for word similarity, which improves evaluation reliability by redesigning the annotation task and the performance measure. We created two datasets for Hebrew and showed a high inter-rater agreement. Finally, we showed that the

---

[1] We used code.google.com/p/word2vec implementation, with window size of 2 and dimensionality of 200.

(A)	1st	2nd	3rd	4th
singer : artist	○	○	●	○
singer : person	○	○	○	●
singer : musician	●	○	○	○
singer : performer	○	●	○	○

(B)	1st	2nd	3rd	4th
singer : dancer	●	○	○	○
singer : chef	○	○	●	○
singer : official	○	○	○	●
singer : painter	○	●	○	○

Figure 1: The example rankings we supplied to the annotators as a part of the questionnaires instructions (translated from Hebrew). Example (A) appeared in the hyponym-hypernym questionnaires, while (B) appeared in the cohyponyms questionnaire.

	Hyp.	Cohyp.
Inter-rater agreement	0.646	0.659
w2v correlation	0.451	0.587
w2v score (all)	0.718	0.864
w2v score (positive)	0.763	0.822
w2v score (distractor)	0.625	0.833
w2v score (random)	0.864	0.967

Table 2: The hyponym-hypernym dataset agreement (0.646) compares favorably with the agreement for nouns pairs reported by Hill et al (2015) (0.612), and it is much higher than the correlation score of the word2vec model. Notice that useful insights can be gained from the per-comparison-type analysis, like the model's difficulty to distinguish hyponym-hypernym pairs from other relations.

dataset can be used for a finer-grained analysis of the model quality. A future work can be applying this method to other languages and relation types.

Acknowledgements

The work was supported by the Israeli Science Foundation (grant number 1555/15). We thank Omer Levy for useful discussions.

References

Eneko Agirre, Enrique Alfonseca, Keith Hall, Jana Kravalova, Marius Paşca, and Aitor Soroa. 2009. A study on similarity and relatedness using distributional and wordnet-based approaches. In *Proceedings of Human Language Technologies: The 2009 Annual Conference of the North American Chapter of the Association for Computational Linguistics*, pages 19–27. Association for Computational Linguistics.

Elia Bruni, Gemma Boleda, Marco Baroni, and Nam-Khanh Tran. 2012. Distributional semantics in technicolor. In *Proceedings of the 50th Annual Meeting of the Association for Computational Linguistics: Long Papers-Volume 1*, pages 136–145. Association for Computational Linguistics.

Lev Finkelstein, Evgeniy Gabrilovich, Yossi Matias, Ehud Rivlin, Zach Solan, Gadi Wolfman, and Eytan Ruppin. 2001. Placing search in context: The concept revisited. In *Proceedings of the 10th international conference on World Wide Web*, pages 406–414. ACM.

Hershey H Friedman and Taiwo Amoo. 1999. Rating the rating scales. *Friedman, Hershey H. and Amoo, Taiwo (1999)." Rating the Rating Scales." Journal of Marketing Management, Winter*, pages 114–123.

Avishai Henik and Limor Kaplan. 1988. Category content: Findings for categories in hebrew and a comparison to findings in the us. *Psychologia: Israel Journal of Psychology*.

Felix Hill, Roi Reichart, and Anna Korhonen. 2015. Simlex-999: Evaluating semantic models with (genuine) similarity estimation. *Computational Linguistics*.

Thang Luong, Richard Socher, and Christopher D Manning. 2013. Better word representations with recursive neural networks for morphology. In *CoNLL*, pages 104–113. Citeseer.

Tomas Mikolov, Kai Chen, Greg Corrado, and Jeffrey Dean. 2013. Efficient estimation of word representations in vector space. *arXiv preprint arXiv:1301.3781*.

Herbert Rubenstein and John B Goodenough. 1965. Contextual correlates of synonymy. *Communications of the ACM*, 8(10):627–633.

O Rubinsten, D Anaki, A Henik, S Drori, and Y Faran. 2005. Free association norms in the hebrew language. *Word norms in Hebrew*, pages 17–34.

Correlation-based Intrinsic Evaluation of Word Vector Representations

Yulia Tsvetkov♠ **Manaal Faruqui**♠ **Chris Dyer**♣♠
♠Carnegie Mellon University ♣Google DeepMind
{ytsvetko,mfaruqui,cdyer}@cs.cmu.edu

Abstract

We introduce QVEC-CCA—an intrinsic evaluation metric for word vector representations based on correlations of learned vectors with features extracted from linguistic resources. We show that QVEC-CCA scores are an effective proxy for a range of extrinsic semantic and syntactic tasks. We also show that the proposed evaluation obtains higher and more consistent correlations with downstream tasks, compared to existing approaches to intrinsic evaluation of word vectors that are based on word similarity.

1 Introduction

Being linguistically opaque, vector-space representations of words—word embeddings—have limited practical value as standalone items. They are effective, however, in representing meaning—through individual dimensions and combinations of thereof—when used as features in downstream applications (Turian et al., 2010; Lazaridou et al., 2013; Socher et al., 2013; Bansal et al., 2014; Guo et al., 2014, *inter alia*). Thus, unless it is coupled with an extrinsic task, intrinsic evaluation of word vectors has little value in itself. The main purpose of an intrinsic evaluation is to serve as a *proxy* for the downstream task the embeddings are tailored for. This paper advocates a novel approach to constructing such a proxy.

What are the desired properties of an intrinsic evaluation measure of word embeddings? First, retraining models that use word embeddings as features is often expensive. A *computationally efficient* intrinsic evaluation that *correlates with extrinsic scores* is useful for faster prototyping. Second, an intrinsic evaluation that enables *interpretation* and analysis of properties encoded by vector

dimensions is an auxiliary mechanism for analyzing how these properties affect the target downstream task. It thus facilitates refinement of word vector models and, consequently, improvement of the target task. Finally, an intrinsic evaluation that approximates a range of related downstream tasks (e.g., semantic text-classification tasks) allows to assess *generality* (or specificity) of a word vector model, without actually implementing all the tasks.

Tsvetkov et al. (2015) proposed an evaluation measure—QVEC—that was shown to correlate well with downstream semantic tasks. Additionally, it helps shed new light on how vector spaces encode meaning thus facilitating the interpretation of word vectors. The crux of the method is to correlate distributional word vectors with linguistic word vectors constructed from rich linguistic resources, annotated by domain experts. QVEC can easily be adjusted to specific downstream tasks (e.g., part-of-speech tagging) by selecting task-specific linguistic resources (e.g., part-of-speech annotations). However, QVEC suffers from two weaknesses. First, it is not invariant to linear transformations of the embeddings' basis, whereas the bases in word embeddings are generally arbitrary (Szegedy et al., 2014). Second, it produces an unnormalized score: the more dimensions in the embedding matrix the higher the score. This precludes comparison of models of different dimensionality. In this paper, we introduce QVEC-CCA, which simultaneously addresses both problems, while preserving major strengths of QVEC.[1]

2 QVEC and QVEC-CCA

We introduce QVEC-CCA—an intrinsic evaluation measure of the quality of word embeddings. Our method is a modification of QVEC—an evalua-

---

[1] https://github.com/ytsvetko/qvec

Proceedings of the 1st Workshop on Evaluating Vector Space Representations for NLP, pages 111–115,
Berlin, Germany, August 12, 2016. ©2016 Association for Computational Linguistics

tion based on alignment of embeddings to a matrix of features extracted from a linguistic resource (Tsvetkov et al., 2015). We review QVEC, and then describe QVEC-CCA.

QVEC. The main idea behind QVEC is to quantify the linguistic content of word embeddings by maximizing the correlation with a manually-annotated linguistic resource. Let the number of common words in the vocabulary of the word embeddings and the linguistic resource be N. To quantify the semantic content of embeddings, a semantic/syntactic linguistic matrix $\mathbf{S} \in \mathbb{R}^{P \times N}$ is constructed from a semantic/syntactic database, with a column vector for each word. Each word vector is a distribution of the word over P linguistic properties, based on annotations of the word in the database. Let $\mathbf{X} \in \mathbb{R}^{D \times N}$ be embedding matrix with every row as a dimension vector $\mathbf{x} \in \mathbb{R}^{1 \times N}$. D denotes the dimensionality of word embeddings. Then, $\mathbf{S}$ and $\mathbf{X}$ are aligned to maximize the cumulative correlation between the aligned dimensions of the two matrices. Specifically, let $\mathbf{A} \in \{0, 1\}^{D \times P}$ be a matrix of alignments such that $a_{ij} = 1$ iff $\mathbf{x}_i$ is aligned to $\mathbf{s}_j$, otherwise $a_{ij} = 0$. If $r(\mathbf{x}_i, \mathbf{s}_j)$ is the Pearson's correlation between vectors $\mathbf{x}_i$ and $\mathbf{s}_j$, then QVEC is defined as:

$$\text{QVEC} = \max_{\mathbf{A}: \sum_j a_{ij} \leq 1} \sum_{i=1}^{X} \sum_{j=1}^{S} r(\mathbf{x}_i, \mathbf{s}_j) \times a_{ij}$$

The constraint $\sum_j a_{ij} \leq 1$, warrants that one distributional dimension is aligned to at most one linguistic dimension.

QVEC-CCA. To measure correlation between the embedding matrix $\mathbf{X}$ and the linguistic matrix $\mathbf{S}$, instead of cumulative dimension-wise correlation we employ canonical correlation analysis (Hardoon et al., 2004, CCA). CCA finds two sets of basis vectors, one for $\mathbf{X}^\top$ and the other for $\mathbf{S}^\top$, such that the correlations between the projections of the matrices onto these basis vectors are maximized. Formally, CCA finds a pair of basis vectors $\mathbf{v}$ and $\mathbf{w}$ such that

$$\text{QVEC-CCA} = \text{CCA}(\mathbf{X}^\top, \mathbf{S}^\top)$$
$$= \max_{\mathbf{v}, \mathbf{w}} r(\mathbf{X}^\top \mathbf{v}, \mathbf{S}^\top \mathbf{w})$$

Thus, QVEC-CCA ensures invariance to the matrices' bases' rotation, and since it is a single correlation, it produces a score in $[-1, 1]$.

3 Linguistic Dimension Word Vectors

Both QVEC and QVEC-CCA rely on a matrix of linguistic properties constructed from a manually crafted linguistic resource. Linguistic resources are invaluable as they capture generalizations made by domain experts. However, resource construction is expensive, therefore it is not always possible to find an existing resource that captures exactly the set of optimal lexical properties for a downstream task. Resources that capture more coarse-grained, general properties can be used instead, for example, WordNet for semantic evaluation (Fellbaum, 1998), or Penn Treebank (Marcus et al., 1993, PTB) for syntactic evaluation. Since these properties are not an exact match to the task, the intrinsic evaluation tests for a necessary (but possibly not sufficient) set of generalizations.

Semantic vectors. To evaluate the semantic content of word vectors, Tsvetkov et al. (2015) exploit supersense annotations in a WordNet-annotated corpus—SemCor (Miller et al., 1993). The resulting supersense-dimension matrix has 4,199 rows (supersense-annotated nouns and verbs that occur in SemCor at least 5 times[2]), and 41 columns: 26 for nouns and 15 for verbs. Example vectors are shown in table 1.

WORD	NN.ANIMAL	NN.FOOD	$\cdots$	VB.MOTION
fish	0.68	0.16	$\cdots$	0.00
duck	0.31	0.00	$\cdots$	0.69
chicken	0.33	0.67	$\cdots$	0.00

Table 1: Linguistic dimension word vector matrix with semantic vectors, constructed using SemCor.

Syntactic vectors. Similar to semantic vectors, we construct syntactic vectors for all words with 5 or more occurrences in the training part of the PTB. Vector dimensions are probabilities of the part-of-speech (POS) annotations in the corpus. This results in 10,865 word vectors with 45 interpretable columns, each column corresponds to a POS tag from the PTB; a snapshot is shown in table 2.

4 Experiments

Experimental setup. We replicate the experimental setup of Tsvetkov et al. (2015):

---

[2]We exclude sparser word types to avoid skewed probability estimates of senses of polysemous words.

WORD	PTB.NN	PTB.VB	$\cdots$	PTB.JJ
spring	0.94	0.02	$\cdots$	0.00
fall	0.49	0.43	$\cdots$	0.00
light	0.52	0.02	$\cdots$	0.41

Table 2: Linguistic dimension word vector matrix with syntactic vectors, constructed using PTB.

- We first train 21 word vector models: variants of CBOW and Skip-Gram models (Mikolov et al., 2013); their modifications CWindow, Structured Skip-Gram, and CBOW with Attention (Ling et al., 2015b; Ling et al., 2015a); GloVe vectors (Pennington et al., 2014); Latent Semantic Analysis (LSA) based vectors (Church and Hanks, 1990); and retrofitted GloVe and LSA vectors (Faruqui et al., 2015).

- We then evaluate these word vector models using existing *intrinsic* evaluation methods: QVEC and the proposed QVEC-CCA, and also word similarity tasks using the WordSim353 dataset (Finkelstein et al., 2001, WS-353), MEN dataset (Bruni et al., 2012), and SimLex-999 dataset (Hill et al., 2014, SimLex).[3]

- In addition, the same vectors are evaluated using *extrinsic* text classification tasks. Our semantic benchmarks are four binary categorization tasks from the 20 Newsgroups (20NG); sentiment analysis task (Socher et al., 2013, Senti); and the metaphor detection (Tsvetkov et al., 2014, Metaphor).

- Finally, we compute the Pearson's correlation coefficient r to quantify the linear relationship between the intrinsic and extrinsic scorings. The higher the correlation, the better suited the intrinsic evaluation to be used as a proxy to the extrinsic task.

We extend the setup of Tsvetkov et al. (2015) with two syntactic benchmarks, and evaluate QVEC-CCA with the syntactic matrix. The first task is POS tagging; we use the LSTM-CRF model (Lample et al., 2016), and the second is dependency parsing (Parse), using the stack-LSTM model of Dyer et al. (2015).

Results. To test the efficiency of QVEC-CCA in capturing the semantic content of word vectors, we evaluate how well the scores correspond to the scores of word vector models on semantic benchmarks. QVEC and QVEC-CCA employ the semantic supersense-dimension vectors described in §3.

In table 3, we show correlations between intrinsic scores (word similarity/QVEC/QVEC-CCA) and extrinsic scores across semantic benchmarks for 300-dimensional vectors. QVEC-CCA obtains high positive correlation with all the semantic tasks, and outperforms QVEC on two tasks.

	20NG	Metaphor	Senti
WS-353	0.55	0.25	0.46
MEN	0.76	0.49	0.55
SimLex	0.56	0.44	0.51
QVEC	0.74	0.75	0.88
QVEC-CCA	0.77	0.73	0.93

Table 3: Pearson's correlations between word similarity/QVEC/QVEC-CCA scores and the downstream text classification tasks.

In table 4, we evaluate QVEC and QVEC-CCA on syntactic benchmarks. We first use linguistic vectors with dimensions corresponding to part-of-speech tags (denoted as PTB). Then, we use linguistic vectors which are a concatenation of the semantic and syntactic matrices described in §3 for words that occur in both matrices; this setup is denoted as PTB+SST.

		POS	Parse
	WS-353	-0.38	0.68
	MEN	-0.32	0.51
	SimLex	0.20	-0.21
PTB	**QVEC**	0.23	0.39
	QVEC-CCA	0.23	0.50
PTB+SST	**QVEC**	0.28	0.37
	QVEC-CCA	0.23	0.63

Table 4: Pearson's correlations between word similarity/QVEC/QVEC-CCA scores and the downstream syntactic tasks.

Although some word similarity tasks obtain high correlations with syntactic applications, these results are inconsistent, and vary from a high negative to a high positive correlation. Conversely, QVEC and QVEC-CCA consistently obtain moderate-to-high positive correlations with the downstream tasks.

Comparing performance of QVEC-CCA in PTB and PTB+SST setups sheds light on the importance of linguistic signals captured by the linguistic matrices. Appending supersense-annotated columns to the linguistic matrix which already contains POS-annotated columns does not affect correlations of QVEC-CCA with the POS tagging task,

---

[3] We employ an implementation of a suite of word similarity tasks at wordvectors.org (Faruqui and Dyer, 2014).

since the additional linguistic information is not relevant for approximating how well dimensions of word embeddings encode POS-related properties. In the case of dependency parsing—the task which encodes not only syntactic, but also semantic information (e.g., captured by subject-verb-object relations)—supersenses introduce relevant linguistic signals that are not present in POS-annotated columns. Thus, appending supersense-annotated columns to the linguistic matrix improves correlation of QVEC-CCA with the dependency parsing task.

5 Conclusion

We introduced QVEC-CCA—an approach to intrinsic evaluation of word embeddings. We also showed that both QVEC and QVEC-CCA are not limited to semantic evaluation, but are general approaches, that can evaluate word vector content with respect to desired linguistic properties. Semantic and syntactic linguistic features that we use to construct linguistic dimension matrices are rather coarse, thus the proposed evaluation can approximate a range of downstream tasks, but may not be sufficient to evaluate finer-grained features. In the future work we propose to exploit existing semantic, syntactic, morphological, and typological resources (e.g., universal dependencies treebank (Agić et al., 2015) and WALS (Dryer and Haspelmath, 2013)), and also multilingual resources (e.g., Danish supersenses (Martínez Alonso et al., 2015)) to construct better linguistic matrices, suited for evaluating vectors used in additional NLP tasks.

Acknowledgments

This work was supported by the National Science Foundation through award IIS-1526745. We thank Benjamin Wilson for helpful comments.

References

Željko Agić, Maria Jesus Aranzabe, Aitziber Atutxa, Cristina Bosco, Jinho Choi, Marie-Catherine de Marneffe, Timothy Dozat, Richárd Farkas, Jennifer Foster, Filip Ginter, Iakes Goenaga, Koldo Gojenola, Yoav Goldberg, Jan Hajič, Anders Trærup Johannsen, Jenna Kanerva, Juha Kuokkala, Veronika Laippala, Alessandro Lenci, Krister Lindén, Nikola Ljubešić, Teresa Lynn, Christopher Manning, Héctor Alonso Martínez, Ryan McDonald, Anna Missilä, Simonetta Montemagni, Joakim Nivre, Hanna Nurmi, Petya Osenova, Slav Petrov, Jussi Piitulainen, Barbara Plank, Prokopis Prokopidis, Sampo Pyysalo, Wolfgang Seeker, Mojgan Seraji, Natalia Silveira, Maria Simi, Kiril Simov, Aaron Smith, Reut Tsarfaty, Veronika Vincze, and Daniel Zeman. 2015. Universal dependencies 1.1. LINDAT/CLARIN digital library at Institute of Formal and Applied Linguistics, Charles University in Prague.

Mohit Bansal, Kevin Gimpel, and Karen Livescu. 2014. Tailoring continuous word representations for dependency parsing. In *Proc. of ACL*.

Elia Bruni, Gemma Boleda, Marco Baroni, and Nam-Khanh Tran. 2012. Distributional semantics in technicolor. In *Proc. of ACL*.

Kenneth Ward Church and Patrick Hanks. 1990. Word association norms, mutual information, and lexicography. *Computational Linguistics*, 16(1):22–29.

Matthew S. Dryer and Martin Haspelmath, editors. 2013. *WALS Online*. Max Planck Institute for Evolutionary Anthropology. http://wals.info/.

Chris Dyer, Miguel Ballesteros, Wang Ling, Austin Matthews, and Noah A. Smith. 2015. Transition-based dependency parsing with stack long short-term memory. In *Proc. of ACL*.

Manaal Faruqui and Chris Dyer. 2014. Community evaluation and exchange of word vectors at word-vectors.org. In *Proc. of ACL (Demonstrations)*.

Manaal Faruqui, Jesse Dodge, Sujay Kumar Jauhar, Chris Dyer, Noah A. Smith, and Eduard Hovy. 2015. Retrofitting word vectors to semantic lexicons. In *Proc. of NAACL*.

Christiane Fellbaum, editor. 1998. *WordNet: an electronic lexical database*. MIT Press.

Lev Finkelstein, Evgeniy Gabrilovich, Yossi Matias, Ehud Rivlin, Zach Solan, Gadi Wolfman, and Eytan Ruppin. 2001. Placing search in context: the concept revisited. In *Proc. of WWW*.

Jiang Guo, Wanxiang Che, Haifeng Wang, and Ting Liu. 2014. Revisiting embedding features for simple semi-supervised learning. In *Proc. of EMNLP*.

David R Hardoon, Sandor Szedmak, and John Shawe-Taylor. 2004. Canonical correlation analysis: An overview with application to learning methods. *Neural Computation*, 16(12):2639–2664.

Felix Hill, Roi Reichart, and Anna Korhonen. 2014. SimLex-999: Evaluating semantic models with (genuine) similarity estimation. *CoRR*, abs/1408.3456.

Guillaume Lample, Miguel Ballesteros, Sandeep Subramanian, Kazuya Kawakami, and Chris Dyer. 2016. Neural architectures for named entity recognition. In *Proc. of NAACL*.

Angeliki Lazaridou, Eva Maria Vecchi, and Marco Baroni. 2013. Fish transporters and miracle homes: How compositional distributional semantics can help NP parsing. In *Proc. of EMNLP*.

Wang Ling, Lin Chu-Cheng, Yulia Tsvetkov, Silvio Amir, Ramon Fermandez, Chris Dyer, Alan W Black, and Isabel Trancoso. 2015a. Not all contexts are created equal: Better word representations with variable attention. In *Proc. of EMNLP*.

Wang Ling, Chris Dyer, Alan Black, and Isabel Trancoso. 2015b. Two/too simple adaptations of word2vec for syntax problems. In *Proc. of NAACL*.

Mitchell P Marcus, Mary Ann Marcinkiewicz, and Beatrice Santorini. 1993. Building a large annotated corpus of English: The penn treebank. *Computational Linguistics*, 19(2):313–330.

Héctor Martínez Alonso, Anders Johannsen, Sussi Olsen, Sanni Nimb, Nicolai Hartvig Sørensen, Anna Braasch, Anders Søgaard, and Bolette Sandford Pedersen. 2015. Supersense tagging for Danish. In *Proc. of NODALIDA*, page 21.

Tomas Mikolov, Kai Chen, Greg Corrado, and Jeffrey Dean. 2013. Efficient estimation of word representations in vector space. In *Proc. of ICLR*.

George A. Miller, Claudia Leacock, Randee Tengi, and Ross T. Bunker. 1993. A semantic concordance. In *Proc. of HLT*, pages 303–308.

Jeffrey Pennington, Richard Socher, and Christopher D. Manning. 2014. GloVe: Global vectors for word representation. In *Proc. of EMNLP*.

Richard Socher, Alex Perelygin, Jean Wu, Jason Chuang, Christopher D. Manning, Andrew Y. Ng, and Christopher Potts. 2013. Recursive deep models for semantic compositionality over a sentiment treebank. In *Proc. of EMNLP*.

Christian Szegedy, Wojciech Zaremba, Ilya Sutskever, Joan Bruna, Dumitru Erhan, Ian Goodfellow, and Rob Fergus. 2014. Intriguing properties of neural networks. In *Proc. of ICLR*.

Yulia Tsvetkov, Leonid Boytsov, Anatole Gershman, Eric Nyberg, and Chris Dyer. 2014. Metaphor detection with cross-lingual model transfer. In *Proc. of ACL*, pages 248–258.

Yulia Tsvetkov, Manaal Faruqui, Wang Ling, Guillaume Lample, and Chris Dyer. 2015. Evaluation of word vector representations by subspace alignment. In *Proc. of EMNLP*, pages 2049–2054.

Joseph Turian, Lev Ratinov, and Yoshua Bengio. 2010. Word representations: a simple and general method for semi-supervised learning. In *Proc. of ACL*.

Evaluating word embeddings with fMRI and eye-tracking

Anders Søgaard
University of Copenhagen
soegaard@hum.ku.dk

Abstract

The workshop CfP assumes that down-stream evaluation of word embeddings is impractical, and that a valid evaluation metric for pairs of word embeddings can be found. I argue below that if so, the only meaningful evaluation procedure is comparison with measures of *human word processing in the wild*. Such evaluation is non-trivial, but I present a practical procedure here, evaluating word embeddings as features in a multi-dimensional regression model predicting brain imaging or eye-tracking word-level aggregate statistics.

What's the meaning of embeddings? In order to decide how to evaluate word embeddings, we first need to decide what word embeddings are supposed to encode. If we assume that word embeddings are primarily representations of the *meaning* of words, it makes sense to consult lexical semantic theories.

Here's a very, very, very (very, ...) crude characterization of lexical semantics: Researchers disagree whether words are defined by their co-occurrences (Firth, 1957), the contexts in which they are used (Wittgenstein, 1953), how they are organized in the brain (Miller and Fellbaum, 1992), or the referents they denote in the real world (Montague, 1973). I realize this is a ridiculously simplistic reduction of modern lexical semantics, but I think it suffices for our discussion of how best to evaluate word embeddings.[1]

Any metrics here? From (one or more of) these theories we want to derive a valid evaluation metric. In my view, *a valid metric satisfies two principles: (i) that it measures what we want to measure (adequacy), and (ii) that it cannot easily be*

---

[1] See the discussion in the last paragraph.

hacked. What I mean by (i) is that we want word embeddings to capture the meaning of words; and by (ii), that the reason we want to play the evaluation game is because it isn't obvious what the meaning of a word is. If the meaning of a word was given directly by its character sequence, I would not be writing this paper, and this workshop would not have been proposed. The question then is, do any of the four theories above provide us with a valid metric for the general quality of word embeddings?

Below, I argue that none of the four theories leave us with fully valid evaluation metrics, except maybe COGNITIVE LEXICAL SEMANTICS. I suggest evaluating embeddings by direct comparison with brain-imaging and eye-tracking data rather than word association norms, as an alternative approach to COGNITIVE LEXICAL SEMANTICS. I show that state-of-the-art embeddings correlate poorly with such data, but argue that this is nevertheless the only valid metric left on the table, if downstream evaluation is not an option – and that, practically, we can evaluate embeddings by the error of a multi-dimensional regression model predicting brain imaging or eye-tracking data using the embeddings as features.

Co-occurrence theory In CO-OCCURRENCE THEORY, the meaning of a word is defined by its co-occurrences with other words – e.g., the meaning of *big* is given by its co-occurrence with words such as *house* and *small*, i.e., its value in a co-occurrence matrix. Word embeddings should therefore predict lexical co-occurrences, which can be evaluated in terms of perplexity or word error rate. This was how embeddings were evaluated in the early papers, e.g., (Mikolov et al., 2010). But note that constructing co-occurrence matrices is also an integral part of standard approaches to *inducing* embeddings (Levy et al., 2015). In

Proceedings of the 1st Workshop on Evaluating Vector Space Representations for NLP, pages 116–121,
Berlin, Germany, August 12, 2016. ©2016 Association for Computational Linguistics

fact for any definition of a word's *company*, we can built co-occurrence matrices tailored to maximize our objective. The associated metrics can thus be "hacked" in the sense that the encodings used for evaluation, can also be used for induction. Just like with other intrinsic evaluation metrics in unsupervised learning, co-occurrence-based evaluation easily bites its own tail. As soon as we have defined a word's *company*, the quality of the embeddings depends solely on the quality of the data. The evaluation strategy becomes the induction strategy, and the validity of the embeddings is by postulate, not by evidence. In other words, the metric can be hacked. Note that whether such a metric is *adequate* (measuring meaning) remains an open question.

Sprachspiel theory In SPRACHSPIEL THEORY, the meaning of a word is defined by its usage, i.e., the situations in which it is used. In Wittgenstein's words, *only someone who already knows how to do something with it, can significantly ask a name.* Obviously, it is hard to parameterize contexts, but explicit semantic analysis (Gabrilovich and Markovitch, 2009) presents a simple approximation, e.g., thinking of Wikipedia sites as contexts. Learning word representations from inverted indexings of Wikipedia is encoding a situational lexical semantics, albeit in a somewhat simplistic way. The meaning of *big*, for example, is defined by the Wikipedia entries it occurs in, i.e., its value in a term-document (or term-topic or term-frame or ...) matrix. The question then is: How well do our embeddings distinguish between different contexts? See earlier work on using embeddings for document classification, for example. However, such an encoding has also been proposed as an approach to *inducing* embeddings (Søgaard et al., 2015). While this proposal adopts a specific encoding of term-document matrices, similar encodings can be built for any definition of a *Sprachspiel*. Any such metric can thus be "hacked" or build into the model, directly. Note, again, that whether such a metric is *adequate* (measuring meaning) remains an open question.

Cognitive lexical semantics How well does our embeddings align with our mental representations of words? Obviously, we do not have direct access to our mental representations, and most researchers have relied on word associations norms

instead.[2] In matrix terms, COGNITIVE LEXICAL SEMANTICS defines the meaning of a word as a vector over vertices in an ontology or a mental lexicon. The hypothesis is that our mental lexicon is organized as a undirected, colored, weighted network, and the meaning of words are defined by the edges connecting them to other words. The meaning of *big*, for example, is in a synonym relation with *large*, an antonym of *small*, etc. Such networks are typically informed by word association norms and corpus linguistic evidence. Using Wordnets for evaluating word embeddings was recently proposed by Tsvetkov et al. (2015).

However, again, Faruqui and Dyer (2015) recently proposed this as a learning strategy, encoding words by their occurrence in Wordnet. Using mental lexica as gold standard annotation thus suffers from the same problem as defining the meaning of words by their co-occurrences or distributions over situations or documents; the derived metrics can be hacked. Also, there's a number of problems with using Wordnets and the like for evaluating word embeddings. The most obvious ones are low coverage and low inter-annotator agreement in such resources. Moreover, as shown by Juergens (2014), some inter-annotator disagreements are not random (errors), but reflect different, linguistically motivated choices. There are different ways to structure word meanings that lead to different semantic networks. Different lexicographic theories suggest different ways to do this. This means that our resources are theoretically biased. After all, while psycholinguistic priming effects and word association norms suggest that semantically similar words are retrieved faster than orthographically similar words, there is to the best of my knowledge no bullet-proof evidence that our brain does not order words alphabetically (or some other obscure way) in the mental lexicon.

Do we have alternatives? Our limited understanding of the brain makes evaluating COGNITIVE LEXICAL SEMANTICS non-trivial — at least if we want to go beyond lexicographic representations of the mental lexicon. If we accept lexicographic resources as approximations of the mental lexicon, we can use these resources for training, as

---

[2]See Faruqui et al. (2016; Batchkarov et al. (2016; Chiu et al. (2016) for critiques of using word association norms. The problem with word association norms is inadequacy (and statistical power): They conflate several types of similarity, e.g., synonymy and antonymy, and they are culture-specific.

well as evaluation, in the same way as we do evaluation in other supervised learning problems. If we don't, we have to resort to alternatives. Below we consider one, namely direct evaluation against brain imaging (and eye tracking) data.

Denotational semantics At first sight, DENOTATIONAL SEMANTICS seems to assume discrete word representations (sets). Obviously, however, some words have overlapping sets of referents. Can we evaluate our embeddings by how well they predict such overlaps? DENOTATIONAL SEMANTICS, in matrix terms, defines the meaning of a word as its distribution over a set of referents (e.g., its occurrences in Amazon product descriptions). While learning embeddings of words from their distribution over Amazon product descriptions has, to the best of our knowledge, not yet been proposed, this would be easy to do. DENOTATIONAL SEMANTICS is thus very similar to SPRACHSPIEL THEORY from an evaluation point of view; if we fix the set of referents, e.g., Amazon products, evaluation again becomes similar to evaluation in other supervised learning problems.

Brain imaging, anyone? If we accept the premise in the call for papers for this workshop – that down-stream evaluation of word embeddings is impractical and all over the map – we also accept the conclusion that we are interested in embeddings, not only for practical purposes, but as models of cognitive lexical semantics. It seems that this motivates focusing on evaluation procedures such as correlation with word association norms or evaluation against mental lexica. However, lexicographic resources are sparse and theoretically biased, and word association norms are unreliable. What do we do?

If we could measure the semantic processing associated with a word in brain imaging, this would give us a less biased access to the cognitive lexical semantics of words. If we assume such data is available, there are two possible approaches to evaluating word embeddings against such data:

(a) Studying the correlation between distances in word embedding space and EEG/fMRI/etc. space; or, perhaps more robustly, the P@k predicting nearest neighbors EEG/fMRI/etc. using embeddings.

(b) Evaluating the squared error of a regression model trained to associate the input word embeddings with EEG/fMRI/etc.

Note that we have reasons to think such metrics are not entirely inadequate, since we know humans understand words when they read them. fMRI data, for example, may contain a lot of noise and other types of information, but semantic word processing is bound to the contribute to the signal, one way or the other.

At last, a few experiments I present some initial experiments doing both (a) and (b). We evaluate the Ew30 and SENNA embeddings (Collobert et al., 2011) against fMRI data from Wehbe et al. (2015), using the token-level statistics derived in Barrett et al. (2016), and eye-tracking data from the Dundee Corpus (Barrett and Søgaard, 2015).

My first experiment is a simple one, merely to show how uncorrelated raw fMRI and eye-tracking data are with state-of-the-art embeddings. I deliberately pick a very simple prediction problem. Specifically, we randomly sample 9 words that are shared between the cognitive gold standard data and the two sets of embeddings we wish to evaluate. For each of the 9 words, I compare nearest neighbors, computing P@1 for both our embedding models.

I convert the fMRI data and the eye-tracking data to vectors of aggregate statistics following the suggestions in Barrett and Søgaard (2015) and Barrett et al. (2016). Table 1 presents the nearest neighbors (out of the 9 randomly selected words) in the gold data, as well as the two word embeddings. The P@1 for both embeddings is 2/9. If I increase the size of the candidate set to 50, and do three random runs, scores drop to 4% and 3.3%, respectively. For comparison, the embeddings agree on the nearest neighbors in 9, 10, and 10 words across three random runs. On the other hand, this is expected, since the embedding algorithms have obvious similarities, while the brain imaging data is entirely independent of the embeddings. If I run the same experiment on the gaze data, using a candidate set of 50 random words, scores are even lower (0–1/50). The P@1 agreements between the fMRI data and the eye-tracking recordings across three runs are also very low (0, 2, and 2 in 50).

If I look at the nearest neighbors across the full dataset, manually, the picture is also blurred. Sometimes, the brain imaging data has odd nearest neighbors, say *teachers* for *having*, when Ew30 had *giving*, for example, which is intuitively much closer. In other cases, the gold stan-

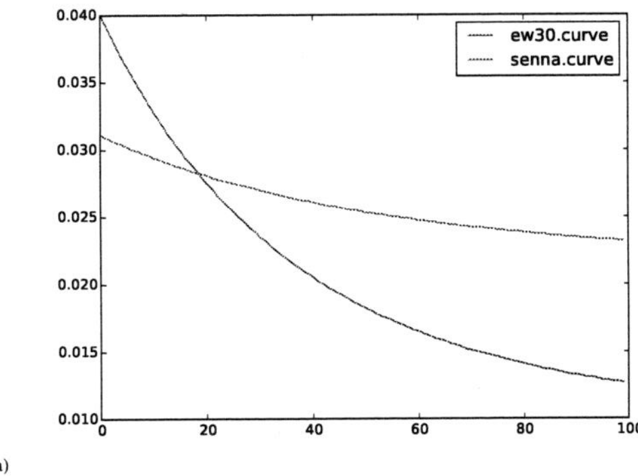 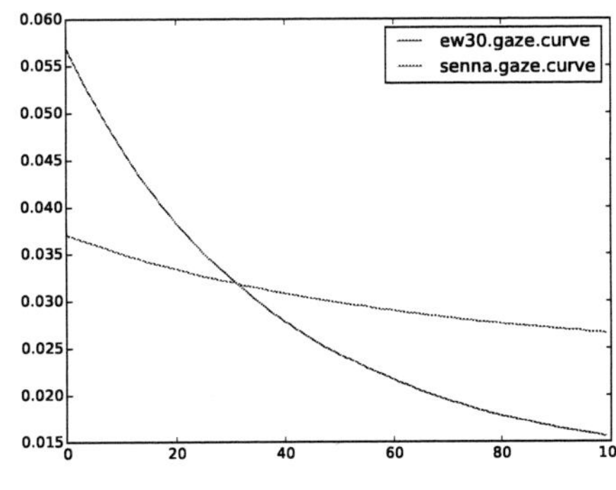

Figure 1: Learning curve fitting state-of-the-art embeddings to token-level fMRI (a) and eye-tracking (b) statistics (x-axis: learning iterations, y-axis: squared mean error)

Target	Nearest neighbors		
	SENNA	Ew30	GOLD
rolling	nervous	pig	pig
madly	out	nervous	house
rise	hold	hold	anytime
house	hold	pig	anytime
nervous	rolling	rolling	hold
hold	house	rise	managed
managed	hold	out	hold
out	madly	managed	pig
pig	rolling	rolling	rolling

Table 1: Nearest neighbors within a random sample of nine words. We underline the nearest neighbors in SENNA and Ew30 embeddings when they agree with the fMRI gold data.

Target	Ew30	GOLD	Okay?
students	teachers	mistake	No
creep	drift	long	No
peace	death	eat	Maybe
tight	nasty	hold	Maybe
squeak	twisted	broke	Yes
admiring	cursing	stunned	Yes
amazed	delighted	impressed	Yes

Table 2: Examples of nearest neighbors (over full dataset) for Ew30 and fMRI embeddings. Manual judgments (**Okay?**) reflect whether the fMRI nearest neighbors made intuitive sense.

dard nearest neighbors are better than state-of-the art, or defendable alternatives. Table 2 lists a few examples, comparing against Ew30, and whether the gold standard makes intuitive sense (to me).

However, it is not clear, *a priori*, that the embeddings should correlate perfectly with brain imaging data. The brain may encode these signals in some transformed way. I therefore ran the following experiment:

For words w in a training split, I train a deep neural regression model to reconstruct the fMRI/gaze vector from the input embedding, which I evaluate by its squared error on a held-out test split. All vectors are normalized to the (0,1)-range, leading to squared distances in the (0,2)-range. The training split is the first 100 words in the common vocabulary (of the two embeddings and the gold standard); the test split the next 100 words. Sampling from the common vocabulary is important; comparisons across different vocabularies is a known problem in the word embeddings literature. I use SGD and a hidden layer with 100 dimensions.

I present a learning curve for the first 100 iterations fitting the embeddings to the fMRI data in Figure 1a. Observe that the Ew30 embeddings give us a much better fit than the SENNA embeddings. Interestingly, the better fit is achieved with fewer dimensions (30 vs. 50). This suggests that the Ew30 embeddings capture more of the differences in the brain imaging data. See the same effect with the eye-tracking data in Figure 1b.

What I am saying ... Under the assumption that downstream evaluation of word embeddings is impractical, I have argued that correlating with human word processing data is the only valid type of evaluation left on the table. Since brain imaging and eye-tracking data are very noisy signals, correlating distances does not provide sufficient statistical power to compare systems. For that reason I have proposed comparing embeddings by testing how useful they are when trying to predict human processing data. I have presented some preliminary experiments, evaluating state-of-the-art embeddings by how useful they are for predicting brain imaging and eye-tracking data using a deep neural regression model. The test is made available at the website:

```
http://cst.dk/anders/fmri-eval/
```

where users can upload pairs of embeddings and obtain learning curves such as the ones above. I believe this type of evaluation is the most meaningful task-independent evaluation of word embeddings possible right now. Note that you can also do nearest neighbor queries (and t-SNE visualizations) with the output of such a model.

More advanced theories? Our proposal was in part motivated by a crude simplification of lexical semantics. Of course more advanced theories exist. For example, Marconi (1997) says lexical competence involves both an inferential aspect, i.e., learning a semantic network of synonymy and hyponymy relations, as well as a referential aspect, which is in charge of naming and application. In this framework, a word is defined by its edges in a semantic network *and* its denotation and/or the situations in which it can be used. Technically, however, this is a simple concatenation of the vectors described above. Again, the derived metrics are easily hacked. In other words, if Marconi (1997) is right, evaluation reduces to settling on the definition of the semantic network and of denotation or language games, and finding representative data. From a metrics point of view, any evaluation based on such a theory would be a vicious circle.

Acknowledgments

This work was supported by ERC Starting Grant No. 313695, as well as research grant from the Carlsberg Foundation.

References

Maria Barrett and Anders Søgaard. 2015. Reading behavior predicts syntactic categories. In *CoNLL*.

Maria Barrett, Joachim Bingel, and Anders Søgaard. 2016. Extracting token-level signals of syntactic processing from fmri - with an application to pos induction. In *ACL*.

Miroslav Batchkarov, Thomas Kober, Jeremy Reffin, Julie Weeds, and David Weir. 2016. A critique of word similarity as a method for evaluating distributional semantic models. In *RepEval*.

Billy Chiu, Anna Korhonen, and Sampo Pyysalo. 2016. Intrinsic evaluation of word vectors fails to predict extrinsic performance. In *RepEval*.

Ronan Collobert, Jason Weston, Léon Bottou, Michael Karlen, Koray Kavukcuoglu, and Pavel Kuksa. 2011. Natural language processing (almost) from scratch. *The Journal of Machine Learning Research*, 12:2493–2537.

Manaal Faruqui and Chris Dyer. 2015. Non-distributional word vector representations. In *ACL*.

Manaal Faruqui, Yulia Tsvetkov, Pushpendre Rastogi, and Chris Dyer. 2016. Problems with evaluation of word embeddings using word similarity tasks. In *RepEval*.

John Firth. 1957. *Papers in Linguistics 1934-1951*. Oxford University Press.

Evgeniy Gabrilovich and Shaul Markovitch. 2009. Wikipedia-based semantic interpretation for natural language processing. *Journal of Artificial Intelligence Research*, pages 443–498.

David Juergens. 2014. An analysis of ambiguity in word sense annotations. In *LREC*.

Omer Levy, Yoav Goldberg, and Ido Dagan. 2015. Improving distributional similarity with lessons learned from word embeddings. *TACL*, 3:211–225.

Diego Marconi. 1997. *Lexical Competence*. MIT Press.

Tomas Mikolov, Martin Karafiat, Lukas Burget, Jan Cernocky, and Sanjeev Khudanpur. 2010. Recurrent neural network based language model. In *INTERSPEECH*.

George Miller and Christiane Fellbaum. 1992. Semantic networks of English. In *Lexical and conceptual semantics*. Blackwell.

Richard Montague. 1973. The proper treatment of quantification in ordinary English. In *Formal philosophy*. Yale University Press.

Anders Søgaard, Željko Agić, Héctor Martínez Alonso, Barbara Plank, Bernd Bohnet, and Anders Johannsen. 2015. Inverted indexing for cross-lingual nlp. In *ACL*.

Yulia Tsvetkov, Manaal Faruqui, Wang Ling, Guillaume Lample, and Chris Dyer. 2015. Evaluation of word vector representations by subspace alignment. In *EMNLP*.

Leila Wehbe, Brian Murphy, Partha Talukdar, Alona
Fyshe, Aaditya Ramdas, and Tom Mitchell. 2015.
Simultaneously uncovering the patterns of brain regions involved in different story reading subpro-
cesses. *PLoS ONE*, 10(3).

Ludwig Wittgenstein. 1953. *Philosophical Investiga-
tions*. Blackwell Publishing.

Defining Words with Words: Beyond the Distributional Hypothesis

Iuliana-Elena Parasca*   Andreas Lukas Rauter*   Jack Roper*   Aleksandar Rusinov*
Guillaume Bouchard   Sebastian Riedel   Pontus Stenetorp
{iuliana.parasca,andreas.rauter,jack.roper,aleksandar.rusinov}.13@ucl.ac.uk
{g.bouchard,s.riedel,p.stenetorp}@cs.ucl.ac.uk
Department of Computer Science, University College London

Abstract

The way humans define words is a powerful way of representing them. In this work, we propose to measure word similarity by comparing the overlap in their definition. This highlights linguistic phenomena that are complementary to the information extracted from standard context-based representation learning techniques. To acquire a large amount of word definitions in a cost-efficient manner, we designed a simple interactive word game, *Word Sheriff*. As a byproduct of game play, it generates short word sequences that can be used to uniquely identify words. These sequences can not only be used to evaluate the quality of word representations, but it could ultimately give an alternative way of learning them, as it overcomes some of the limitations of the distributional hypothesis. Moreover, inspecting player behaviour reveals interesting aspects about human strategies and knowledge acquisition beyond those of simple word association games, due to the conversational nature of the game. Lastly, we outline a vision of a *communicative evaluation* setting, where systems are evaluated based on how well a given representation allows a system to communicate with human and computer players.

1   Introduction

The distributional hypothesis (Harris, 1954) is at the core of many modern Natural Language Processing (NLP) techniques. It is based on the following assumption:

Words are similar if they have similar contexts.

While powerful, the assumption of context is not always convenient, nor satisfactory. For example, antonyms (black vs. white) and hypernyms (laptop vs. computer) tend to appear in the same context, but they cannot naively replace each other. Similarly, implicit or prior knowledge is difficult to capture by only referring to word contexts. One rarely writes that a banana is yellow, while this is one of the main adjectives one would use when defining it.

In this paper, we describe a novel and complementary framework to capture information that is difficult to obtain by exploiting the distributional hypothesis. It is based on a *relaxed* variant of a dictionary-based hypothesis that assumes that words are the same if they have the same definition. We soften our dictionary-based definition by introducing the notion of "similar definition":

Words are similar if they have similar definitions.

The issue with using word definitions is that it depends on the ability for people to define words. In principle, coming up with proper coherent definitions is costly, as it requires multiple linguistic experts. However, if what we aim to capture is *the ability to identify a word*, we can come up with a more cost-effective data acquisition technique. Our key contribution is the use of crowdsourcing and gamification to show that creating a simple interactive game can generate a huge amount of "short definitions" at very low cost, with the potential to lead to an exciting new data source to evaluate or improve existing word representations. What we mean by "short definition" is a short sequence of words that enables a human to uniquely identify a word.

We will now describe such a game, *Word Sheriff*, which is based on the interaction between a narrator and several guessers, the narrator being a human who implicitly creates definitions. Be-

---

*Contributed equally to this work.

Proceedings of the 1st Workshop on Evaluating Vector Space Representations for NLP, pages 122–126,
Berlin, Germany, August 12, 2016. ©2016 Association for Computational Linguistics

fore going into the details of the game, we should point out that there are many variants or alternative "definition games" that could be designed in a similar spirit, the main idea being that "word definitions matter" because there is some unwritten knowledge that is hard to capture by a static analysis of already existing textual data.

2 Word Sheriff

Our game is loosely based on the Pyramid game show franchise (Stewart, 1973), and for each round, one player (narrator) is presented with a target word or phrase known only to herself. The player must then give the partners (guessers) a series of clues in order to lead them to guess the correct word. After receiving each clue, guessers are allowed to make one guess. The game terminates when one of the guessers find the target word. To incentivise the narrator to use a minimal number of salient clues, the total number of allowed clues is decided beforehand by the narrator, where a lower number of clues lead to a higher reward. An initial web-based prototype of the game was created by four undergraduate students as a part of a project-based course over eight weeks.

Illustrations of successful and unsuccessful game sessions are shown in Tables 1 and 2. In the first session, the narrator decided on limiting herself to 2 clues as she thought that `banana` is easily uniquely identifiable by `yellow` and `fruit`. In fact, this was somewhat risky, as `lemon` would have been an equally correct answer. While in the second session, a larger number of clues were selected by the narrator, yet the guessers did not arrive at the target word `weather`. Interestingly, the narrator used a syntactic clue `noun` that was supposed to guide the guessers to the right type of word. This shows the two-way communicative aspect of the game, as this word was probably chosen because both guessers were proposing adjectives in the second round. Another interesting aspect of the game appears in the first round, where Guesser 1 proposed a word with an opposite meaning (`sun` when `rain` is given as the first clue), and Guesser 2 tried to complete a common n-gram (`rain jacket`).

3 Initial Limited Release

By analysing the logs generated by the game played by human players, we can make interesting linguistic insights and observe player behavioural

Round	Narrator's clue	Guesser 1	Guesser 2
1a	fruit		
1b		orange	apple
2a	yellow		
2b		lemon	**banana**

Table 1: Successful game in 2 rounds for `banana`

Round	Narrator's clue	Guesser 1	Guesser 2
1a	rain		
1b		sun	jacket
2a	sunny		
2b		cloudy	windy
3a	noun		
3b		cloud	umbrella

Table 2: Unsuccessful try (3 rds., `weather`)

patterns. Ultimately, in order to be successful in the game, any player, human or computer, must be able to account for the linguistic phenomena that we observe.

To seed our game, we annotated 241 words with clues to be used as gold data for bots that could be introduced if not enough players were online to start a game. We then performed a limited release over a handful of days within our computer science department, where members could play the game freely. All in all, 246 games were played by roughly 100 individual players, where 85% stated that they would consider playing the game again when answering a voluntary anonymous survey.

4 Data Analysis

To better understand what linguistic phenomena that can be observed when playing our game, we qualitatively analysed the annotations collected from the players during our initial limited release. For brevity, we only report phenomena that are difficult to account for using the distributional hypothesis, namely:

- **Hypernymy**: One of the most common strategies is to use two clues involving one hypernym and one distinguishable feature, such as `animal` + `horn` for `rhinoceros` or `country` + `oslo` for `norway`. Perhaps surprisingly, we did not observe any hyponym relations, but this might be due to the limited amount of data analysed.

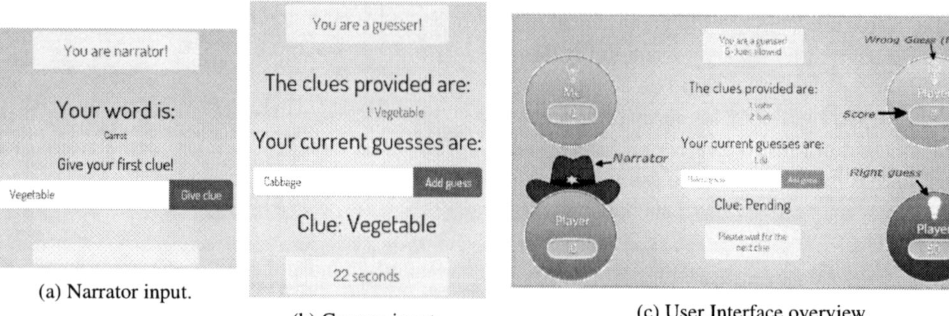

(a) Narrator input.

(b) Guesser input.

(c) User Interface overview.

Figure 1: Screenshots of our web-based prototype.

	1st	2nd	3rd
hyena	animal	laugh	dog
wasabi	japanese	spice	
sausage	meat	pig	
anaesthesiologist	doctor	sleep	

Table 3: Compositional strategies.

- **Antonymy**: When observing the guesses given after the first clue, it was interesting to see that players sometimes strategically use antonyms, such a `win` $\mapsto$ `lose`. We speculate that experienced players will tend to use antonymy more often than beginners, as it has the potential to uniquely identify a word using single clue, but this intuition would have to be statistically validated on a larger dataset.

- **Prior Knowledge**: Many clue words are related to the target words based on prior knowledge about the world, such as the physical proximity, functional properties or other types of common sense knowledge. One interesting example appears when the target word is `mouth`: guessers tend to use the *Container/Containee* relation and propose `teeth` or `tongue` as clues. Another interesting example is `guacamole`, for which some clues are `avocado` and `burrito`, which are related to the subject or the object of the relation *IsIngredientOf*. Another clue is `condiment`, which relate to the *Typical Usage* of the target word.

The previous observations were mainly focusing on individual words, but another interesting aspect is the compositional nature of the clue words. In Table 3 we report several examples of compositional strategies used by the narrators. This strategy is primarily enabled by the conversational nature of our game, which unlike traditional word association games allow for more than a single response.

5 Related work

For NLP, games have been proposed for numerous tasks such as anaphora resolution (Hladká et al., 2009) and word sense disambiguation (Jurgens and Navigli, 2014). From the literature, Verbosity (von Ahn et al., 2006) is the game most closely related to ours. However, unlike Verbosity our game does not impose ontological restrictions on the input given by the narrator since the end result of the annotations produced by our game does not seek conform with an ontology. Our game also has an adversarial component (guesser-guesser), which we argue is essential for player enjoyment (Prensky, 2007).

Despite a plethora of proposed games, the ones that remain available online have a waning or non-existing player base, why? Our hypothesis is that this is due to the games constraining player creativity to conform with annotation guidelines, leading to less enjoyment, or because of attempts to mimic existing games and adding seemingly unrelated annotation elements to it, to which the player naturally asks the question "Why should I play a variant with a convoluted annotation element, as opposed to a variant without it?".

Thus, we took inspiration from Boyd-Graber et al. (2012) that gathered annotations using an online quiz bowl game and found that the annotators needed no financial incentives and even im-

124

plemented their own version of the game once the authors had taken their version offline.[1] Our starting-point was thus, can we build upon an existing game that is enjoyable in its own right and with only minor modifications make it sustainable and yield annotations that are useful for evaluating NLP methods?

There are clear parallels between our game and word association games that date back several hundred years and has been of interest to the field of psycholinguistics. One can thus see our goal to be a natural extension of word associations work such as Nelson et al. (2004). In regards to using dictionary definitions, there is the work of Hill et al. (2016), that used dictionary definitions to learn word representations.

6 Future Directions and Challenges

Given the promising results of our prototype implementation and data acquired from our initial limited release, we believe that there are several interesting directions to take our work:

- In our initial release we did not account for the demographic background of our players. An interesting experiment would be to collect such data and inspect it to see if players with different backgrounds would use different explanations.

- Since the data we collected indicate that our model can avoid several pitfalls of the distributional hypothesis, it would seem that retrofitting existing word representations could in fact lead to better word representations for both intrinsic and extrinsic tasks.

- Ultimately, what we find to be the most exiting application would be to use our data and game to perform what we term *communicative evaluation*. Most evaluation of NLP systems is performed in a setting where a system is presented with an input and is asked to *infer* some aspect of the input such as its sentiment, topic, or linguistic structure. However, a key aspect of language is that its purpose is communication, something which our game captures in that players are not only asked to infer the intent of the narrator but also to *communicate* the meaning of the target word when they themselves act as the narrator. Given a representation, a system should

be able to learn to perform both the guesser and narrator role, evaluating how well the representation aids the communicative task. This is similar to existing work in computer to computer communication, where two systems learn to communicate about the world, but our setting is different in that as long as a portion of the data is given by human players the way of communicating that is learnt is grounded in human communication.

However, we do believe that there are several hurdles to overcome if we are to succeed in our efforts and we highlight two issues in particular:

- Firstly, our game being a multi-player game, we are reliant on a large player base in order to be sustainable. Not only is it necessary for a significant number of players to be online at any given point in time, it can also be argued that the quality of our annotations are reliant on the players coming from diverse backgrounds, so as not to bias our data.

- Secondly, running a large-scale online game requires large-scale infrastructure. Such infrastructure would also need to me maintained over a large period of time, potentially longer than what a research grant may offer.

Our strategy to overcome these issues is to seek partnership with a commercial actor that can give us access to a wider audience and provide infrastructure. Such a commercial actor would be compensated by more immediate access to the data generated by the players of the game and by the value the game itself can provide for its users, for example as an educational application for language learners.

7 Conclusions

In this work, we showed how to generate an interesting dataset that captures linguistic phenomena such as antonymy, hypernymy and common sense knowledge that are difficult to capture by standard approaches based on the distributional hypothesis. Not only is this data complementary to existing word-similarity datasets, but they can come at nearly no cost as their are obtained as a by-product of a game that is actually very fun to play.

Apart from direct applications of such datasets to psycholinguistics, there are several applications for which the data generated by "definition games", but it could be useful in applications

---

[1] Personal communication.

where prior knowledge plays an important role, such as question answering involving reasoning about the physical world. It is also likely that it will help to improve machine translation by using the word with the right definition, when there is no one-to-one correspondence between words in the two different languages.

Lastly, we outlined future directions that we seek to take our research in and described several challenges and how we seek to overcome them.

Acknowledgments

This work was supported by a Marie Curie Career Integration Award and an Allen Distinguished Investigator Award. We would like to thank the over one hundred players that took part in the initial limited release of our game, Jordan Boyd-Graber for answering questions regarding their online quiz bowl game, and the anonymous reviewers for their helpful feedback.

References

[Boyd-Graber et al.2012] Jordan Boyd-Graber, Brianna Satinoff, He He, and Hal Daume III. 2012. Besting the quiz master: Crowdsourcing incremental classification games. In *Proceedings of the 2012 Joint Conference on Empirical Methods in Natural Language Processing and Computational Natural Language Learning*, pages 1290–1301, Jeju Island, Korea, July. Association for Computational Linguistics.

[Harris1954] Zellig S Harris. 1954. Distributional structure. *Word*, 10(2-3):146–162.

[Hill et al.2016] Felix Hill, Kyunghyun Cho, and Anna Korhonen. 2016. Learning distributed representations of sentences from unlabelled data. *arXiv preprint arXiv:1602.03483*.

[Hladká et al.2009] Barbora Hladká, Jiří Mírovský, and Pavel Schlesinger. 2009. Play the language: Play coreference. In *Proceedings of the ACL-IJCNLP 2009 Conference Short Papers*, pages 209–212. Association for Computational Linguistics.

[Jurgens and Navigli2014] D. Jurgens and R. Navigli. 2014. It's all fun and games until someone annotates: Video games with a purpose for linguistic annotation. *Transactions of the Association for Computational Linguistics*, 2:449–464.

[Nelson et al.2004] Douglas L Nelson, Cathy L McEvoy, and Thomas A Schreiber. 2004. The university of south florida free association, rhyme, and word fragment norms. *Behavior Research Methods, Instruments, & Computers*, 36(3):402–407.

[Prensky2007] M. Prensky. 2007. *Fun, Play and Games: What Makes Games Engaging*. Paragon House, St Paul, MN, USA.

[Stewart1973] Bob Stewart. 1973. The $10,000 Pyramid.

[von Ahn et al.2006] Luis von Ahn, Mihir Kedia, and Manuel Blum. 2006. Verbosity: a game for collecting common-sense facts. In *Proceedings of the SIGCHI conference on Human Factors in computing systems*, pages 75–78. ACM.

A Proposal for Linguistic Similarity Datasets Based on Commonality Lists

Dmitrijs Milajevs
Queen Mary University of London
London, UK
d.milajevs@qmul.ac.uk

Sascha Griffiths
Queen Mary University of London
London, UK
s.griffiths@qmul.ac.uk

Abstract

Similarity is a core notion that is used in psychology and two branches of linguistics: theoretical and computational. The similarity datasets that come from the two fields differ in design: psychological datasets are focused around a certain topic such as fruit names, while linguistic datasets contain words from various categories. The later makes humans assign low similarity scores to the words that have nothing in common and to the words that have contrast in meaning, making similarity scores ambiguous. In this work we discuss the similarity collection procedure for a multi-category dataset that avoids score ambiguity and suggest changes to the evaluation procedure to reflect the insights of psychological literature for word, phrase and sentence similarity. We suggest to ask humans to provide a list of commonalities and differences instead of numerical similarity scores and employ the structure of human judgements beyond pairwise similarity for model evaluation. We believe that the proposed approach will give rise to datasets that test meaning representation models more thoroughly with respect to the human treatment of similarity.

1 Introduction

Similarity is the degree of resemblance between two objects or events (Hahn, 2014) and plays a crucial role in psychological theories of knowledge and behaviour, where it is used to explain such phenomena as classification and conceptualisation. *Fruit* is a *category* because it is a practical generalisation. Fruits are sweet and constitute deserts, so when one is presented with an unknown fruit, one can hypothesise that it is served toward the end of a dinner.

Generalisations are extremely powerful in describing a language as well. The verb *runs* requires its subject to be singular. *Verb*, *subject* and *singular* are categories that are used to describe English grammar. When one encounters an unknown word and is told that it is a verb, one will immediately have an idea about how to use it assuming that it is used similarly to other English verbs.

The semantic formalisation of similarity is based on two ideas. The occurrence pattern of a word *defines* its meaning (Firth, 1957), while the difference in occurrence between two words *quantifies* the difference in their meaning (Harris, 1970). From a computational perspective, this motivates and guides development of similarity components that are embedded into natural language processing systems that deal with tasks such as word sense disambiguation (Schütze, 1998), information retrieval (Salton et al., 1975; Milajevs et al., 2015), machine translation (Dagan et al., 1993), dependency parsing (Hermann and Blunsom, 2013; Andreas and Klein, 2014), and dialogue act tagging (Kalchbrenner and Blunsom, 2013; Milajevs and Purver, 2014).

Because it is difficult to measure performance of a single (similarity) component in a pipeline, datasets that focus on similarity are popular among computational linguists. Apart from a pragmatic attempt to alleviate the problems of evaluating similarity components, these datasets serve as an empirical test of the hypotheses of Firth and Harris, bringing together our understanding of human mind, language and technology.

Two datasets, namely MEN (Bruni et al., 2012) and SimLex-999 (Hill et al., 2015), are currently widely used. They are designed especially for meaning representation evaluation and surpass datasets stemming from psychology (Tversky and Hutchinson, 1986), information retrieval

Proceedings of the 1st Workshop on Evaluating Vector Space Representations for NLP, pages 127–133,
Berlin, Germany, August 12, 2016. ©2016 Association for Computational Linguistics

(Finkelstein et al., 2002) and computational linguistics (Rubenstein and Goodenough, 1965) in quantity by having more entries and, in case of SimLex-999, attention to the evaluated relation by distinguishing similarity from relatedness. The datasets provide similarity (relatedness) scores between word pairs.

In contrast to linguistic datasets which contain randomly paired words from a broad selection, datasets that come from psychology contain entries that belong to a single category such as *verbs of judging* (Fillenbaum and Rapoport, 1974) or *animal terms* (Henley, 1969). The reason for category oriented similarity studies is that "stimuli can only be compared in so far as they have already been categorised as identical, alike, or equivalent at some higher level of abstraction" (Turner et al., 1987). Moreover, because of the *extension effect* (Medin et al., 1993), the similarity of two entries in a context is less than the similarity between the same entries when the context is extended. "For example, *black* and *white* received a similarity rating of 2.2 when presented by themselves; this rating increased to 4.0 when *black* was simultaneously compared with *white* and *red* (*red* only increased 4.2 to 4.9)" (Medin et al., 1993). In the first case *black* and *white* are more dissimilar because they are located on the extremes of the greyscale, but in the presence of *red* they become more similar because they are both monochromes.

Both MEN and SimLex-999 provide pairs that do not share any similarity to control for false positives, and they do not control for the comparison scale. This makes similarity judgements ambiguous as it is not clear what low similarity values mean: incomparable notions, contrast in meaning or even the difference in comparison context. SimLex-999 assigns low similarity scores to the incomparable pairs (0.48, *trick* and *size*) and to antonymy (0.55, *smart* and *dumb*), but *smart* and *dumb* have relatively much more in common than *trick* and *size*!

The present contribution investigates how a similarity dataset with multiple categories should be built and considers what sentence similarity means in this context.

2 Dataset Construction

Human similarity judgements To build a similarity dataset that contains non-overlapping categories, one needs to avoid comparison of incomparable pairs. However, that itself requires an a priori knowledge of item similarity or belongingness to a category, making the problem circular.

To get out of this vicious circle, one might erroneously refer to an already existing taxonomy such as WordNet (Miller, 1995). But in case of similarity, as Turney (2012) points out, categories that emerge from similarity judgements are different from taxonomies. For example, *traffic* and *water* might be considered to be similar because of a functional similarity exploited in hydrodynamic models of traffic, but their lowest common ancestor in WordNet is *entity*.

Since there is no way of deciding upfront whether there is a similarity relation between two words, the data collection procedure needs to test for both: relation existence and its strength. Numerical values, as has been shown in the introduction, do not fit this role due to ambiguity. One way to avoid the issue is to avoid asking humans for numerical similarity judgements, but instead to ask them to list commonalities and differences between the objects. As one might expect, similarity scores correlate with the number of listed commonalities (Markman and Gentner, 1991; Markman and Gentner, 1996; Medin et al., 1993). For incomparable pairs, the commonality list should be empty, but the differences will enumerate properties that belong to one entity, but not to another (Markman and Gentner, 1991; Medin et al., 1993).

Verbally produced features (norms) for empirically derived conceptual representation of McRae et al. (2005) is a good example of what and how the data should be collected. But in contrast to McRae et al. (2005)—where explicit comparison of concepts was avoided—participants should be asked to produce commonalities as part of similarity comparison.

The entries in the dataset So far, we have proposed a similarity judgement collection method that is robust to incomparable pairings. It also naturally gives rise to categories, because the absence of a relation between two entries means the absence of a common category. It still needs to be decided which words to include in the dataset.

To get a list of words that constitute the dataset, one might think of categories such as *sports, fruits, vegetables, judging verbs, countries, colours* and so on. Note, that at this point its acceptable to think of categories, because later the arbitrary category assignments will be reevaluated. Once the list of categories is ready, each of them is populated with category instances, e.g. *plum, banana* and *lemon* are all *fruits*.

When the data is prepared, humans are asked to provide commonalities and differences between all pairs of every group. First, all expected similarities are judged, producing a dataset that can be seen as a merged version of category specific datasets. At this point, a good similarity model should provide meaning representation that are easily split to clusters: *fruit* members and *sport* members have to be separable.

Intra-category comparisons should be also performed, but because it is impractical to collect all possible pairwise judgements between the number of words of magnitude of hundreds, a reasonable sample should be taken. The intra-category comparisons will lead to unexpected category pairings, such as *food* that contains *vegetables* and *fruits*, so the sampling procedure might be directed by the discovery of comparable pairs: when a *banana* and *potato* are said to be similar, *fruits* and *vegetables* members should be more likely to be assessed.

Given the dynamic nature of score collection, we suggest setting up *a game with a purpose* (see Venhuizen et al. (2013) an example) where players are rewarded for contributing their commonality lists. Another option would be to crowdsource the human judgements (Keuleers and Balota, 2015).

Evaluation beyond proximity Human judgements validate the initial category assignment of items and provide new ones. If a category contains a superordinate, similarity judgements arrange category members around it (Tversky and Hutchinson, 1986). For example, similarity judgements given by humans arrange fruit names around the word *fruit* in such a way that it is their nearest neighbour, making *fruit* the *focal point* of the category of *fruits*.

As an additional evaluation method, the model should be able to retrieve focal points. Therefore, a precaution should be taken before human judgement collection. If possible, categories should contain a superordinate.

Similarity evaluation needs to focus on how well a model is able to recover human similarity intuitions expressed as groupings, possibly around their focal points. We propose to treat it as a soft multi-class clustering problem (White et al., 2015), where two entities belong to the same class if there is a similarity judgement for them (e.g. *apple* and *banana* are similar because they are *fruits*) and the strength is proportional to the number of such judgements, so we could express that *apple* is more a *fruit* than it is a *company*.

In contrast to the current evaluation based on correlation, models also need to be tested on the geometric arrangement of subordinates around the focal points, as only the proximity based evalua-tion does not capture this (Tversky and Hutchinson, 1986).

3 Sentence Similarity

The question of sentence similarity is more complex because sentences in many ways are different entities than words. Or are they? Linguistics has recently often pointed toward a continuum which exists between words and sentences (Jackendoff, 2012). Jackendoff and Pinker (2005), for example, point out that there is good evidence that "human memory must store linguistic expressions of all sizes." These linguistic expressions of variable size are often called *constructions*. Several computational approaches to constructions have been proposed (Gaspers et al., 2011; Chang et al., 2012), but to the authors' best knowledge they do not yet feature prominently in natural language processing.

To be able to measure the similarity of phrases and sentences in the proposed framework, we need to be able to identify what could serve as commonalities between them. So what are they? First of all, words, sentences and other constructions draw attention to *states of affairs* around us. Also, sentences are similar to others with respect to the functions they perform (Winograd, 1983, p. 288).

Prototype effects As Tomasello (2009) points out, speakers of English can make sense of phrases like *X floosed Y the Z* and *X was floosed by Y*. This is due to their similarity to sentences such as *John gave Mary the book* and *Mary was kissed by John* respectively. Thus, *X floosed Y the Z* is clearly a *transfer of possession* or *dative* (Bresnan et al., 2007).

The amount in which sentences are similar, at least to a certain extent, corresponds to the function of a given sentence (the ideational function (Winograd, 1983, p. 288) especially). Tomasello (1998) points out that sentence-level constructions show *prototype effects* similar to those discussed above for lexical systems (e.g. colours). Consider the following sentences:

- *John gave Mary the book.* is a example of an *Agent Causes Transfer* construction. These usually are build around words such as *give, pass, hand, toss, bring, etc.*
- *John promised Mary the book.* is a example of an *Conditional transfer* construction. These usually are build around words such as *promise, guarantee, owe, etc.*

As soon as one has such a prototype network, one can actually decide sentence similarity as one can say with respect to what prototypes sentences and utterances are similar. In this case, a common sentence prototype serves the same role as commonality between words.

Similarity in context However, prototype categories work on the semantic-grammatical level, and might be handled by *similarity in context*: a noun phrase can be similar to a noun as in *female lion* and *lioness*, and to another noun phrases as in *yellow car* and *cheap taxi*. The same similarity principle can be applied to phrases as to words. In this case, similarity is measured in context, but it is still a comparison of the phrases' head words of which meaning is modified by arguments they appear with (Kintsch, 2001; Mitchell and Lapata, 2008; Mitchell and Lapata, 2010; Dinu and Lapata, 2010; Baroni and Zamparelli, 2010; Thater et al., 2011; Séaghdha and Korhonen, 2011). With verbs this idea can be applied to compare transitive verbs with intransitive. For example, *to cycle* is similar to *to ride a bicycle*.

Sentential similarity might be treated as the similarity of the heads in the contexts. That is, the similarity between *sees* and *notices* in *John sees Mary* and *John notices a woman*. This approach abstracts away from grammatical differences between the sentences and concentrates on semantics and fits the proposed model as the respect for the head, which is a lexical entity, has to be found (Corbett and Fraser, 1993).

Attention attraction But still, what about pragmatics? As Steels (2008) points out, sentences and words direct attention and do not always directly point or refer to entities and actions in the world. For example, he points to the fact that if a person asks another person to *pass the wine* they are actually asking for the *bottle*. The speaker just attracts attention to an object of perception in a given situation.

Grammaticalisaton and lexicalisaton There are several ways in which a sentence can both be *grammaticalised* and *lexicalised*. For example, *No* and *I've seen John eating them* are similar sentences because they lexicalise the same answer to the question *Do we have cookies?* More generally, this gives rise to dialogue act tags: for another way of utterance categorisation, refer to the work of Kalchbrenner and Blunsom (2013) and Milajevs and Purver (2014).

Thus, questions which the sentences answer, are valid respects for similarity explanation, as well as entailment, paraphrase (White et al., 2015) or spatial categories (Ritter et al., 2015). This also mo-

tivates the approach of treating sentences on their own and encoding the meaning of a sentence into a vector in such a way that similar sentences are clustered together (Coecke et al., 2010; Baroni et al., 2014; Socher et al., 2012; Wieting et al., 2015; Hill et al., 2016).

Discourse fit If one conceptualises sentence similarity with respect to a discourse, then one might ask how different sentences fit in to such a discourse. Griffiths et al. (2015) tried to construct two versions of the same dialogue using a bottom-up method. They deconstructed a certain dialogue in a given domain—a receptionist scenario—into *greetings*, *directions* and *farewells*. They used a small custom made corpus for this purpose and created the two dialogues by having people rate the individual utterances by friendliness. The resulting two dialogues were surprisingly uneven. The dialogue was supposed to give instructions to a certain location within a building. The "friendly version" was very elaborated and consisted of several sentences:

(1) The questionnaire is located in room Q2-102. That is on the second floor. If you turn to your right and walk down the hallway. At the end of the floor you will find the stairs. Just walk up the stairs to the top floor and go through the fire door. The room is then straight ahead.

The sentence which served the same purpose in the "neutral version" was a fairly simple sentence:

(2) The questionnaire is located in Q2-102.

Often the same function of a given sentence in a dialogue can be performed by as little as one word or several phrases or a different sentence or even a complete story.

Language sub-systems and strategies Steels (2010) introduces the idea of language sub-systems and language strategies. A language sub-system are the means of expressing certain related or similar meanings. Examples of such sub-systems include:

- Lexical systems which express colours.
- Morphological devices to encode tenses.
- Usage of word order to express relations between agent and patient.

The later is an illustration of a language strategy. In English agent-patient relations are mainly encoded by syntax whereas German would use intonation and a combination or articles and case to convey the same information. Russian, in contrast, will use morphological devices for the same purpose. Hence, for some purposes the entities which are similar may not be of clearly delineated categories such as "word" or "sentence" but may be of chunks of language which belong to the same sub-system.

Above we identified seven criteria by which sentence similarity can be compared. The instructions for the sentence similarity judgement tasks may incorporate the criteria as hints for human participants during data collection.

4 Conclusion

In this contribution we discussed the notion of similarity from an interdisciplinary perspective. We contrasted properties of the similarity relation described in the field of psychology with the characteristics of similarity datasets used in computational linguistics. This lead to the recommendations on how to improve the later by removing low score ambiguity in a multi-category similarity dataset.

In the future, a multi-category similarity dataset should be build that allow evaluation of vector space models of meaning by not only measuring proximity between the points, but also their arrangement with respect to clusters. The same ideas can be used to build phrase- and sentence-level datasets. However, we leave the exact sentence similarity criteria selection for future work in this area.

On a broader perspective, this work highlights psychological phenomena that being incorporated into the models of meaning are expected to improve their performance.

Acknowledgements

We thank the anonymous reviewers for their comments. Support from EPSRC grant EP/J002607/1 is gratefully acknowledged by Dmitrijs Milajevs. Sascha Griffiths is supported by ConCreTe: the project ConCreTe acknowledges the financial support of the Future and Emerging Technologies (FET) programme within the Seventh Framework Programme for Research of the European Commission, under FET grant number 611733.

References

Jacob Andreas and Dan Klein. 2014. How much do word embeddings encode about syntax? In *Proceedings of the 52nd Annual Meeting of the Association for Computational Linguistics (Volume 2: Short Papers)*, pages 822–827, Baltimore, Maryland, June. Association for Computational Linguistics.

Marco Baroni and Roberto Zamparelli. 2010. Nouns are vectors, adjectives are matrices: Representing adjective-noun constructions in semantic space. In *Proceedings of the 2010 Conference on Empirical Methods in Natural Language Processing*, EMNLP '10, pages 1183–1193, Stroudsburg, PA, USA. Association for Computational Linguistics.

Marco Baroni, Raffaela Bernardi, and Roberto Zamparelli. 2014. Frege in space: A program of compositional distributional semantics. *LiLT (Linguistic Issues in Language Technology)*, 9.

Joan Bresnan, Anna Cueni, Tatiana Nikitina, and R Harald Baayen. 2007. Predicting the dative alternation. pages 69–94. Royal Netherlands Academy of Arts and Sciences, Amsterdam.

Elia Bruni, Gemma Boleda, Marco Baroni, and Nam-Khanh Tran. 2012. Distributional semantics in technicolor. In *Proceedings of the 50th Annual Meeting of the Association for Computational Linguistics: Long Papers - Volume 1*, ACL '12, pages 136–145, Stroudsburg, PA, USA. Association for Computational Linguistics.

Nancy C Chang, Joachim De Beule, and Vanessa Micelli. 2012. Computational Construction Grammar: Comparing ECG and FCG. In Luc Steels, editor, *Computational Issues in Fluid Construction Grammar*, pages 259–288. Springer Verlag, Berlin.

Bob Coecke, Mehrnoosh Sadrzadeh, and Stephen Clark. 2010. Mathematical foundations for a compositional distributional model of meaning. *CoRR*, abs/1003.4394.

Greville G Corbett and Norman M Fraser. 1993. *Heads in grammatical theory*. Cambridge University Press.

Ido Dagan, Shaul Marcus, and Shaul Markovitch. 1993. Contextual word similarity and estimation from sparse data. In *Proceedings of the 31st Annual Meeting on Association for Computational Linguistics*, ACL '93, pages 164–171, Stroudsburg, PA, USA. Association for Computational Linguistics.

Georgiana Dinu and Mirella Lapata. 2010. Measuring distributional similarity in context. In *Proceedings of the 2010 Conference on Empirical Methods in Natural Language Processing*, EMNLP '10, pages 1162–1172, Stroudsburg, PA, USA. Association for Computational Linguistics.

Samuel Fillenbaum and Amnon Rapoport. 1974. Verbs of judging, judged: A case study. *Journal of Verbal Learning and Verbal Behavior*, 13(1):54 – 62.

Lev Finkelstein, Evgeniy Gabrilovich, Yossi Matias, Ehud Rivlin, Zach Solan, Gadi Wolfman, and Eytan Ruppin. 2002. Placing search in context: The concept revisited. *ACM Trans. Inf. Syst.*, 20(1):116–131, January.

John R. Firth. 1957. A Synopsis of Linguistic Theory, 1930-1955. *Studies in Linguistic Analysis*, pages 1–32.

Judith Gaspers, Philipp Cimiano, Sascha S Griffiths, and Britta Wrede. 2011. An unsupervised algorithm for the induction of constructions. In *2011 IEEE International Conference on Development and Learning (ICDL)*, pages 1–6. IEEE, August.

Sascha Griffiths, Friederike Eyssel, Anja Philippsen, Christian Pietsch, and Sven Wachsmuth. 2015. Perception of Artificial Agents and Utterance Friendliness in Dialogue. In Maha Salem, Astrid Weiss, Paul Baxter, and Kerstin Dautenhahn, editors, *Proceedings of the Fourth Symposium on "New Frontiers in Human-Robot Interaction"*, pages 46 – 53, Canterbury, UK. AISB.

Ulrike Hahn. 2014. Similarity. *Wiley Interdisciplinary Reviews: Cognitive Science*, 5(3):271–280.

Zellig S. Harris, 1970. *Papers in Structural and Transformational Linguistics*, chapter Distributional Structure, pages 775–794. Springer Netherlands, Dordrecht.

Nancy M. Henley. 1969. A psychological study of the semantics of animal terms. *Journal of Verbal Learning and Verbal Behavior*, 8(2):176 – 184.

Karl Moritz Hermann and Phil Blunsom. 2013. The role of syntax in vector space models of compositional semantics. In *Proceedings of the 51st Annual Meeting of the Association for Computational Linguistics (Volume 1: Long Papers)*, pages 894–904, Sofia, Bulgaria, August. Association for Computational Linguistics.

Felix Hill, Roi Reichart, and Anna Korhonen. 2015. Simlex-999: Evaluating semantic models with genuine similarity estimation. *Comput. Linguist.*, 41(4):665–695, December.

Felix Hill, Kyunghyun Cho, and Anna Korhonen. 2016. Learning distributed representations of sentences from unlabelled data. *CoRR*, abs/1602.03483.

Ray Jackendoff and Steven Pinker. 2005. The nature of the language faculty and its implications for evolution of language (Reply to Fitch, Hauser, and Chomsky). *Cognition*, 97(2):211–225.

Ray Jackendoff. 2012. Language. In Keith Frankish and William Ramsey, editors, *The Cambridge Handbook of Cognitive Science*. Cambridge University Press, Cambridge, MA.

Nal Kalchbrenner and Phil Blunsom. 2013. Recurrent convolutional neural networks for discourse compositionality. In *Proceedings of the Workshop on Continuous Vector Space Models and their Compositionality*, pages 119–126, Sofia, Bulgaria, August. Association for Computational Linguistics.

Emmanuel Keuleers and David A. Balota. 2015. Megastudies, crowdsourcing, and large datasets in psycholinguistics: An overview of recent developments. *The Quarterly Journal of Experimental Psychology*, 68(8):1457–1468. PMID: 25975773.

Walter Kintsch. 2001. Predication. *Cognitive Science*, 25(2):173 – 202.

Arthur B. Markman and Dedre Gentner. 1991. Commonalities, differences and the alignment of conceptual frames during similarity judgments. In *Proceedings of the 13th Annual Meeting of the Cognitive Science Society, USA*, pages 287–292.

Arthur B. Markman and Dedre Gentner. 1996. Commonalities and differences in similarity comparisons. *Memory & Cognition*, 24(2):235–249.

Ken McRae, George S. Cree, Mark S. Seidenberg, and Chris McNorgan. 2005. Semantic feature production norms for a large set of living and nonliving things. *Behavior Research Methods*, 37(4):547–559.

Douglas L Medin, Robert L Goldstone, and Dedre Gentner. 1993. Respects for similarity. *Psychological review*, 100(2):254.

Dmitrijs Milajevs and Matthew Purver. 2014. Investigating the contribution of distributional semantic information for dialogue act classification. In *Proceedings of the 2nd Workshop on Continuous Vector Space Models and their Compositionality (CVSC)*, pages 40–47, Gothenburg, Sweden, April. Association for Computational Linguistics.

Dmitrijs Milajevs, Mehrnoosh Sadrzadeh, and Thomas Roelleke. 2015. IR Meets NLP: On the Semantic Similarity Between Subject-Verb-Object Phrases. In *Proceedings of the 2015 International Conference on Theory of Information Retrieval*, ICTIR '15, pages 231–240, New York, NY, USA. ACM.

George A. Miller. 1995. Wordnet: A lexical database for english. *Commun. ACM*, 38(11):39–41, November.

Jeff Mitchell and Mirella Lapata. 2008. Vector-based models of semantic composition. In *Proceedings of ACL-08: HLT*, pages 236–244, Columbus, Ohio, June. Association for Computational Linguistics.

Jeff Mitchell and Mirella Lapata. 2010. Composition in distributional models of semantics. *Cognitive Science*, 34(8):1388–1429.

Samuel Ritter, Cotie Long, Denis Paperno, Marco Baroni, Matthew Botvinick, and Adele Goldberg. 2015. Leveraging preposition ambiguity to assess compositional distributional models of semantics. In *Proceedings of the Fourth Joint Conference on Lexical and Computational Semantics*, pages 199–204, Denver, Colorado, June. Association for Computational Linguistics.

Herbert Rubenstein and John B. Goodenough. 1965. Contextual correlates of synonymy. *Commun. ACM*, 8(10):627–633, October.

G. Salton, A. Wong, and C. S. Yang. 1975. A vector space model for automatic indexing. *Commun. ACM*, 18(11):613–620, November.

Hinrich Schütze. 1998. Automatic word sense discrimination. *Comput. Linguist.*, 24(1):97–123, March.

Diarmuid Ó Séaghdha and Anna Korhonen. 2011. Probabilistic models of similarity in syntactic context. In *Proceedings of the Conference on Empirical Methods in Natural Language Processing*, EMNLP '11, pages 1047–1057, Stroudsburg, PA, USA. Association for Computational Linguistics.

Richard Socher, Brody Huval, Christopher D. Manning, and Andrew Y. Ng. 2012. Semantic compositionality through recursive matrix-vector spaces. In *Proceedings of the 2012 Joint Conference on Empirical Methods in Natural Language Processing and Computational Natural Language Learning*, EMNLP-CoNLL '12, pages 1201–1211, Stroudsburg, PA, USA. Association for Computational Linguistics.

Luc Steels. 2008. The symbol grounding problem has been solved, so what's next? In Manuel de Vega, Arthur M Glenberg, and Arthur C Graesser, editors, *Symbols and Embodiment: Debates on Meaning and Cognition*, pages 223–244. Oxford University Press, Oxford.

Luc Steels. 2010. Can Evolutionary Linguistics Become a Science? *Journal for Evolutionary Linguistics*, 1(1).

Stefan Thater, Hagen Fürstenau, and Manfred Pinkal. 2011. Word meaning in context: A simple and effective vector model. In *Proceedings of 5th International Joint Conference on Natural Language Processing*, pages 1134–1143, Chiang Mai, Thailand, November. Asian Federation of Natural Language Processing.

Michael Tomasello. 1998. The return of constructions. *Journal of Child Language*, 25(02):431–442.

Michael Tomasello. 2009. *The cultural origins of human cognition*. Harvard University Press, Cambridge, MA.

John C Turner, Michael A Hogg, Penelope J Oakes, Stephen D Reicher, and Margaret S Wetherell. 1987. *Rediscovering the social group: A self-categorization theory*. Basil Blackwell.

Peter D Turney. 2012. Domain and function: A dual-space model of semantic relations and compositions. *Journal of Artificial Intelligence Research*, pages 533–585.

Amos Tversky and J. Wesley Hutchinson. 1986. Nearest neighbor analysis of psychological spaces. *Psychological Review*, 93(1):3 – 22.

Noortje Venhuizen, Valerio Basile, Kilian Evang, and Johan Bos. 2013. Gamification for word sense labeling. In *Proceedings of the 10th International Conference on Computational Semantics (IWCS 2013) – Short Papers*, pages 397–403, Potsdam, Germany.

Lyndon White, Roberto Togneri, Wei Liu, and Mohammed Bennamoun. 2015. How well sentence embeddings capture meaning. In *Proceedings of the 20th Australasian Document Computing Symposium*, ADCS '15, pages 9:1–9:8, New York, NY, USA. ACM.

John Wieting, Mohit Bansal, Kevin Gimpel, and Karen Livescu. 2015. From paraphrase database to compositional paraphrase model and back. *arXiv preprint arXiv:1506.03487*.

Terry Winograd. 1983. *Language as a cognitive process (Vol. 1): Syntax*. Addison-Wesley, Reading, MA.

Probing for semantic evidence of composition by means of simple classification tasks

Allyson Ettinger[1], Ahmed Elgohary[2], Philip Resnik[1,3]
[1]Linguistics, [2]Computer Science, [3]Institute for Advanced Computer Studies
University of Maryland, College Park, MD
{aetting, resnik}@umd.edu, elgohary@cs.umd.edu

Abstract

We propose a diagnostic method for probing specific information captured in vector representations of sentence meaning, via simple classification tasks with strategically constructed sentence sets. We identify some key types of semantic information that we might expect to be captured in sentence composition, and illustrate example classification tasks for targeting this information.

1 Introduction

Sentence-level meaning representations, when formed from word-level representations, require a process of composition. Central to evaluation of sentence-level vector representations, then, is evaluating how effectively a model has executed this composition process.

In assessing composition, we must first answer the question of what it means to do composition well. On one hand, we might define effective composition as production of sentence representations that allow for high performance on a task of interest (Kiros et al., 2015; Tai et al., 2015; Wieting et al., 2015; Iyyer et al., 2015). A limitation of such an approach is that it is likely to produce overfitting to the characteristics of the particular task.

Alternatively, we might define effective composition as generation of a meaning representation that makes available all of the information that we would expect to be extractable from the meaning of the input sentence. For instance, in a representation of the sentence "The dog didn't bark, but chased the cat", we would expect to be able to extract the information that there is an event of chasing, that a dog is doing the chasing and a cat is being chased, and that there is no barking event (though there is a semantic relation between *dog*

and *bark*, albeit modified by negation, which we likely want to be able to extract as well). A model able to produce meaning representations that allow for extraction of these kinds of key semantic characteristics—semantic roles, event information, operator scope, etc—should be much more generalizable across applications, rather than targeting any single application at the cost of others.

With this in mind, we propose here a linguistically-motivated but computationally straightforward diagnostic method, intended to provide a targeted means of assessing the specific semantic information that is being captured in sentence representations. We propose to accomplish this by constructing sentence datasets controlled and annotated as precisely as possible for their linguistic characteristics, and directly testing for extractability of semantic information by testing classification accuracy in tasks defined by the corresponding linguistic characteristics. We present the results of preliminary experiments as proof-of-concept.

2 Existing approaches

The SICK entailment dataset (Marelli et al., 2014) is a strong example of a task-based evaluation metric, constructed with a mind to systematic incorporation of linguistic phenomena relevant to composition. SICK is one of the most commonly used benchmark tasks for evaluating composition models (Kiros et al., 2015; Tai et al., 2015; Wieting et al., 2015). However, conclusions that we can draw from this dataset are limited for a couple of reasons. First, certain cues in this dataset allow for strong performance without composition (for example, as Bentivogli et al. (2016) point out, 86.4% of sentence pairs labeled as CONTRADICTION can be identified simply by detecting the presence of negation; a similar obser-

134

vation is made by Lai and Hockenmaier (2014)), which means that we cannot draw firm composition conclusions from performance on this task. Furthermore, if we want to examine the extent to which specific types of linguistic information are captured, SICK is limited in two senses. First, SICK sentences are annotated for transformations performed between sentences, but these annotations lack coverage of many linguistic characteristics important to composition (e.g., semantic roles). Second, even within annotated transformation categories, distributions over entailment labels are highly skewed (e.g., 98.9% of the entailment labels under the "add modifier" transformation are ENTAILMENT), making it difficult to test phenomenon- or transformation-specific classification performance.

In an alternative approach, Li et al. (2015) use visualization techniques to better examine the particular aspects of compositionality captured by their models. They consider recurrent neural network composition models trained entirely for one of two tasks—sentiment analysis and language modeling—and employ dimensionality reduction to visualize sentiment neighborhood relationships between words or phrases before and after applying modification, negation, and clause composition. They also visualize the saliency of individual tokens with respect to the prediction decision made for each of their tasks.

In comparison, our proposal aims to provide generic (task-independent) evaluation and analysis methods that directly quantify the extractability of specific linguistic information that a composition model should be expected to capture. Our proposed evaluation approach follows a similar rationale to that of the diagnostic test suite TSNLP (Balkan et al., 1994) designed for evaluating parsers on a per-phenomenon basis. As highlighted by Scarlett and Szpakowicz (2000) the systematic fine-grained evaluation of TSNLP enables precise pinpointing of parsers' limitations, while ensuring broad coverage and controlled evaluation of various linguistic phenomena and syntactic structures. Our proposal aims at initiating work on developing similar test suites for evaluating semantic composition models.

3 Probing for semantic information with targeted classification tasks

The reasoning of our method is as follows: if we take a variety of sentences—each represented by a composed vector—and introduce a classification scheme requiring identification of a particular type of semantic information for accurate sentence classification, then by testing accuracy on this task, we can assess whether the composed representations give access to the information in question. This method resembles that used for decoding human brain activation patterns in cognitive neuroscience studies of language understanding (Frankland and Greene, 2015), as well as work in NLP that has previously made use of classification accuracy for assessing information captured in vector representations (Gupta et al., 2015).

In order to have maximum confidence in our interpretation of performance in these tasks, our sentences must have sufficient diversity to ensure that there are no consistently correlating cues that would allow for strong performance without capturing the relevant compositional information. Relatedly, we want to ensure that the classification tasks cannot be solved by memorization (rather than actual composition) of phrases.

3.1 Dataset construction

The goal in constructing the sentence dataset is to capture a wide variety of syntactic structures and configurations, so as to reflect as accurately as possible the diversity of sentences that systems will need to handle in naturally-occurring text—while maintaining access to detailed labeling of as many relevant linguistic components of our data as possible. Ideally, we want a dataset with enough variation and annotation to allow us to draw data for all of our desired classification tasks from this single dataset.

For our illustrations here, we restrict our structural variation to that available from active/passive alternations, use of relative clauses at various syntactic locations, and use of negation at various syntactic locations. This allows us to demonstrate decent structural variety without distracting from illustration of the semantic characteristics of interest. Many more components can be added to increase complexity and variation, and to make sentences better reflect natural text. More detailed discussion of considerations for construction of the actual dataset is given in Section 5.

3.2 Semantic characteristics

There are many types of semantic information that we might probe for with this method. For our purposes here, we are going to focus on two basic types, which are understood in linguistics to be fundamental components of meaning, and which have clear ties to common downstream applications: semantic role and scope.

The importance of semantic role information is well-recognized both in linguistics and in NLP—for the latter in the form of tasks such as abstract meaning representation (AMR) (Banarescu et al., 2013). Similarly, the concept of scope is critical to many key linguistic phenomena, including negation—the importance of which is widely acknowledged in NLP, in particular for applications such as sentiment analysis (Blunsom et al., 2013; Iyyer et al., 2015). Both of these information types are of course critical to computing entailment.

3.3 Example classification tasks

Once we have identified semantic information of interest, we can design classification tasks to target this information. We illustrate with two examples.

Semantic role　If a sentence representation has captured semantic roles, a reasonable expectation would be extractability of the entity-event relations contained in the sentence meaning. So, for instance, we might choose *professor* as our entity, *recommend* as our event, and AGENT as our relation—and label sentences as positive if they contain *professor* in the AGENT relation with the verb *recommend*. Negative sentences for this task could in theory be any sentence lacking this relation—but it will be most informative to use negative examples containing the relevant lexical items (*professor*, *recommend*) without the relation of interest, so that purely lexical cues cannot provide an alternative classification heuristic.

Examples illustrating such a setup can be seen in Table 1. In this table we have included a sample of possible sentences, varying only by active/passive alternation and placement of relative clauses, and holding lexical content fairly constant. The verb *recommend* and its agent have been bolded for the sake of clarity.

An important characteristic of the sentences in Table 1 is their use of long-distance dependencies, which cause cues based on linear order and word adjacency to be potentially misleading. Notice, for instance, that sentence 5 of the positive label column contains the string *the school recommended*, though *school* is not the agent of *recommended*—rather, the agent of *recommended* is located at the beginning of the sentence. We believe that incorporation of such long-distance dependencies is critical for assessing whether systems are accurately capturing semantic roles across a range of naturally-occurring sentence structures (Rimell et al., 2009; Bender et al., 2011).

This example task can obviously be extended to other relations and other entities/events as desired, with training and test data adjusted accordingly. We will remain agnostic here as to the optimal method of selecting relations and entities/events for classification tasks; in all likelihood, it will be ideal to choose and test several different combinations, and obtain an average accuracy score. Note that if we structure our task as we have suggested here—training and testing only on sentences containing certain selected lexical items—then the number of examples at our disposal (both positive and negative) will be dependent in large part on the number of syntactic structures covered in the dataset. This emphasizes again the importance of incorporating broad structural diversity in the dataset construction.

Negation scope　Negation presents somewhat of a challenge for evaluation. How can we assess whether a representation captures negation properly, without making the task as simple as detecting that negation is present in the sentence?

One solution that we propose is to incorporate negation at various levels of syntactic structure (corresponding to different negation scopes), which allows us to change sentence meaning while holding lexical content relatively constant. One way that we might then assess the negation information accessible from the representation would be to adapt our classification task to focus not on a semantic role relation *per se*, but rather on the event described by the sentence meaning. For instance, we might design a task in which sentences are labeled as positive if they describe an event in which a professor performs an act of recommending, and negative otherwise.

The labeling for several sentences under this as well as the previous classification scheme are given in Table 2. In the first sentence, when negation falls in the relative clause (*that did not like the school*)—and therefore has scope only over *like the school*—*professor* is the agent of *recommend*,

Positive label	Negative label
the professor recommended the student	**the student recommended** the professor
the administrator was **recommended** by **the professor**	the professor was **recommended** by **the administrator**
the school hired the researcher that **the professor recommended**	the school hired the professor that **the researcher recommended**
the school hired **the professor** that **recommended** the researcher	the school hired the professor that was **recommended** by **the researcher**
the professor that liked the school **recommended** the researcher	**the school** that hired the professor **recommended** the researcher

Table 1: Labeled data for professor-as-agent-of-recommend task (*recommend* verb and its actual agent have been bolded).

and the professor entity does perform an act of recommending. In the second sentence, however, negation has scope over *recommend*, resulting in a meaning in which the professor, despite being agent of *recommend*, is not involved in performing a recommendation. By incorporating negation in this way, we allow for a task that assesses whether the effect of negation is being applied to the correct component of the sentence meaning.

4 Preliminary experiments

As proof-of-concept, we have conducted some preliminary experiments to test that this method yields results patterning in the expected direction on tasks for which we have clear predictions about whether a type of information could be captured.

Experiments Settings

We compared three sentence embedding methods: 1) Averaging GloVe vectors (Pennington et al., 2014), 2) Paraphrastic word averaging embeddings (Paragram) trained with a compositional objective (Wieting et al., 2015). and 3) Skip-Thought embeddings (ST) (Kiros et al., 2015).[1] For each task, we used a logistic regression classifier with train/test sizes of 1000/500.[2] The classification accuracies are summarized in Table 4.

We used three classification tasks for preliminary testing. First, before testing actual indicators of composition, as a sanity check we tested whether classifiers could be trained to recognize the simple presence of a given lexical item, specifically *school*. As expected, we see that all three models are able to perform this task with 100% accuracy, suggesting that this information is well-captured and easily accessible. As an extension of this sanity check, we also trained classifiers to

recognize sentences containing a token in the category of "human". To test for generalization across the category, we ensured that no human nouns appearing in the test set were included in training sentences. All three models reach a high classification performance on this task, though Paragram lags behind slightly.

Finally, we did a preliminary experiment pertaining to an actual indicator of composition: semantic role. We constructed a simple dataset with structural variation stemming only from active/passive alternation, and tested whether models could differentiate sentences with *school* appearing in an agent role from sentences with *school* appearing as a patient. All training and test sentences contained the lexical item "school", with both active and passive sentences selected randomly from the full dataset for inclusion in training and test sets. Note that with sentences of this level of simplicity, models can plausibly use fairly simple order heuristics to solve the classification task, so a model that retains order information (in this case, only ST) should have a good chance of performing well. Indeed, we see that ST reaches a high level of performance, while the two averaging-based models never exceed chance-level performance.

5 Discussion

We have proposed a diagnostic method for directly targeting and assessing specific types of semantic information in composed sentence representations, guided by considerations of the linguistic information that one might reasonably expect to be extractable from properly composed sentence meaning representations.

Construction of the real dataset to meet all of our desired criteria promises to be a non-trivial task, but we expect it to be a reasonable one. A carefully-engineered context-free-grammar-based

---

[1]We used the pretrained models provided by the authors. GloVe and Paragram embeddings are of size 300 while Skip-Thought embeddings are of size 2400.

[2]We tuned each classifier with 5-fold cross validation.

sentence	prof-ag-of-rec	prof-recommends
the professor that *did not* like the school **recommended** the researcher	TRUE	TRUE
the professor that liked the school *did not* **recommend** the researcher	TRUE	FALSE
the school that liked the professor **recommended** the researcher	FALSE	FALSE

Table 2: Sentence labeling for two classification tasks: "contains *professor* as AGENT of *recommend*" (column 2), and "sentence meaning involves professor performing act of recommending" (column 3).

Task	GloVe	Paragram	ST
Has-school	100.0	100.0	100.0
Has-human	99.9	90.5	99.0
School-as-agent	47.98	48.57	91.15

Table 3: Percentage correct on has-school, has-human, and has-school-as-agent tasks.

generative process should allow us to cover a good deal of ground with respect to syntactic variation as well as annotation of linguistic characteristics. Human involvement in annotation should become necessary only if we desire annotation of linguistic characteristics that do not follow deterministically from syntactic properties.

One example of such a characteristic, which merits discussion of its own, is sentence plausibility. A clear limitation of automated sentence generation in general is the inability to control for plausibility of the generated sentences. We acknowledge this limitation, but would argue that for the purposes of evaluating composition, the presence of implausible sentences is not only acceptable—it is possibly advantageous. It is acceptable for the simple reason that composition seems to operate independently of plausibility: consider, for instance, a sentence such as *blue giraffes interrogate the apple*, which we are able to compose to extract a meaning from, despite its nonsensical nature. Arguments along this vein have been made in linguistics since Chomsky (1957) illustrated (with the now-famous example *colorless green ideas sleep furiously*) that sentences can be grammatical—structurally interpretable—without having a sensible meaning.

As for the potential advantage, the presence of implausible sentences in our dataset may be desirable for the following reason: in evaluating whether a system is able to perform composition, we are in fact interested in whether it is able to compose completely novel phrases. To evaluate this capacity accurately, we will want to assess systems' composition performance on phrases that they have never encountered. Elgohary and Carpuat (2016) meet this need by dis-

carding all training sentences that include any observed bigrams in their evaluation sentences. With implausible sentences, we can substantially reduce the likelihood that systems will have been trained on the phrases encountered during the classification evaluation—while remaining agnostic as to the particulars of those systems' training data. It would be useful, in this case, to have annotation of the plausibility levels of our sentences, in order to ascertain whether performance is in fact aided by the presence of phrases that may reasonably have occurred during composition training. Possible approaches to estimating plausibility without human annotation include using n-gram statistics on simple argument/predicate combinations (Rashkin et al., 2016) or making use of selectional preference modeling (Resnik, 1996; Erk, 2007; Séaghdha, 2010).

A final note: learning low-dimensional vector representations for sentences is bound to require a trade-off between the coverage of encoded information and the accessibility of encoded information—some semantic characteristics may be easily extractable at the cost of others. We have not, in this proposal, covered all semantic characteristics of interest, but it will ultimately be valuable to develop a broad-coverage suite of classification tasks for relevant information types, to obtain an assessment that is both fine-grained and comprehensive. This kind of holistic assessment will be useful for determining appropriate models for particular tasks, and for determining directions for model improvement.

Acknowledgments

This work was supported in part by an NSF Graduate Research Fellowship under Grant No. DGE 1322106. Any opinions, findings, and conclusions or recommendations expressed are those of the authors and do not necessarily reflect the views of the NSF. This work benefited from the helpful comments of two anonymous reviewers, and from discussions with Marine Carpuat, Alexander Williams and Hal Daumé III.

References

Lorna Balkan, Doug Arnold, and Siety Meijer. 1994. Test suites for natural language processing. *Translating and the Computer*, pages 51–51.

Laura Banarescu, Claire Bonial, Shu Cai, Madalina Georgescu, Kira Griffitt, Ulf Hermjakob, Kevin Knight, Philipp Koehn, Martha Palmer, and Nathan Schneider. 2013. Abstract meaning representation for sembanking. In *Proceedings of the 7th Linguistic Annotation Workshop and Interoperability with Discourse*, pages 178–186.

Emily M Bender, Dan Flickinger, Stephan Oepen, and Yi Zhang. 2011. Parser evaluation over local and non-local deep dependencies in a large corpus. In *Proceedings of the Conference on Empirical Methods in Natural Language Processing*, pages 397–408.

Luisa Bentivogli, Raffaella Bernardi, Marco Marelli, Stefano Menini, Marco Baroni, and Roberto Zamparelli. 2016. SICK through the SemEval glasses. lesson learned from the evaluation of compositional distributional semantic models on full sentences through semantic relatedness and textual entailment. *Language Resources and Evaluation*, pages 1–30.

Phil Blunsom, Edward Grefenstette, and Karl Moritz Hermann. 2013. "not not bad" is not "bad": A distributional account of negation. In *Proceedings of the 2013 Workshop on Continuous Vector Space Models and their Compositionality*.

Noam Chomsky. 1957. *Syntactic structures*. Mouton & Co.

Ahmed Elgohary and Marine Carpuat. 2016. Learning monolingual compositional representations via bilingual supervision. In *Proceedings of the Annual Meeting of the Association for Computational Linguistics*.

Katrin Erk. 2007. A simple, similarity-based model for selectional preferences. In *Proceedings of the Annual Meeting of the Association for Computational Linguistics*, pages 216–223.

Steven M Frankland and Joshua D Greene. 2015. An architecture for encoding sentence meaning in left mid-superior temporal cortex. *Proceedings of the National Academy of Sciences*, 112(37):11732–11737.

Abhijeet Gupta, Gemma Boleda, Marco Baroni, and Sebastian Padó. 2015. Distributional vectors encode referential attributes. In *Proceedingsof the Conference on Empirical Methods in Natural Language Processing*.

Mohit Iyyer, Varun Manjunatha, Jordan Boyd-Graber, and Hal Daumé III. 2015. Deep unordered composition rivals syntactic methods for text classification. In *Proceedings of the 53rd Annual Meeting of the Association for Computational Linguistics and the 7th International Joint Conference on Natural Language Processing*, pages 1681–1691.

Ryan Kiros, Yukun Zhu, Ruslan R Salakhutdinov, Richard Zemel, Raquel Urtasun, Antonio Torralba, and Sanja Fidler. 2015. Skip-thought vectors. In *Advances in Neural Information Processing Systems*, pages 3276–3284.

Alice Lai and Julia Hockenmaier. 2014. Illinois-lh: A denotational and distributional approach to semantics. *Proc. SemEval*.

Jiwei Li, Xinlei Chen, Eduard Hovy, and Dan Jurafsky. 2015. Visualizing and understanding neural models in nlp. *arXiv preprint arXiv:1506.01066*.

Marco Marelli, Stefano Menini, Marco Baroni, Luisa Bentivogli, Raffaella Bernardi, and Roberto Zamparelli. 2014. A SICK cure for the evaluation of compositional distributional semantic models. In *Language Resources and Evaluation*, pages 216–223.

Jeffrey Pennington, Richard Socher, and Christopher D Manning. 2014. Glove: Global vectors for word representation. In *EMNLP*, volume 14, pages 1532–1543.

Hannah Rashkin, Sameer Singh, and Yejin Choi. 2016. Connotation frames: A data-driven investigation. In *Proceedings of the Annual Meeting of the Association for Computational Linguistics*.

Philip Resnik. 1996. Selectional constraints: An information-theoretic model and its computational realization. *Cognition*, 61(1):127–159.

Laura Rimell, Stephen Clark, and Mark Steedman. 2009. Unbounded dependency recovery for parser evaluation. In *Proceedings of the Conference on Empirical Methods in Natural Language Processing*, pages 813–821.

Elizabeth Scarlett and Stan Szpakowicz. 2000. The power of the tsnlp: lessons from a diagnostic evaluation of a broad-coverage parser. In *Advances in Artificial Intelligence*, pages 138–150. Springer.

Diarmuid O Séaghdha. 2010. Latent variable models of selectional preference. In *Proceedings of the Annual Meeting of the Association for Computational Linguistics*, pages 435–444.

Kai Sheng Tai, Richard Socher, and Christopher D Manning. 2015. Improved semantic representations from tree-structured long short-term memory networks. In *Proceedings of the Annual Meeting of the Association for Computational Linguistics*.

John Wieting, Mohit Bansal, Kevin Gimpel, and Karen Livescu. 2015. Towards universal paraphrastic sentence embeddings. *arXiv preprint arXiv:1511.08198*.

SLEDDED: A Proposed Dataset of Event Descriptions for Evaluating Phrase Representations

Laura Rimell
Computer Laboratory
University of Cambridge
laura.rimell@cl.cam.ac.uk

Eva Maria Vecchi
Computer Laboratory
University of Cambridge
eva.vecchi@cl.cam.ac.uk

Abstract

Measuring the semantic relatedness of phrase pairs is important for evaluating compositional distributional semantic representations. Many existing phrase relatedness datasets are limited to either lexical or syntactic alternations between phrase pairs, which limits the power of the evaluation. We propose SLEDDED (Syntactically and LExically Divergent Dataset of Event Descriptions), a dataset of event descriptions in which related phrase pairs are designed to exhibit minimal lexical and syntactic overlap; for example, *a decisive victory — won the match clearly*. We also propose a subset of the data aimed at distinguishing event descriptions from related but dissimilar phrases; for example, *vowing to fight to the death — a new training regime for soldiers*, which serves as a proxy for the tasks of narrative generation, event sequencing, and summarization. We describe a method for extracting candidate pairs from a corpus based on occurrences of event nouns (e.g. *war*) and a two-step annotation process consisting of expert annotation followed by crowdsourcing. We present examples from a pilot of the expert annotation step.

1 Introduction

Measuring the semantic relatedness of phrase pairs is an important means of evaluation for vector space representations, particularly in Compositional Distributional Semantics (CDS). However, existing phrase relatedness datasets are not often designed to test lexical and syntactic divergence simultaneously. On the one hand are datasets which hold syntactic structure fixed while vary-ing lexical items, e.g. the adjective-noun dataset of Mitchell and Lapata (2010) (1) and the subject-verb-object dataset of Kartsaklis and Sadrzadeh (2014) (2).

(1)   a.   *new information*
       b.   *further evidence*

(2)   a.   *programme offer support*
       b.   *service provide help*

Such datasets are useful for examination of targeted syntactic structures, especially in type-based CDS models, but fail to challenge CDS models to compose longer phrases with realistic sentence structure.

On the other hand, the datasets with the most complex and varied syntactic structures tend to exhibit a great deal of lexical overlap across the highly-related pairs, e.g. MSRPar (Dolan et al., 2004) (3) and SICK (Marelli et al., 2014b) (4).

(3)   a.   *The unions also staged a five-day strike in March that forced all but one of Yale's dining halls to close.*
       b.   *The unions also staged a five-day strike in March; strikes have preceded eight of the last 10 contracts.*

(4)   a.   *A hiker is on top of the mountain and is doing a joyful dance.*
       b.   *A hiker is on top of the mountain and is dancing.*

This phenomenon is not intentional, but a function of the data collection methodology. However, the high degree of lexical overlap makes it difficult to evaluate CDS models, since lexical overlap baselines are challenging to beat (Rus et al., 2014); and non-compositional or semi-compositional methods can perform better than fully compositional ones (Marelli et al., 2014a).

While sentence pairs with high lexical overlap may be common in some tasks – extractive sum-

Proceedings of the 1st Workshop on Evaluating Vector Space Representations for NLP, pages 140–144,
Berlin, Germany, August 12, 2016. ©2016 Association for Computational Linguistics

marization of multiple similar news stories, for example – we believe that datasets with this characteristic are not able to make clear distinctions between CDS models. We therefore propose a new dataset exhibiting both lexical and syntactic variation across related phrases.

2 Proposal

We propose SLEDDED (Syntactically and LExically Divergent Dataset of Event Descriptions), a phrase relatedness dataset in which semantically related phrase pairs are carefully curated to exhibit both syntactic and lexical divergence. Specifically, we propose to base the related pairs on *event descriptions*, where one description is centered around a *non-deverbal event noun* and its counterpart centered around a *verb*. Example noun-verb pairs are shown in Figure 1.

victory – win
ceremony – celebrate
meal – eat
war – fight

Figure 1: Example pairs of non-deverbal event nouns and counterpart verbs (idealized, not from corpus data).

Non-deverbal event nouns describe events, but in contrast to deverbal nouns such as *celebration* or *fighting*, are not morphologically derived from verbs. The use of non-deverbal event nouns ensures that related nouns and verbs cannot be trivially equated by stemming. In the proposed dataset, we aim for minimal shared lemmas in every phrase pair. Example phrase pairs are shown in Figure 2.

a decisive victory – won the match clearly
graduation ceremony – celebrated her degree
a delicious meal – ate pasta bolognese
war between neighbors – fought over borders

Figure 2: Example pairs of short phrases (idealized, not from corpus data).

Although related phrases similar to those described here can be found within many large paraphrase datasets, they are not readily separable from other kinds of related pairs. We believe that more focused datasets like SLEDDED can provide a good complement to larger, less controlled paraphrase datasets.

SLEDDED is aimed primarily at providing a new challenge for CDS. We expect vector addition to be a challenging baseline, as it has been for many other tasks, since simple addition captures word relatedness without regard to syntax. Composition with Recursive Neural Networks (RNNs) may also do well. We consider the dataset to be a particular challenge for type-based (e.g. tensors) and syntax-based (e.g. tree kernels) composition methods. We also propose a subset of confounders that require a distinction between relatedness and similarity for events, that can serve as a proxy for tasks such as narrative generation or event sequencing, and may be challenging for all models; see Section 3.4.

3 Methods

In this section we describe our proposed method for building SLEDDED, and present examples from a pilot involving corpus data extraction and expert annotation.

We choose to extract target phrases from a corpus rather than elicit phrases by crowdsourcing, since we expect the notion of event nouns to be confusing for non-experts, and also expect a wider range of realistic examples from corpus data. We considered several existing methods for automatic extraction of paraphrases that are lexically or syntactically divergent; however, none are exactly suited for our proposed dataset. Bunescu and Mooney (2007) use named entity pairs as anchors for diverse expressions of semantic relations, e.g. *Pfizer buys Rinat, Pfizer paid several hundred million dollars for Rinat, Pfizer Expands With Acquisition of Rinat*. We do not wish to use named entity anchors and this format limits the dataset to binary relations. Xu et al. (2014) use multi-instance learning to jointly model word and sentence relatedness in Twitter data, but require a large corpus of crowdsourced sentence similarity judgements. We do not want to invest in large numbers of sentence-level judgements when it is not certain how many word alignments involving event nouns could be subsequently learned.

Instead, we choose to capitalize on the fact that event nouns can co-refer with verbal descriptions of events, either anaphorically (backwards referring) or cataphorically (forwards referring). An example would be *The two countries **fought** savagely over their borders. The **war** lasted for years.* Identifying such pairs falls within the task of event coreference resolution (Bagga and Baldwin, 1999; Chen and Ji, 2009; Bejan and Harabagiu, 2014), but focuses on cases where one event mention is a noun. Moreover, we do not care about optimal clusterings of event mentions, but rather a set of candidates for related nouns and verbs, which can be manually filtered to create the dataset. For our pilot, we used a simple supervised method to identify event nouns, following Bel et al. (2010), and investigated the adjacent sentences for co-referring verbs.

3.1 Event Nouns

Our goal was a wide variety of event nouns covering various topics. We began with a small seed set of 73 positives (event nouns) and 94 negatives (non-event nouns), manually curated by Bel et al. (2010). We expanded the seed set using FrameNet (Fillmore and Baker, 2010), labeling nouns belonging to the *activity* or *process* classes as positive, and nouns belonging to the *entity* or *locale* classes as negative. This combination resulted in 1028 seed nouns, half positive and half negative (after downsampling the negatives).

We then bootstrapped additional nouns using the NYT portion of the Gigaword Corpus (Graff et al., 2005) by training an SVM on our seed set, using 126 syntactic features. This approach is similar to that of Bel et al. (2010), who trained a decision tree classifier with a dozen features. We made use of linguistic features previously found useful for identifying non-deverbal event nouns (Resnik and Bel, 2009; Bel et al., 2010), including the ability to occur as the subject of aspectual verbs (*the ceremony* **lasted** *for an hour*, *the meal* **began** *at 7:00*) and the object of temporal prepositions (**during** *the war*). The SVM achieved 78% accuracy using cross-validation on the seed set.

We used the SVM to classify 500 frequent nouns from NYT Gigaword that were not in our seed set. Of these, 286 were predicted as negative and 214 positive; we manually edited the positives down to 185. The resulting 699 positives were used for corpus extraction, and the 800 negatives will be used for confounders.

3.2 Corpus Extraction

After preprocessing NYT Gigaword, sentences containing positive event nouns were extracted. Expert annotators will see the extracted target sentences in random order, and each target sentence will be accompanied by its immediately preceding and following sentences, which will be inspected for co-referring verbs.

3.3 Two-Stage Annotation

Positive examples are still sparse among our candidate pairs. This leads us to propose a two-stage annotation process where the initial candidates are filtered by experts, after which the relatedness ratings are obtained by crowdsourcing. The goal of the first phase is for experts to choose phrase pairs that exhibit lexical and syntactic divergence, and appear to have moderate to high relatedness. The experts also shorten full sentences to phrases of at most 10 words.

Expert annotation can be a bottleneck for dataset creation. However, in cases where the source data is unbalanced, expert annotation can actually increase the potential size of the dataset, since funds are not wasted on crowdsourcing to rule out a large number of negatives. As mentioned above, the initial expert filtering also ensures high quality examples despite the potentially difficult concept of non-deverbal event nouns.

The authors have performed a short pilot of the expert annotation stage. In a couple of hours we produced approximately fifty positive examples, suggesting that in less than a month of part-time expert annotation we could produce a dataset of a few thousand pairs (including confounders; see Section 3.4) to proceed to crowdsourcing. The annotation guidelines developed for this pilot are shown in Figure 3. On a sample of the data we obtained inter-annotator agreement of 0.89, reported as $2P(A) - 1$ for unbalanced data (Eugenio and Glass, 2004). Table 1 provides a sample of phrase pairs that the annotators considered moderately or highly related.

3.4 Confounders

We propose two sets of confounders. The first set consists of standard low-relatedness pairs, created by shuffling related pairs, by pairing event nouns with unrelated adjacent sentences (the unrelated pairs from the expert annotation stage), and by pairing phrases centered around non-event nouns with adjacent sentences. Non-event noun phrases can be extracted from the corpus using our negatives list from (Bel et al., 2010), FrameNet, and bootstrapping. The data passed along for crowdsourcing will consist of the positives from expert annotation along with an equal number of confounders.

- Target sentence S_{targ} contains an event noun or noun phrase.
- Mark as a positive pair if S_{prev} or S_{next} contains a verb or verb phrase which is related in meaning to the noun or noun phrase in S_{targ}.
- Short phrases around the noun or verb can be considered in the relatedness decision.
  - Noun phrase can include an adjectival or nominal modifier, or short PP, which identifies the relevant sense (e.g. *welfare program* vs. *TV program*).
  - Event noun must be the head of the noun phrase, e.g. *earned income*, not *income tax*.
  - Verb phrase can include an object, other argument, or short PP, which identifies the relevant sense (e.g. *provide aid*).
- The noun (phrase) and verb (phrase) must be topically similar, but do not need to be paraphrases (e.g. *disease/diagnosis, disease/donate organ, trial/convict* are positives).
- Do not include antonymous related items, e.g. *loss/win*.
- Do not include cases where the noun and verb share a root, e.g. *fight/fight, presumption/presume*.
- Shorten the two sentences to phrases of maximum 10 words.

Figure 3: Annotation guidelines used for pilot expert annotation.

the comfort of a KLM **flight** from Belfast	they **returned** to their home in Northern Ireland
the peso **crisis** erupted	Mexican stocks **slipped**
he heads an **outreach program**	he **works with refugees**
starting a **workout program**	**walk** at a medium pace for an hour
we have won this **war**	vowing to **fight** to the death
passengers in New York have no **choice**	passengers can **decide** whether to avoid Kennedy
the **political battle** underlined the role that settlements play	Cabinet members **argued** that construction projects might be in jeopardy
enjoy a sound **meal**	**nibble** on snacks
Clinton gave a **speech**	the White House **announced** its members
the son died of heart **disease**	**donate** an organ for a family
a first-round playoff **loss**	**win** one last Super Bowl

Table 1: Sample candidates for highly and moderately related phrase pairs as judged by the authors, from pilot annotation. The counterpart noun and verb, with modifiers when relevant, are in bold.

The second proposed set of confounders is aimed at evaluating whether CDS models can distinguish between *relatedness* and *similarity* with regard to event descriptions. Here, we choose phrases centered around a common argument of a verb, but where the phrase does not describe the same event. For example, *the two countries* **fought** *savagely* might be paired with *many* **soldiers** *required training*, rather than *the* **war** *lasted for years*; or *we* **ate** *at a new restaurant* might be paired with *the art of making* **pizza**, rather than *the* **meal** *was delicious*. We conceive this as an alternative subset of the data, where the task is to assign a lower score to the phrases containing a non-event noun, a much harder task than simple relatedness. This task is a proxy for downstream applications such as event sequencing, narrative generation, and summarization, where it is necessary to identify when multiple phrases describe the same

event. We emphasize that this confounder set is speculative; we expect that its development will be complex and will introduce interesting problems which will undoubtedly result in modifications to the approach as we work with the data.

4   Conclusion

SLEDDED is a targeted dataset of event descriptions which focuses on semantic relatedness under lexical and syntactic divergence. Although SLEDDED is aimed primarily at CDS, it would also be suitable for evaluating representations used for tasks such as Recognizing Textual Entailment (RTE) or Machine Translation (MT). We believe phrase relatedness tasks have continued potential for evaluating the next generation of vector space representations, if they are carefully designed to isolate the behavior of different representations under specific linguistic conditions.

Acknowledgments

This work is supported by ERC Starting Grant DisCoTex (306920). We thank David Weir and the participants in the IWCS 2015 Advances in Distributional Semantics Workshop for their suggestions on a previous version of this proposal, and the anonymous reviewers for their helpful comments.

References

Amit Bagga and Breck Baldwin. 1999. Cross-document event coreference: Annotations, experiments, and observations. In *Proceedings of the ACL Workshop on Coreference and its Applications*, page 18, College Park, MD.

Cosmin Adrian Bejan and Sanda Harabagiu. 2014. Unsupervised event coreference resolution. *Computational Linguistics*, 40:311–347.

Núria Bel, Maria Coll, and Gabriela Resnik. 2010. Automatic detection of non-deverbal event nouns for quick lexicon production. In *Proceedings of the 23rd International Conference on Computational Linguistics (COLING 2010)*, pages 46–52, Beijing, China.

Razvan C. Bunescu and Raymond J. Mooney. 2007. Learning to extract relations from the web using minimal supervision. In *Proceedings of the 45th Annual Meeting of the Association for Computational Linguistics*, pages 576–583.

Zheng Chen and Heng Ji. 2009. Graph-based event coreference resolution. In *Proceedings of the 2009 Workshop on Graph-based Methods for Natural Language Processing (TextGraphs-4)*, pages 54–57, Singapore.

William Dolan, Chris Quirk, and Chris Brockett. 2004. Unsupervised construction of large paraphrase corpora: Exploiting massively parallel news sources. In *Proceedings of the 20th International Conference on Computational Linguistics*.

Barbara Di Eugenio and Michael Glass. 2004. The kappa statistic: A second look. *Computational Linguistics*, 30:95–101.

C. J. Fillmore and C. Baker. 2010. A frames approach to semantic analysis. In *The Oxford Handbook of Linguistic Analysis*, pages 791–816. Oxford University Press, Oxford.

David Graff, Junbo Kong, Ke Chen, and Kazuaki Maeda. 2005. English gigaword second edition. LDC2005T12.

Dimitri Kartsaklis and Mehrnoosh Sadrzadeh. 2014. A study of entanglement in a categorical framework of natural language. In *Proceedings of the 11th Workshop on Quantum Physics and Logic (QPL)*, Kyoto, Japan.

Marco Marelli, Luisa Bentivogli, Marco Baroni, Raffaella Bernardi, Stefano Menini, and Roberto Zamparelli. 2014a. SemEval-2014 task 1: Evaluation of compositional distributional semantic models on full sentences through semantic relatedness and textual entailment. In *Proceedings of SemEval*, pages 1–8.

Marco Marelli, Stefano Menini, Marco Baroni, Luisa Bentivogli, Raffaella Bernardi, and Roberto Zamparelli. 2014b. A SICK cure for the evaluation of compositional distributional semantic models. In *Proceedings of LREC*.

Jeff Mitchell and Mirella Lapata. 2010. Composition in distributional models of semantics. *Cognitive Science*, 34(8):1388–1429.

Gabriela Resnik and Núria Bel. 2009. Automatic detection of non-deverbal event nouns in spanish. In *Proceedings of GL2009: 5th International Conference on Generative Approaches to the Lexicon*, Pisa.

Vasile Rus, Rajendra Banjade, and Mihai Lintean. 2014. On paraphrase identification corpora. In *Proceedings of the Ninth International Conference on Language Resources and Evaluation (LREC)*, Reykjavik, Iceland.

Wei Xu, Alan Ritter, Chris Callison-Burch, William B. Dolan, and Yangfeng Ji. 2014. Extracting lexically divergent paraphrases from twitter. *TACL*, 2:435–448.

Sentence Embedding Evaluation Using Pyramid Annotation

Tal Baumel

Dept. of Computer Science
Ben-Gurion University
Beer-Sheva, Israel

talbau@cs.bgu.ac.il

Raphael Cohen

Dept. of Computer Science
Ben-Gurion University
Beer-Sheva, Israel

cohenrap@cs.bgu.ac.il

Michael Elhadad

Dept. of Computer Science
Ben-Gurion University
Beer-Sheva, Israel

elhadad@cs.bgu.ac.il

Abstract

Word embedding vectors are used as input for a variety of tasks. Choosing the right model and features for producing such vectors is not a trivial task and different embedding methods can greatly affect results. In this paper we re-purpose the "Pyramid Method" annotations used for evaluating automatic summarization to create a benchmark for comparing embedding models when identifying paraphrases of text snippets containing a single clause. We present a method of converting pyramid annotation files into two distinct sentence embedding tests. We show that our method can produce a good amount of testing data, analyze the quality of the testing data, perform test on several leading embedding methods, and finally explain the downstream usages of our task and its significance.

1 Introduction

Word vector embeddings [Mikolov *et al.* 2013] have become a standard building block for NLP applications. By representing words using continuous multi-dimensional vectors, applications take advantage of the natural associations among words to improve task performance. For example, POS tagging [Al Rfou *et al.* 2014], NER [Passos *et al.* 2014], parsing [Bansal *et al.* 2014], Semantic Role Labeling [Herman *et al.* 2014] or sentiment analysis [Socher *et al.* 2011] - have all been shown to benefit from word embeddings, either as additional features in existing supervised machine learning architectures, or as exclusive word representation features. In deep learning applications, word embeddings are typically used as pre-trained initial layers in deep architectures, and have been shown to improve performance on a wide range of tasks as well (see for example, [Cho *et al.*, 2014; Karpathy and Fei-Fei 2015; Erhan *et al*,. 2010]).

One of the key benefits of word embeddings is that they can bring to tasks with small annotated datasets and small observed vocabulary, the capacity to generalize to large vocabularies and to smoothly handle unseen words, trained on massive scale datasets in an unsupervised manner.

Training word embedding models is still an art with various embedding algorithms possible and many parameters that can greatly affect the results of each algorithm. It remains difficult to predict which word embeddings are most appropriate to a given task, whether fine tuning of the embeddings is required, and which parameters perform best for a given application.

We introduce a novel dataset for comparing embedding algorithms and their settings on the specific task of comparing short clauses. The current state-of-the-art paraphrase dataset [Dolan and Brockett, 2005] is quite small with 4,076 sentence pairs (2,753 positive). The Stanford Natural Language Inference (SNLI) (Bowman *et al.*, 2015) corpus contains 570k sentences pairs labeled with one of the tags: entailment, contradiction, and neutral. SNLI improves on previous paraphrase datasets by eliminating indeterminacy

Proceedings of the 1st Workshop on Evaluating Vector Space Representations for NLP, pages 145–149,
Berlin, Germany, August 12, 2016. ©2016 Association for Computational Linguistics

of event and entity coreference which make human entailment judgment difficult. Such indeterminacies are avoided by eliciting descriptions of the same images by different annotators.

We repurpose manually created data sets from automatic summarization to create a new paraphrase dataset with 197,619 pairs (8,390 positive and challenging distractors in the negative pairs). Like SNLI, our dataset avoids semantic indeterminacy because the texts are generated from the same news reports – we thus obtain definite entailment judgments but in the richer domain of news report as opposed to image descriptions. The propositions in our dataset are on average 12.1 words long (as opposed to about 8 words for the SNLI hypotheses).

In addition to paraphrase, our dataset captures a notion of centrality - the clause elements captured are Summary Content Units (SCU) which are typically shorter than full sentences and intended to capture proposition-level facts. As such, the new dataset is relevant for exercising the large family of "Sequence to Sequence" (seq2seq) tasks involving the generation of short text clauses [Sutskever *et al.* 2014].

The paper is structured as follows: §2 describes the pyramid method; §3 describes the process for generating a paraphrase dataset from a pyramid dataset; in §4, we evaluate a number of algorithms on the new benchmark and in §5, we explain the importance of the task.

2 The Pyramid Method

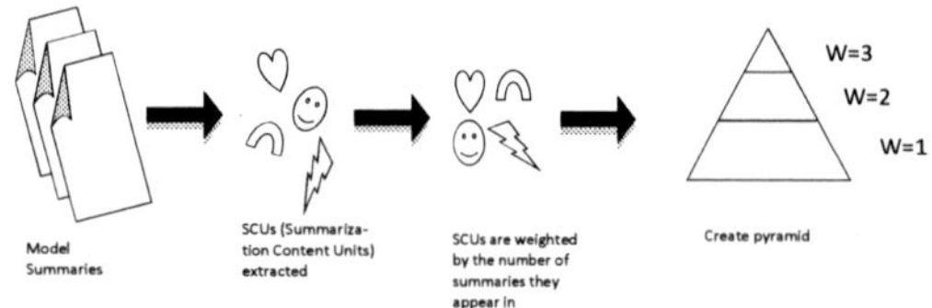

Figure 1: Pyramid Method Illustration

The Pyramid Method (Nenkova and Passonneau, 2004) is a summarization evaluation scheme designed to achieve consistent score while taking into account human variation in content selection and formulation. This evaluation method is manual and can be applied to both manual and auto-matic summarization. It has been included as a main evaluation technique in all DUC datasets since 2005 (Passonneau *et al.*, 2006).

In order to use the method, a pyramid file must first be created manually (Fig. 1):

- Create a set of model (gold) summaries

- Divide each summary into Summary Content Units (SCUs) – SCUs are key facts extracted from the manual summarizations, they are no longer than a single clause

- A pyramid file is created where each SCU is given a score by the number of summaries in which it is mentioned (*i.e.*, SCUs mentioned in 3 summaries will obtain a score of 3)

After the pyramid is created, it can be used to evaluate a new summary:

- Find all the SCUs in the summary

- Sum the score of all the found SCUs and divide it by the maximum score that the same amount of SCUs can achieve

SCUs are extracted from different source summaries, written by different authors. When counting the number of occurrences of an SCU, annotators effectively create clusters of text snippets that are judged semantically equivalent in the context of the source summaries. SCUs actually refer to clusters of text fragments from the summaries and a label written by the pyramid annotator describing the meaning of the SCU.

In our evaluation, we divert the pyramid file from its original intention of summarization evaluation, and propose to use it as a proposition paraphrase dataset.

3 Repurposing Pyramid Annotations

We define two types of tests that can be produced from a pyramid file: a binary decision test and a ranking test. For the binary decision test, we collect pairs of different SCUs from manual summaries and the label given to the SCU by annotators. The binary decision consists of deciding whether the pair is taken from the same SCU. In order to make the test challenging and still achievable, we add the following constraints on pair selection:

- Both items must contain at least 3 words;

- For non-paraphrase pairs, both items must match on more than 3 words;

- Both items must not include any pronouns;

- The pair must be lexically varied (at least one content word must be different across the items)

Non-paraphrase pair: 'Countries worldwide sent Equipment', 'Countries worldwide sent Relief Workers'	Paraphrase pair: 'countries worldwide sent money equipment', 'rescue equipment poured in from around the world'

Figure 2: Binary test pairs example

For the ranking test, we generate a set of multiple choice questions by taking as a question an SCU appearance in the text and the correct answer is another appearance of the same SCU in the test. To create synthetic distractors, we use the 3 most lexically similar text segments from distinct SCUs:

Morris Dees co-founded the SPLC:
1. **Morris Dees was co-founder of the Southern Poverty Law Center (SPLC) in 1971 and has served as its Chief Trial Counsel and Executive Director**
2. Dees and the SPLC seek to destroy hate groups through multi-million dollar civil suits that go after assets of groups and their leaders
3. Dees and the SPLC have fought to break the organizations by legal action resulting in severe financial penalties
4. The SPLC participates in tracking down hate groups and publicizing their activities in its Intelligence Report

Figure 3: Ranking test example question

Using DUC-2007, 2006 and 2005 pyramid files (all contain news stories), we created 8,755 questions for the ranking test and for the binary test we generated 8,390 positive pairs, 189,229 negative pairs for a total 197,619 pairs. The propositions in the dataset contain 95,286 words (6,882 unique).

4 Baseline Embeddings Evaluation

In order to verify that this task indeed is sensitive to differences in word embeddings, we evaluated 8 different word embeddings on the task as a baseline: Random, None (One-Hot em-

bedding), word2vec (Mikolov *et al.*, 2013) trained on Google News and two models trained on Wikipedia with different window sizes (Levy and Goldberg 2014), word2vec trained with Wikipedia dependencies (Levy and Goldberg 2014), GloVe (Pennington *et al.*, 2014) and Open IE based embeddings (Stanovsky *et al.*, 2015). For all of the embeddings, we measured sentence similarity as the cosine similarity[1] of the normalized sum of all the words in the sentences.

For the binary decision test, we evaluated the embedding by finding a threshold for answering where a pair is a paraphrase that maximizes the F-measure (trained over 10% the dataset and tested on the rest) of the embedding decision. For the rank test, we computed the percentage of questions where the correct answer achieved the highest similarity score and the MRR measure (Craswell, 2009).

Results are summarized in Table 1.

	Binary Test (F-measure)	Ranking Test (Success Rate)	Ranking Test (Mean reciprocal rank)
Random-Baseline	0.04059	24.662%	0.52223
One-Hot	0.26324	63.973%	0.77202
word2vec-BOW (google-news)	0.42337	**66.960%**	**0.78933**
word2vec-BOW2 (Wikipedia)	0.39450	61.684%	0.75274
word2vec-BOW5 (Wikipedia)	0.40387	62.886%	0.76292
word2vec-Dep	0.39097	60.025%	0.74003
GloVe	0.37870	63.000%	0.76389
Open IE Embedding	**0.42516**	65.667%	0.77847

Table 1: Different embedding performance on binary and ranking tests.

The OpenIE Embedding model scored the highest for the binary test (0.42 F). Word2vec model trained on google news achieved the best success rate in the ranking test (precision@1 of 66.9%),

---

[1] Using spaCy for tokenization

significantly better than the word2vec model trained on Wikipedia (62.8%). MRR for ranking was dominated by word2vec with 0.41.

5 Task Significance

The task of identifying paraphrases specifically extracted from pyramids can aid NLP sub-fields such as:

- **Automatic Summarization**: Identifying paraphrases can both help identifying salient information in multi-document summarization and evaluation by recreating pyramid files and applying them on automatic summaries;

- **Textual Entailment**: Paraphrases are bi-directional entailments;

- **Sentence Simplification**: SCUs capture the central elements of meaning in observable long sentences.

- **Expansion of Annotated Datasets**: Given an annotated dataset (*e.g.,* aligned translations), unannotated sentences could be annotated the same as their paraphrases

6 Conclusion

We presented a method of using pyramid files to generate paraphrase detection tasks. The suggested task has proven challenging for the tested methods, as indicated by the relatively low F-measures reported in Table 1 on most models. Our method can be applied on any pyramid annotated dataset so the reported numbers could increase by using other datasets such as TAC 2008, 2009, 2010, 2011 and 2014[2]. We believe that the improvement that this task can provide to downstream applications is a good incentive for further research.

---

[2] http://www.nist.gov/tac/tracks/index.html

Acknowledgments

This work was supported by the Lynn and William Frankel Center for Computer Sciences, Ben-Gurion University. We thank the reviewers for extremely helpful advice. We would also like to thanks the reviewers for their insight.

References

Al-Rfou, R., Perozzi, B. and Skiena, S., 2013. Polyglot: Distributed word representations for multilingual nlp. arXiv preprint arXiv:1307.1662.

Bansal, M., Gimpel, K. and Livescu, K., 2014. Tailoring Continuous Word Representations for Dependency Parsing. In ACL (2) (pp. 809-815).

Bowman, S.R., Angeli, G., Potts, C. and Manning, C.D., 2015. A large annotated corpus for learning natural language inference. arXiv preprint arXiv:1508.05326.

Craswell, N., 2009. Mean reciprocal rank. In Encyclopedia of Database Systems (pp. 1703-1703). Springer US

Cho, K., Van Merriënboer, B., Gulcehre, C., Bahdanau, D., Bougares, F., Schwenk, H. and Bengio, Y., 2014. Learning phrase representations using RNN encoder-decoder for statistical machine translation. arXiv preprint arXiv:1406.1078.

Dolan, W.B. and Brockett, C., 2005, October. Automatically constructing a corpus of sentential paraphrases. In Proc. of IWP.

Erhan, D., Bengio, Y., Courville, A., Manzagol, P.A., Vincent, P. and Bengio, S., 2010. Why does unsupervised pre-training help deep learning?. The Journal of Machine Learning Research, 11, pp.625-660.

Goldberg, Y. and Levy, O., 2014. word2vec explained: Deriving mikolov et al.'s negative-sampling word-embedding method. arXiv preprint arXiv:1402.3722.

Hermann, K.M., Das, D., Weston, J. and Ganchev, K., 2014, June. Semantic Frame Identification with Distributed Word Representations. In ACL (1) (pp. 1448-1458).

Levy, O. and Goldberg, Y., 2014. Dependency-Based Word Embeddings. In ACL (2) (pp. 302-308).

Mikolov, T., Yih, W.T. and Zweig, G., 2013, June. Linguistic Regularities in Continuous Space Word Representations. In HLT-NAACL (pp. 746-751). Vancouver

Nenkova, A. and Passonneau, R., 2004. Evaluating content selection in summarization: The pyramid method.

Passonneau, R., McKeown, K., Sigelman, S. and Goodkind, A., 2006. Applying the pyramid method in the 2006 Document Understanding Conference.

Passos, A., Kumar, V. and McCallum, A., 2014. Lexicon infused phrase embeddings for named entity resolution. arXiv preprint arXiv:1404.5367.

Pennington, J., Socher, R. and Manning, C.D., 2014, October. Glove: Global Vectors for Word Representation. In EMNLP (Vol. 14, pp. 1532-1543).

Karpathy, A. and Fei-Fei, L., 2015. Deep visual-semantic alignments for generating image descriptions. In Proceedings of the IEEE Conference on Computer Vision and Pattern Recognition (pp. 3128-3137).

Socher, R., Pennington, J., Huang, E.H., Ng, A.Y. and Manning, C.D., 2011, July. Semi-supervised recursive autoencoders for predicting sentiment distributions. In Proceedings of the Conference on Empirical Methods in Natural Language Processing (pp. 151-161). Association for Computational Linguistics.

Stanovsky, G., Dagan, I, and Mausam, 2015. Open IE as an Intermediate Structure for Semantic Tasks. Proceedings of the 53rd Annual Meeting of the Association for Computational Linguistics (ACL 2015)

Author Index

Association for Computational Linguistics
209 N. Eighth Street
Stroudsburg, Pennsylvania 18360

ISBN 978-1-5108-2770-7